Christina Koning is a novelist and journalist. She is a book reviewer for *The Times*, Book Editor for *Cosmopolitan* and has worked extensively for the *Guardian*, the *Independent* and the *Observer*. She contributed to the *Oxford Guide to Twentieth-Century Literature*. She has two children and lives in London.

GOOD READING GUIDE TO CHILDREN'S BOOKS

Inspire your child with a lifelong love of books

Christina Koning

IN ASSOCIATION WITH **SHE** MAGAZINE

BLOOMSBURY

First published in 1997 by
Bloomsbury Publishing Plc
38 Soho Square
London W1V 5DF

A copy of the CIP entry for this book is available from the
British Library

ISBN 07475 3198 6

1 3 5 7 9 10 8 6 4 2

Typeset by Hewer Text Composition Services, Edinburgh
Printed by Clays Ltd, St Ives plc

For my children, Anna and James

Contents

Acknowledgements

I should like to thank Pam Girdwood, of Southwark Library Educational Services, for her invaluable advice. I should also like to thank my children, Anna and James, for giving me some of the best ideas in the book, and for helping me with all the bits I wasn't certain about.

Introduction

We are living, so received wisdom has it, in a post-literate age. Films, television and video fulfil our need for fiction; computers answer all the questions we would once have addressed to works of reference. Bombarded from all sides by the multimedia stimuli of the modern world, we have no need for books. Books, in a word, are obsolete.

Most people over thirty would probably disagree with that statement, if only because we are old enough to remember a time before the personal computer became ubiquitous, and when libraries were places where people went to read, not merely to get out of the cold. But for the generation that has grown up in a world dominated by the wonders of information technology and computer graphics, the idea that the two-thousand-year tradition of reading is coming to an end must seem almost inevitable. After all, what can books teach us that computers can't?

Leaving aside the debate between the relative merits of turning a page or scrolling up a computer screen, I do not see why books and computers have to be mutually exclusive. Surely the whole point about living in a pluralistic, multimedia age is having the freedom to choose how one wants to acquire – or access – one's information? Computers are wonderful machines, which can on occasion (for example, when one is writing a book) make life a lot easier. But to my mind there are few pleasures which can equal that of opening a novel for the first time, of smelling the intoxicating scent of newly printed paper, and of knowing that, for no more than the price of a cinema ticket, one is invited to enter another world.

And that, for me, is the heart of the matter. For while one can be overwhelmed by the high-voltage emotions and technical wizardry of films, and entertained by the slick imitation of real life put across by television, in neither case is one offered the same degree of insight into individual thoughts and feelings which can be found in the novels of Jane Austen, or in the plays of Shakespeare, or the poems of John Keats. Reading is still the best way of discovering how it feels to be someone else, and of developing, with that intuitive sympathy, a greater understanding of oneself.

Which brings me to the subject of children's books. It is one of the ironies of living in our post-literate, technological age that at a time when there is increasing concern about levels of literacy in general, and falling standards of reading and writing in schools, more children's books are being published than ever before (over 7,000 new titles a year in Britain alone). Where once children's book publishing might have been regarded as a somewhat sleepy back-water, it is now big business, with publishers competing aggressively for the biggest share of the market. Children's books – as is obvious the minute you walk into any bookshop – are being marketed as if they were computer games – with bolder covers, snappier blurbs and lots of fun features that pop up and fold out, to make reading more entertaining.

When confronted with so much exciting diversity, it can be difficult to know what to buy. Most parents will have had the experience of going into a bookshop with the intention of finding something which will inspire their child to read, only to be overwhelmed by the feeling that they don't know where to begin. Should they stick with the tried-and-tested favourites of their own youth – or should they take a chance on an unfamiliar author? Is it better to buy something which is comfortably within the child's reading capabilities – or should one try to stretch him or her a little, by choosing something more difficult?

One of the aims of this book is to try to make that process of selection easier, by offering the kind of broad guidelines I have found useful in choosing books for my own children. Throughout I emphasize that these are *only* guidelines, not hard-and-fast rules. Although, for the sake of convenience, I have grouped the books according to age, I should like to stress that these are merely approximate groupings. As most parents will already know, and teachers and librarians will confirm, many children read outside their reading category – both above and below. It is one of the advantages of reading that, while one can always read *on*, one can also read *back*.

HOW TO USE THIS BOOK

The book is divided into five chapters, of which four are concerned with fiction and one with reference books (a subject which really requires a book in its own right). A final section consists of brief biographical entries on outstanding contributors to children's literature. In the introduction to each chapter, I have outlined the kind of challenges and occasional difficulties a child might expect to encounter at a given stage of his or her reading career, and to suggest how these might be dealt with. In selecting books to review for each age group, I have set out to offer a mixture of established classics and the best contemporary writing currently available for children. Inevitably – since length does not permit this to be a comprehensive survey – there will be omissions, although I hope that some of these will be covered in the 'read-on' suggestions at the end of each review. Where one of these suggested titles is reviewed elsewhere in the guide, I have marked it with an asterisk. In each case, I have given the date of first publication but the publisher of the most recent edition.

ILLUSTRATION

No book on children's literature would be complete without referring to the many superb artists and illustrators working in the field. I have tried to mention as many as possible, particularly in the sections devoted to picture books for younger children, where words and images seem equally important. Elsewhere, I have given special mention to books whose illustrations seemed exceptionally good, or to books (such as those written in comic-strip form) where pictures play a particularly important part.

KEYS

Throughout, I have adopted the Young Book Trust's system of grading books according to both Interest Level, which indicates the age range for which it will have most appeal and which may span several years, and Reading Age – the age at which the child is likely to be able to read the book unaided. For example, a book designed to appeal to three- to six-year-olds may be suitable for a child of five-plus to read independently. These categories are, of course, approximate. In the sections devoted to fiction for older children and reference books, I have assigned Key Stage gradings, to help with selecting books for school projects. These are according to the National Curriculum guidelines set out in the Oxford University Press handbook and are as follows:

Key Stage 1: age 5–7
Key Stage 2: age 7–11
Key Stage 3: age 11–14

INDICES

All the books are listed alphabetically according to title and author. Most titles are also listed under subject – some titles appearing more than once. For example, Arthur Ransome's *Swallows and Amazons* can be found under title, author and in three separate subject categories: Adventure, Families and Pirates. Reference books are dealt with in the same way.

A NOTE ON GENDER

Attentive readers will note that in the introductions to each chapter I have tried, as far as possible, to avoid using the clumsy formulation 'he or she' when referring to the hypothetical young reader. This left me with the choice of assuming my putative child to be male, or following Penelope Leach's example in her ground-breaking books on childcare by referring throughout to 'she' – which is what I have chosen to do. Parents of male children will not, I hope, object to making the appropriate substitution.

As well as passing on some of the basic rules of thumb I have found useful in helping my own children to read, I have tried to convey in this book something of what reading means to me – and why I consider it to be one of the most fulfilling and enjoyable of all human activities. I would go so far as to say that establishing the habit of reading is one of the best things any parent can do for his or her child; nothing else offers such a range of imaginative pleasures or so much intellectual stimulation – all contained within an attractive, portable, user-friendly package. As a writer of fiction, I suppose I have something of a vested interest in promoting the cause of reading – and who better to convince of its importance than the next generation of readers?

First Books, First Words and PreSchool

BABIES: 0–18 MONTHS

With reading, as with most other essential activities, the sooner you start the better. For while a newborn baby is certainly too young to be able to appreciate a book as a physical object, she is already starting to respond to the sound of her mother's voice, and to the many other stimuli – light, colour, texture, smell – which define her world. Every time you talk to your child, or sing to her, or recite a nursery rhyme, you are introducing her to language, and preparing her for the day when she will say – and read – her first words.

So where do you start, when it comes to choosing your child's first books? Well, initially the important things to remember are these:

Babies like putting things in their mouths
Babies like bright colours – especially red
Babies enjoy the repetition of familiar sounds
Babies enjoy surprises

So: a durable format, bold colourful pictures, the repetition of simple but attractive words and a story with an element of unexpectedness are features to look for when choosing a book for your baby. Board books and cloth books, waterproof books and the tougher kind of lift-the-flap and pop-up books are all designed for your baby to get to grips with herself.

Babies love turning the pages of a familiar book and pointing out their favourite pictures or repeating their favourite sounds. What they are doing may seem to be no more than having fun, but it is actually a crucial part of the early learning process. Learning to recognize shapes and colours, repeating sounds and linking pictures with words are important stages in your child's journey towards reading. These skills will also help her to make sense of the world around her.

As well as the robust type of books designed for babies to handle themselves, there are those meant for reading aloud – an important activity in the early months of a baby's development. Nursery rhyme collections, counting games and simple stories all come into their own here. Every time you repeat the words of a much-loved rhyme or read your child a story, you are helping to consolidate the words she already knows, as well as introducing her to new ones. The sooner you establish the habit of a bedtime story, the sooner bedtimes become fun – something to be looked forward to, instead of something to be got through!

18 MONTHS–3 YEARS

When it comes to books – as with everything else – toddlers are impatient to find out all there is to know. They won't be content just to sit beside you on the sofa while you turn the pages – they'll grab the book out of your hands and do it themselves. If the story's a new one, they won't want to wait until you reach the final page before finding out what happens; if it's one they've heard before, they'll be in a hurry to get to the end so that they can go back to the beginning again.

Books for this age group still need to be fairly durable – for obvious reasons – but the pictures and text ought to be complex enough to provide a challenge. Two- and three-year-olds may still enjoy the soothing rhymes and jingles of babyhood, but they are also ready for more sophisticated narratives, which can incorporate counting exercises, alphabet learning and, of course, humour.

Pop-up books, lift-the-flap books and turn-the-wheel books – in fact any book with a hidden surprise – are all perfect for this age.

As your child becomes familiar with a variety of stories, she will start to develop her own tastes. For some children, this means a strongly marked preference for a particular kind of story – stories about elephants, for example – or for a favourite character. One friend's three-year-old drove her to distraction with his passion for *Thomas the Tank Engine* books, insisting on hearing the same stories over and over again until the whole household was heartily sick of them. If this sounds like your child, then remember – it's a stage which does eventually pass. And on the positive side, hearing the same words and phrases repeated again and again is one way your child can learn the vocabulary she needs to begin reading.

NURSERY AND PRESCHOOL (3–4 YEARS)

Between three and four, your child will be developing her abilities across a range of different areas, many of which will be directly connected to acquiring language skills. If she is attending a playgroup or nursery, she will be learning how to express herself through painting and drawing, as well as how to write her name. She will be enjoying role-playing and dressing-up games, experimenting with simple science, and consolidating her number and letter recognition. In addition to all this, she will be spending more time with other children, and developing her social and conversational skills.

Stories and storytelling are of course an important part of pre-school activity, both in the context of nursery school and in the home. Many children are given a simple reading book to take home at around this age, as a way of getting them used to the idea of reading for themselves. These can be part of an actual reading scheme, or merely a picture book the child has enjoyed; most nursery teachers I have spoken to use a bit of both.

There is of course no set age by which a child should learn to read, just as there are no hard-and-fast rules about when children should learn to walk or speak, but in general the age range is between four and seven years. This does not mean that you can expect your child to be a fluent reader by the time she reaches her fourth – or even fifth – birthday, but she will probably recognize quite a lot of words, and may even have started to read simple sentences by the time she starts school.

The thing to remember is that it is not a competition. Children learn at different rates, and a child who shows little interest in anything but the Home Corner in her nursery school may be a fluent reader of adventure stories by the time she is six. As children develop their listening and concentration skills, they respond to more challenging and complex narratives. They may also – as they start to develop their own reading skills – return to earlier and simpler favourites. Don't discourage this. Building confidence is an important part of the reading process, and memorizing a familiar text is one way for your child to feel she is reading properly.

ADVENTURES OF KING ROLLO, THE
. . . .

by David McKee (Sparrow Books, 1979)
Interest level: 2–5/Reading age: 5+

D AVID McKee's gently humorous stories about King Rollo and his friends Queen Gwen, Cook, the magician and Hamlet the cat have retained their popularity with the very young, no doubt partly because they have been adapted for television, but also because of the character of Rollo himself – a king who acts like a little boy. The brightly coloured, stylized illustrations are another plus.

OTHER BOOKS BY DAVID MCKEE
Further Adventures of King Rollo; *Tusk Tusk; *Not Now, Bernard

ADVENTURES OF MOG, THE
. . . .

by Judith Kerr (Collins, 1993)
Interest level: 4–7/Reading age: 6+
PETS

J UDITH Kerr's stories about Mog, the forgetful cat, and the family with which she lives, have delighted children for over twenty years. Mog occasionally gets into scrapes, but things are always happily resolved in the end. In this collection (just three of the many stories available), Mog saves the Thomas family from a burglar, is teased by an unruly baby, and makes an unusual entrance on Christmas Eve.

AHOY THERE, LITTLE POLAR BEAR!
. . . .

by Hans De Beer (North-South Books, 1995)
Interest level: 3–6/Reading age: 6+
BEARS

I N this ingenious pop-up book in the *Little Polar Bear* series, Lars the baby polar bear gets carried away from his home at the North Pole by a passing fishing-boat. He is befriended by a kindly ship's cat before being reunited with his parents. Clever paper-engineering combined with engaging drawings of the characters make this a definite favourite with little ones.

ALL IN ONE PIECE
. . . .

by Jill Murphy (Walker Books, 1987)
Commended for Kate Greenaway Medal
Interest level: 2–5/Reading age: 5+

M R and Mrs Large are getting ready for the office party – with a little help
from their children, Lester, Laura, Luke and the baby. Will they ever
manage to get out of the house in one piece? Jill Murphy's appealing story
about a family of elephants will strike a chord with any parent who has ever
tried to get the jam stains off a best dress before an evening out. The engaging
illustrations are a bonus.

ALL JOIN IN
. . . .

by Quentin Blake (Red Fox, 1990)
Kurt Maschler Award
Interest level: 0–5/Reading age: 5+
POETRY

'I MPORTANT message,' reads a sign in Quentin Blake's distinctively spiky
writing at the beginning of this book, 'YOU CAN JOIN IN TOO.' When
offered Blake's collection of wonderfully onomatopoeic rhymes and anarchic
illustrations, most children will need little further encouragement. The titles
speak (or rather, shout, whistle, roar, hoot, yell) for themselves: 'The Hooter
Song', 'Sorting Out the Kitchen Pans' and, best of all, the superbly noisy title
song all provide the perfect excuse for children to let off steam.

ANIMALS OF FARTHING WOOD, THE
. . . .

by Colin Dann (Reed, 1979 onwards)
Interest level: 4–7/Reading age: 5+
ANIMALS

C OLIN Dann's series of story and picture books about a woodland
community of rabbits, owls, foxes and deer has been enormously
popular with young readers, doubtless because of the television cartoon.
The stories often seem rather predictable, but the Disneyesque simplicity of
the graphics has a certain appeal.

As Quiet as a Mouse
. . . .
by Hilda Offen (Red Fox, 1994)
Interest level: 1–5/Reading age: 5+
POETRY

H ILDA Offen's jolly action rhyme follows a toddler through a series of activities from sneezing to stamping, with an appropriate picture to every one. Young children will have lots of fun joining in the actions and anticipating each new excuse for noise-making.

Avocado Baby
. . . .
by John Burningham (Picture Puffin, 1982)
Interest level: 3–6/Reading age: 5+
BABIES

T HE Hargraveses' new baby is just like the rest of the family – small and weak. Until, that is, he eats his first avocado. Suddenly he starts growing big and strong, so that nothing – and no one – can stop him . . . The idea of a super-strong baby appeals to most young readers – and offers an incentive to try unusual foods!

OTHER BOOKS BY JOHN BURNINGHAM
Courtney; *Cloudland*; *Granpa*; *Mr Gumpy's Outing*; Mr Gumpy's Motor Car; *Come Away from the Water, Shirley*; *Oi! Get Off Our Train*

Babar the Elephant
. . . .
by Jean and Laurent de Brunhof (Methuen, from 1931)
Interest level: 3–6/Reading age: 6+

F IRST published in the early 1930s, Jean de Brunhof's stories about a little elephant, who is adopted by a rich old lady, marries his childhood sweetheart and becomes King of the Elephants, have enjoyed a huge following in the author's native France and elsewhere – as evinced by the recent spate of Babar merchandising: toys, board books and games. The quaint, almost naive style of the illustrations (later imitated by de Brunhof's son, Laurent, who continued producing books in the series after his father's death) adds to the charm.

BABY BOARD BOOKS

by Nick Butterworth (Collins, 1994)
Interest level: 0–4/Reading age: 5+
BABIES

Tᴵᴛʟᴇꜱ include: *When It's Time for Bed, When We Play Together, When There's Work to Do* and *When We Go Shopping*. Nick Butterworth's appealing illustrations of a baby and his cuddly animal friends going about their daily routine – getting up, playing, going to the shops and going to bed – make these sturdy books (designed with little fingers in mind) a pleasure to read. Simple text matches the clear, gently humorous pictures of a small child's day.

OTHER BOOKS BY NICK BUTTERWORTH
*A Year in Percy's Park; **Jasper's Beanstalk*; **The Cross Rabbit*

BABY'S CATALOGUE, THE

by Allan Ahlberg; illustrated by Janet Ahlberg (Puffin, 1982)
Interest level: 1–4/Reading age: 5+
BABIES

Tʜᴇ discovery that their own baby liked nothing better than looking at catalogues prompted Janet and Allan Ahlberg to produce this charming picture book, with its pages of different kinds of mums, dads, brothers, sisters, pets and other familiar aspects of a baby's life, all illustrated in Janet Ahlberg's inimitable soft-focus style.

OTHER BOOKS BY JANET AND ALLAN AHLBERG
*Peepo!; **Each Peach Pear Plum*; **The Jolly Postman*; **Funnybones*; **Burglar Bill*; **Jeremiah in the Dark Woods*

BAD-TEMPERED LADYBIRD, THE
. . . .

by Eric Carle (Picture Puffin, 1977)
Interest level: 3–6/Reading age: 6+
ANIMALS

E RIC Carle's story about a bad-tempered ladybird who tries to pick a fight with everyone he meets, confronting an increasingly disproportionate range of opponents beginning with a wasp and ending with a blue whale, enables young readers to practise their naming and counting skills, as well as learn to tell the time. As the ladybird moves through the book, the sun rises and falls in the sky, and the time at the top of each page changes accordingly.

BEAR UNDER THE STAIRS, THE
. . . .

by Helen Cooper (Picture Corgi, 1993)
Smarties Prize/Shortlisted for Kate Greenaway Award
Interest level: 3–5/Reading age: 5+
ANIMALS • BEARS • FEARS

I s there *really* a bear under the stairs – or is it all in William's imagination? Exquisitely illustrated with the author's pencil-and-wash drawings, this is a story which helps young children come to terms with their fears (whether of the dark or of unspecified monsters), using humour as the key.

OTHER BOOKS BY HELEN COOPER
*Little Monster Did It!

BEDTIME FOR FRANCES
. . . .

by Russell Hoban; illustrated by Garth Williams
(Jonathan Cape, 1960)
Interest level: 3–6/Reading age: 5+
FEARS

F RANCES, the baby badger, cannot get to sleep. She tries reciting her alphabet, she tries pulling the covers over her head. But still she cannot get rid of the idea that there may be a tiger in the room – or something worse . . . Then she hits on a very good way of getting off to sleep. Russell Hoban's appealing story, the first of a series about Frances, explores a common childhood fear with reassuring humour.

OTHER STORIES BY RUSSELL HOBAN
A Birthday for Frances; *Best Friends for Frances*

BUSTER'S DAY
. . . .

by Rod Campbell (Macmillan, 1994)
Interest level: 2–5/Reading age: 5+
BABIES

FOLLOW adventurous baby Buster through his day, in this classic lift-the-flap story, which encourages word-learning by making it fun!

OTHER BOOKS BY ROD CAMPBELL
Dear Zoo; *My Presents*; *Noisy Farm*; *Oh, Dear!*

BUT WHERE IS THE GREEN PARROT?
. . . .

by Thomas and Wanda Zacharias (Macmillan, 1980)
Interest level: 3–5/Reading age: 5+

CAN *you* spot the green parrot hidden in the picture? An ingenious interactive picture book, designed to help young readers concentrate on every page.

CAN YOU SPOT THE SPOTTY DOG?
. . . .

by John Rowe (Hutchinson, 1996)
Interest level: 3–6/Reading age: 5+

CAN you spot the spotty dog hidden on the pebbly beach or the little white owl hidden in the leafy tree, or the jet black cat hidden in the dark wood? It's not as easy as it sounds, but John Rowe's intriguing illustrations make it a lot of fun. This is a book that helps to develop a range of skills, from simple observation to remembering lists.

CAN'T YOU SLEEP, LITTLE BEAR?

by Martin Waddell; illustrated by Barbara Firth
(Walker Books, 1988)
Smarties Prize/Kate Greenaway Medal
Interest level: 3–7/Reading age: 7+
BEARS • FEARS

L ITTLE Bear is afraid of the dark, so Big Bear brings him a tiny lantern to
chase away the dark. Little Bear still can't get to sleep, so Big Bear brings
him a bigger lantern – and then the Biggest Lantern of Them All. Surely now
Little Bear won't be afraid? But even with the darkness inside the cave gone,
there's still the darkness outside, and it looks as if Little Bear won't be able to
sleep after all – until Big Bear has the idea of taking him outside, to really *look*
at the dark . . . Martin Waddell's captivating story confronts childhood fear of
the dark with sensitivity and humour. Barbara Firth's delightful illustrations
underline the reassuring message.

CHILD'S GARDEN OF VERSES, A

by Robert Louis Stevenson (Picture Lions, 1885)
Interest level: 2–8/Reading age: 6+
POETRY

F OR many adults, Stevenson's poems epitomize childhood, in all its
imaginative richness. The pleasures of going 'up in a swing'; of seeing
the 'foreign lands' of the next-door garden from the branches of a tree; of
exploring the seashore and the riverbank and building an explorer's camp
behind the sofa in the sitting room – all these experiences and more are
memorably captured in Stevenson's verse. The enduring popularity of the
poems, over a hundred years after they were first published, may have
something to do with the fact that, although written for children, they
incorporate quite complex and interesting rhythms; or it may be simply
that they deal with universal subjects. Whatever the reason, children love
them – and that is the test of a true classic.

COCKATOOS
. . . .
by Quentin Blake (Jonathan Cape, 1992)
Interest level: 2–6/Reading age: 5 +

QUENTIN Blake is one of the most talented illustrators currently working, and this is one of his most delightful books. Professor Dupont has ten pet cockatoos, who decide to play a trick on him one day by disappearing. Young children love treasure hunts of all kinds – and this book offers plenty of scope for the sharp-eyed. Follow Professor Dupont through the book, as he searches for the missing cockatoos which only we, the readers, can see (and count).

COMING AND GOING
. . . .
by Sarah Garland (Bodley Head, 1995)
Interest level: 3–6/Reading age: 5 +
FAMILIES • SIBLINGS

THIS anthology of four stories about a little girl, her mother and baby brother is illustrated with the author's own witty line-and-wash drawings, which capture the ups and downs of family life with great charm and accuracy. Who could fail to recognize the wonderfully chaotic playschool – or the swimming pool with its mums and toddlers? The text is kept to a bare minimum – usually no more than a sentence or two per page – so that young readers are less likely to feel daunted.

COURTNEY
. . . .
by John Burningham (Red Fox, 1996)
Interest level: 3–6/Reading age: 6 +
PETS

THE children decide they want a dog, so they go to the Lost Dogs' Home to choose one. There they find Courtney, the dog nobody wants. They take him home – to their parents' disapproval – and find that he is a dog of many talents. For not only does Courtney know how to cook and serve a wonderful meal, but he can garden, clean and keep everyone amused with juggling tricks. He even rescues the baby when the house is on fire. But the day comes when Courtney disappears, and the children have to face up to life without him – or do they? Burningham's delightfully eccentric illustrations are, as ever, the secret of of his success – together with his engaging habit of siding with the underdog.

CREATION, THE

Brian Wildsmith (Oxford University Press, 1995)
Interest level: 4–6/Reading age: 5+

G LOWINGLY illustrated in Brian Wildsmith's inimitable style with a range of pop-up spreads, this book provides an unforgettable introduction to the creation story for younger readers.

OTHER BOOKS BY BRIAN WILDSMITH
The Hare and the Tortoise; *The Tunnel*

CROSS RABBIT, THE

by Nick Butterworth (Collins, 1995)
Interest level: 2–5/Reading age: 5+
ANIMALS

A LL the animals in Percy's park are having fun in the snow except for Rabbit, who is feeling cross. As ever, Percy sorts out the problem and everyone is happy. One of a series about Nick Butterworth's most popular character, Percy the Park Keeper.

OTHER BOOKS BY NICK BUTTERWORTH
*A Year in Percy's Park; *Jasper's Beanstalk

DAD! I CAN'T SLEEP

by Michael Foreman (Red Fox, 1996)
Interest level: 2–5/Reading age: 5+
FEARS

L ITTLE Panda can't sleep and keeps asking for a drink – so Dad suggests he should try counting sheep. When this doesn't work, Little Panda tries counting cows, then pigs, then tigers and elephants – but without effect. Finally, when Dad has almost run out of ideas, he thinks of dinosaurs. Surely even Little Panda can't hold out against the sleep-inducing properties of counting stegosauruses and pterodactyls? But Dad has reckoned without his son's persistence – for when he opens the bedroom door, it is full of sheep, cows, elephants and dinosaurs, all asking for a drink! Illustrated with the author's distinctive watercolour paintings, this is a story which will strike a chord with children – and parents – everywhere.

DAY OF RHYMES, A

Selected and illustrated by Sarah Pooley (Red Fox, 1987)
Best Books for Babies Award
Interest level: 0–5/Reading age: 5+
POETRY

F AVOURITE jingles and nursery rhymes are arranged according to different times of the day, with a rhyme – or two – for every event, from getting up to going to bed. Pooley's jolly illustrations help to make this a book children will love to have read to them, and will later enjoy reading for themselves.

DEAR ZOO

by Rod Campbell (Picture Puffin, 1982)
Interest level: 2–5/Reading age: 5+
ANIMALS

O NE of the classic lift-the-flap books, illustrated with the author's bright, distinctive drawings of different types of zoo animals. Which one is *your* favourite?

OTHER BOOKS BY ROD CAMPBELL
Buster's Day; *Noisy Farm*; *Oh, Dear!*; *My Presents*

EACH PEACH PEAR PLUM

by Janet and Allan Ahlberg (Picture Lions, 1978)
Interest level: 2–5/Reading age: 5+

C LASSIC picture book in which familiar characters from nursery rhymes and fairy stories are woven into a delightfully humorous rhyming tale, in which Baby Bunting is saved from falling in the river by the Three Bears, and everyone – including including Tom Thumb, Cinderella, Bo-Peep, Jack and

Jill and the Wicked Witch – ends up back at Mother Hubbard's cottage for tea and plum pie. As in many of the Ahlbergs' books for very young children, repetition plays a part in encouraging visual and verbal recognition. In this case the 'Each peach pear plum' refrain is one most children will get to know by heart – together with the story it accompanies.

OTHER BOOKS BY JANET AND ALLAN AHLBERG
Peepo!; *The Baby's Catalogue*; *The Jolly Postman*; *Funnybones*; *Jeremiah in the Dark Woods*; *Burglar Bill*

Eat Up, Gemma

by Sarah Hayes; illustrated by Jan Ormerod (Walker Books, 1989)
Interest level: 3–5/Reading age: 5+
BABIES

B ABY Gemma won't eat her food – she prefers to play with it. Until one day, her big brother comes up with a clever way of making sure she eats up her dinner . . . Jan Ormerod's sensitive illustrations are the perfect complement to Sarah Hayes's appealing story.

Elephant and the Bad Baby, The

by Elfrida Vipont; illustrated by Raymond Briggs (Puffin, 1969)
Interest level: 3–6/Reading age: 5+
BABIES • HUMOUR

A N elephant goes for a walk and meets a bad baby. They embark on a rumbustious race through the town, which ends with them being chased by all the citizens . . . Rhythm and repetition make this a great book to read aloud – and the humour is also highly enjoyable.

ELMER
....

by David McKee (Red Fox, 1989)
Interest level: 3–6/Reading age: 5+

Dᴀᴠɪᴅ McKee's popular series about a patchwork elephant is as imaginative and funny as all his work. The colourful illustrations are another plus.

OTHER BOOKS BY DAVID MCKEE

Not Now, Bernard; *The Adventures of King Rollo*; *Tusk, Tusk*

FARMER DUCK
....

by Martin Waddell; illustrated by Helen Oxenbury (Walker Books,
1991)
*Smarties Book Prize/British Book Awards Children's Illustrated Book of the
Year/Highly Commended for Kate Greenaway Medal*
Interest level: 3–6/Reading age: 5+
ANIMALS

Iɴ this stylish reworking of Orwell's *Animal Farm*, a lazy farmer lies in bed, while a long-suffering duck does all the work around the farm. Then, one day, the cow and the sheep and the hens have a meeting and decide to do something about it . . . Helen Oxenbury's lyrical and expressive illustrations are amongst the best she has done, capturing the mood of the story as it changes from drab oppressiveness to triumphant optimism. This is a story with a message – but one which is conveyed with subtlety and humour. Clearly laid out text and simple vocabulary make this a good choice for young readers, too.

FLOWER FAIRIES
....

by Cicely Mary Barker (Blackie, from 1923)
Interest level: 3–6/Reading age: 6+
FAIRIES & FAIRY TALES

Fɪʀsᴛ published in the 1920s, Cicely M. Barker's charmingly detailed (and botanically accurate) paintings of wayside and garden flowers – together with their accompanying fairies – have enthralled generations of young children, offering an imaginative introduction to the pleasures of nature study.

BOOKS IN THE SERIES INCLUDE
Flower Fairies of the Spring; *Flower Fairies of the Summer*; *Flower Fairies of the Autumn*; *Flower Fairies of the Winter*

GOODNIGHT, OWL!

by Pat Hutchins (Picture Puffin, 1988)
Interest level: 3–5/Reading age: 5+
ANIMALS

Poor Owl can't sleep, because the other animals and birds keep him awake during the daytime – but at night he comes into his own. Pat Hutchins's boldly graphic illustrations and simple text make this a good choice for new readers.

OTHER BOOKS BY PAT HUTCHINS
Rosie's Walk; *Titch*

GRANPA

by John Burningham (Picture Puffin, 1984)
Winner of Kurt Maschler/Emil Award
Interest level: 4–6
DEATH

A little girl enjoys going to stay with her granpa. He takes her on long walks which turn into voyages of adventure, he reads her stories and lets her help in the garden. But then one day, he falls ill – and the child has to come to terms with the fact that she will not see her beloved granpa again. John Burningham's gently humorous story without words conveys the seriousness of the theme, without ever resorting to sentimentality. This book is an invaluable aid for any parent faced with the sad task of explaining death to a young child.

OTHER BOOKS BY JOHN BURNINGHAM
Mr Gumpy's Outing; *Come Away from the Water, Shirley*; *Oi! Get Off Our Train*

GRASSHOPPER LAUGHS, THE
A FABER BOOK OF FIRST VERSE
. . . .

Edited by Michael Bird; illustrated by Andrew Stooke (Faber &
Faber, 1995)
Interest level: 2–6/Reading age: 6+
POETRY

TRADITIONAL nursery rhymes, chants and lullabys are mingled with verse
from Eastern Europe, the Caribbean, Africa, India and America in
Michael Bird's lively collection, which also includes poems by writers as
diverse as T.S. Eliot, Ted Hughes, John Agard and Grace Nichols.

HAIRY MACLARY
. . . .

by Lynley Dodd (Picture Puffin, 1989)
Interest level: 3–5/Reading age: 5+
ANIMALS ● PETS

LYNLEY Dodd's series about a loveably scruffy dog has won lots of fans.
The stories are told in rhyme, and the illustrations are delightfully
offbeat. For cat lovers, there is a companion series about Slinky Malinki,
the adventurous cat.

HAPPY HEDGEHOG BAND, THE
. . . .

by Martin Waddell; illustrated by Jill Barton (Walker Books, 1991)
Interest level: 2–6/Reading age: 6+
ANIMALS ● MUSIC

IN the middle of Dickon Wood, Harry the Hedgehog starts banging on his
drum. Before long, he is joined by his friends Helen and Norbert and Billy.
The sound of the hedgehog band attracts the other inhabitants of the wood,
who all want to join in the music-making – the only trouble is, they don't have
any instruments. But even without instruments, you can always improvise – in
fact, it's surprising how many different kinds of noises you can make . . .
Waddell's lively tale offers lots of participatory fun.

Harry's Treasure Hunt

by Stephen Thraves; illustrated by Mark Burgess (Collins, 1995)
Interest level: 2–5/Reading age: 5+

O BJECTS are hidden on every page of this ingenious lift-the-flap book, in which young readers can follow one of four different trails to the treasure by turning the coloured wheels behind every page. Helping Harry the Hippo find the present Uncle Henry has left him is not only fun but encourages the development of colour matching, object recognition and basic counting skills.

Hilda Hen's Search

by Mary Wormell (Gollancz, 1994)
Interest level: 2–5/Reading age: 5+
ANIMALS

H ILDA Hen is looking for a safe place to lay her eggs – but it turns out to be harder to find than she thinks! Mary Wormell's bold linocut illustrations perfectly complement this satisfying story.

OTHER BOOKS BY MARY WORMELL
Hilda Hen's Birthday

I Can

by Susan Winter (Dorling Kindersley, 1993)
Interest level: 2–5/Reading age: 5+
SIBLINGS

W ITH its companion volume, *Me Too*, Susan Winter's engaging picture book eloquently depicts both the competitiveness and the warmth of the relationship between an older and a younger child. In *I Can*, the story is told from big brother's point of view: he can dress himself, his little sister can't; he can stand on his head, swim without armbands, paint pictures and do all the things she hasn't yet learned to do – but in a funny way, he quite likes having her around. *Me Too* tells the story from baby sister's angle, with a nicely judged shift of emphasis. The illustrations in both are delightful, and the text simple and clear – ideal for young readers, and for any child coping with a younger 'rival'.

I WANT MY POTTY
. . . .

by Tony Ross (Collins Picture Lions, 1987)
Interest level: 2–4/Reading age: 5+

IN the first in Tony Ross's popular series about a little princess with very decided views, we find her learning to use her potty – at the right time! Other books show her learning the art of table manners and finding out what she wants to be when she grows up. The pictures are appealingly offbeat.

OTHER BOOKS BY TONY ROSS
*Stone Soup

I'M A CAR
. . . .

by Woody (Bloomsbury Children's Books, 1997)
Interest level: 1–4/Reading age: 5+

ANYONE who has ever watched a small boy – or girl – pretending to be a car will recognize the accuracy of this appealing 'Let's pretend' picture book. With each turn of the page, you can see the central character both as he appears in reality and in his imagination.

IF I HAD A DOG
. . . .

by Bernice Lum (Bloomsbury Children's Books, 1995)
Interest level: 1–4/Reading age: 5+
PETS

IF you had a dog, what would you call him? And what kind of things would you teach him to do? Stanley the dog can not only do all the things ordinary dogs can do, but he can dance, and sing, and juggle – and even read . . . Attractively bold graphics and clear, simple text make this an ideal choice for very young readers.

OTHER BOOKS IN THE SERIES
If My Dog Had a Job, If My Dog Could Drive, If My Dog Went on Holiday

IN A MINUTE
. . . .

by Tony Bradman; illustrated by Eileen Browne (Mammoth, 1990)
Interest level: 3–5/Reading age: 5+

Jo, the small heroine of Tony Bradman's attractive series, is impatient to get to the playground. But her family seems to have other ideas. Eventually, just as she is giving up, Patch the dog makes *his* feelings clear – and Jo gets her outing after all!

OTHER BOOKS BY TONY BRADMAN
Wait and See; *Through My Window*; *Dilly the Dinosaur*

IN THE NIGHT KITCHEN
. . . .

by Maurice Sendak (Picture Puffin, 1971)
Interest level: 2–6/Reading age: 5+

WONDERFULLY surreal picture book incorporating the author's own distinctive illustrations, in which Mickey hears a racket in the night and goes downstairs to find the kitchen full of bakers (all of whom bear an uncanny resemblance to Oliver Hardy), busy stirring the batter for the breakfast cake. After successive adventures in which he falls into the batter, and later makes his escape in an aeroplane made out of dough, Mickey ends up back in bed, fast asleep. This is one of those books whose appeal is impossible to categorize, but which has become a firm favourite with generations of children.

IT'S A SHOELACE!
. . . .

by Sue Hendra (Bloomsbury Children's Books, 1996)
Interest level: 3–5/Reading age: 5+

WHAT is the strange green string running through this book? Is it spaghetti? Or a funny kind of toothpaste? Or could it be something even more fun – like a shoelace to practise tying your shoes with? Sue Hendra's ingenious design, which invites young children to 'follow the shoelace' through the book, makes reading – and learning to tie a neat bow – into an enjoyable game.

JASPER'S BEANSTALK

by Nick Butterworth; illustrated by Mick Inkpen
(Hodder & Stoughton, 1992)
Interest level: 2–5/Reading age: 5+

O N Monday Jasper the kitten finds a bean; on Tuesday he plants it, on Wednesday he waters it and so on all through the week – until Monday comes round again. Disappointed that the bean has not yet grown, Jasper digs it up again and throws it away in disgust. Eventually, of course, the bean *does* grow – providing a gentle message about the rewards of patience to end this appealing story.

OTHER BOOKS BY NICK BUTTERWORTH
One Snowy Night; *Baby Board Books* series; *A Year in Percy's Park*

JEREMIAH IN THE DARK WOODS

by Allan Ahlberg; illustrated by Janet Ahlberg (Puffin, 1989)
Interest level: 4–7/Reading age: 5+

W HEN Jeremiah Obadiah Jackanory Jones goes into the Dark Woods in search of his grandmother's stolen tarts, he encounters a whole host of favourite nursery characters, from the Three Bears to the Knave of Hearts, some of whom help and some of whom hinder him in his quest . . . The Ahlbergs' delightful book mixes traditional tales with contemporary humour, in a story designed to encourage young readers to develop their skills.

OTHER BOOKS BY JANET AND ALLAN AHLBERG
Peepo!; *The Baby's Catalogue*; *Each Peach Pear Plum*; *The Jolly Postman*; *Funnybones*; *Burglar Bill*

JUICE THE PIG

by Martine Osborne; illustrated by Axel Scheffler
(Macmillan, 1996)
Interest level: 1–5/Reading age: 6+

J UICE the Pig is very fond of hats. He has big hats, small hats, tall hats and feathery hats. What's more, he'll do anything to keep hold of his favourite hats – even walk into the jaws of a hungry crocodile! But then one day Juice learns that there are more important things than hats, and that sharing things can be as much fun as having them all to yourself. Axel Scheffler's jolly illustrations enhance the appeal of this gentle moral tale.

KIPPER'S TOYBOX
. . . .

by Mick Inkpen (Hodder, 1992)
Interest level: 2–5/Reading age: 5+

S OMETHING has been nibbling at Kipper's toybox – but what? Kipper determines to find out, and to make sure that none of his toys is missing . . .

OTHER BOOKS BY MICK INKPEN
Wibbly Pig; *Threadbear*; *Nothing*; *Penguin Small*; *Jojo's Revenge*

LION IN THE MEADOW, A
. . . .

by Margaret Mahy; illustrated by Jenny Williams
(Picture Puffin, 1969)
Interest level: 2–4/Reading age: 5+
ANIMALS ● FEARS

C LASSIC picture book about a little boy whose mother doesn't believe his story that there is a lion in the meadow behind their house, until the 'dragon' she has given him to chase the lion away turns out to be real, too! Jenny Williams's boldly stylized illustrations enhance the fantastical mood of the story, which offers consoling strategies for dealing with larger-than-life fears.

LITTLE BEAVER AND THE ECHO
. . . .

by Amy MacDonald; illustrated by Sarah Fox-Davies
(Walker Books, 1990)
Interest level: 4–7/Reading age: 6+
ANIMALS ● LONELINESS

L ITTLE Beaver lives alone by a big lake. He wishes more than anything that he could find a friend. One day, he is so sad and lonely that he starts to cry. But then he hears someone else crying too, on the other side of the lake, and decides to see if he can help. On the way, he encounters other animals, who agree to accompany him on his quest. By the end of his journey, he finds he is not as lonely as he thought. Amy MacDonald's sensitively told story addresses the very real problem of what to do when you need to find a friend, and is narrated in clear, uncomplicated language ideal for reading aloud and for new readers. Sarah Fox-Davies's delicate watercolour illustrations enhance the book's simple but direct appeal.

LITTLE BEAR'S TROUSERS
. . . .
by Jane Hissey (Red Fox, 1987)
Interest level: 2–6/Reading age: 6+
BEARS

LITTLE Bear has lost his trousers and is looking everywhere for them. Maybe some of the other toys can help? But Camel couldn't use them as hump-warmers and so gave them to Sailor, to make a sail for his boat. Sailor passed them on to Dog, to carry his bones in, and Dog gave them to Rabbit, to use as ear-warmers . . . Jane Hissey's nostalgically detailed illustrations of old-fashioned toys in household settings enhance the gentle humour of her story – one of a highly popular series.

LITTLE MONSTER DID IT!
. . . .
by Helen Cooper (Doubleday, 1995)
Interest level: 2–6/Reading age: 5
BABIES • SIBLINGS

A small girl copes with her anxieties about a new baby by blaming her friend 'Little Monster' (actually a favourite soft toy) when things mysteriously go wrong. Hot-water bottles leak, washbasins overflow, the video breaks and the baby is kept awake – all the fault of Little Monster. But just when it seems as if things will never settle down, Little Monster (and his young owner) decide that baby brother isn't so bad after all . . . An ideal present for a resentful sibling, to help cope with those new baby blues.

OTHER BOOKS BY HELEN COOPER
The Bear under the Stairs

LITTLE MONSTERS
. . . .

by Jan Pienkowski (Orchard Books, 1986)
Interest level: 2–6/Reading age: 5+
MONSTERS

B RILLIANT paper-engineering, combined with Pienkowski's dazzlingly colourful and imaginative inventions, makes this a classic of its kind. Young children love seeing each monster pop out – with the final surprise of the mirror-image on the last page! How many monsters can *you* find?

MAISY'S HOUSE
. . . .

by Lucy Cousins (Walker Books, 1995)
Interest level: 1–5/Reading age: 5+

L UCY Cousins's colourful books about Maisy the little mouse have already become established favourites with preschool children for their boldly stylish illustrations and engaging stories. In this pop-up version, the book becomes a house; other stories are presented in a more conventional format, incorporating simple text.

OTHER BOOKS BY LUCY COUSINS
Maisy Goes to Bed; *Maisy Goes Swimming*; *Maisy Goes to Playschool*; *Maisy's ABC*

MAX'S CHRISTMAS
. . . .

by Rosemary Wells (Collins, 1986)
Interest level: 3–6/Reading age: 5+

I T's Christmas Eve, and Max the baby rabbit and his sister Ruby are getting ready for bed. Max wants to stay up and see Santa Claus, but Ruby tells him he has to go to sleep – 'because nobody ever sees Santa Claus'. Eventually, after a long wait, Max does see Santa – or *does* he? One of a series of appealing picture story books for young readers, featuring the characters familiar from Wells's popular baby board books.

OTHER BOOKS BY ROSEMARY WELLS
Max's Dragon Shirt; *Max's Chocolate Chicken*

MAX'S FIRST WORD

by Rosemary Wells (Ernest Benn, 1979)
Interest level: 1–4/Reading age: 5+

FIRST in a much-loved series of board books featuring Max, the baby rabbit, and his big sister Ruby. In this one, Ruby encourages Max to say his first word, offering him various words to try – only to find that he has his own ideas about learning to talk! The delightful humour in these stories is instantly appealing, as are the charmingly expressive illustrations.

OTHER BOOKS IN THE SERIES
Max's Toys; *Max's Ride*; *Max's New Suit*; *Max's Bedtime*; *Max's Bath*; *Max's Breakfast*

MEG AND MOG

by Helen Nicoll; illustrated by Jan Pienkowski
(Heinemann, 1972)
Interest level: 2–4/Reading age: 5+
WITCHES

HELEN Nicoll's humorous stories about an incompetent witch and her friend Owl, combined with Jan Pienkowski's brilliantly colourful illustrations, have made this series one of the most popular for young readers. Children are fascinated by witches and witchcraft – especially when the magic is tempered by down-to-earth fun.

OTHER BOOKS IN THE SERIES
Mog at the Zoo; *Meg's Castle*; *Meg's Car*; *Meg's Veg*; *Mog's Mumps*

MIFFY

by Dick Bruna (Mammoth, from 1955)
Interest level: 1–4/Reading age: 5+

MIFFY the baby rabbit has been a favourite with the very young since the first books about her adventures started to appear over forty years ago. Bruna's distinctive style of illustration, using bold areas of flat colour and simple but striking shapes, revolutionized children's book design at the time and has been widely copied since. As well as the *Miffy* series, Dick Bruna has also produced alphabet and counting books, including the perennially popular *B is for Bear*.

MISTER MAGNOLIA
. . . .

by Quentin Blake (Random Century, 1980)
Interest level: 2–5/Reading age: 5+

L OVEABLY eccentric Mr Magnolia is a very happy man. He can juggle, play the trumpet and ride his scooter. He has a fine collection of newts and owls. Only one thing is missing which would make his happiness complete – a new boot. This is one of Quentin Blake's best-loved original works, as much for its engagingly anarchic pictures as for its quirky rhymes.

OTHER BOOKS BY QUENTIN BLAKE
How Tom Beat Captain Najork and His Hired Sportsmen, with Russell Hoban; *The Enormous Crocodile*, with Roald Dahl; *Mrs Armitage on Wheels*; *All Join In*; *Cockatoos*

MORRIS'S DISAPPEARING BAG
. . . .

by Rosemary Wells (Picture Puffin, 1975)
Interest level: 3–5/Reading age: 5+
SIBLINGS

I T's Christmas morning and Morris, the baby rabbit, is very excited about opening his presents. At first, he's happy with the new bear he's been given – but later, when he tries to share his new toy with his older brothers and sisters, they aren't interested. Worse than this, they won't share their exciting new toys with him. Then Morris finds a parcel which no one else has unwrapped. Inside is a magic Disappearing Bag ... Rosemary Wells's humorous story will appeal to any sibling who has ever wished their older brothers and sisters would disappear – even if it's only for an hour.

MR GUMPY'S OUTING

by John Burningham (Picture Puffin, 1970)
Interest level: 3–5/Reading age: 5+
ANIMALS

IT is a beautiful day, and Mr Gumpy decides to take a punt up the river. But then he finds that all his animal friends want to come along, too. Will they all fit in the punt, without capsizing it? First published over twenty-five years ago, John Burningham's gently humorous story and distinctively quirky illustrations have made this book and its sequel a favourite with young readers. The use of repetition – as in the steadily growing list of animals – is good reading practice.

OTHER BOOKS BY JOHN BURNINGHAM

Mr Gumpy's Motor Car; *Courtney*; *Cloudland*; *Avocado Baby*; *Granpa*; *Come Away from the Water, Shirley*; *Oi! Get Off Our Train*

MY CAT LIKES TO HIDE IN BOXES

by Eve Sutton; illustrated by Lynley Dodd (Picture Puffin, 1973)
Interest level: 2–4/Reading age: 5+
PETS

CATS from different countries around the world may like to do all kinds of clever and exotic things, but *my* cat – an ordinary stay-at-home kind of cat – likes to hide in boxes! Simple rhyming text with lots of repetition and appealingly comic illustrations make this a popular bedtime choice, as well as a good text for a young reader.

NOISY FARM

by Rod Campbell (Picture Puffin, 1990)
Interest level: 2–5/Reading age: 5+
ANIMALS

IN this attractive lift-the-flap picture book, small readers can follow Sam the dog around the farm, finding the hidden baby animals on every page and learning new sounds.

OTHER BOOKS BY ROD CAMPBELL

Buster's Day; *My Presents*; *Dear Zoo*; *Oh, Dear!*

NOISY NORA
. . . .

by Rosemary Wells (Picture Lions, 1976)
Interest level: 3–6/Reading age: 5+
SIBLINGS

C LASSIC picture story, told in rhyme, about a little mouse who gets tired of waiting while her parents' attention is given to elder sister and baby brother. One day, when all her attempts at getting herself noticed fail, Nora decides she's had enough. 'I'm leaving – and I'm never coming back,' she tells her family. With Nora gone, the house suddenly seems very quiet – but fortunately, she decides to give them all one more chance . . . Wells's story gently points up the difficulties of being a middle child.

NURSERY RHYMES
. . . .

Illustrated by Nicola Bayley (Puffin, 1975)
Interest level: 1–4/Reading age: 5+
POETRY

N ICOLA Bayley's intricately detailed illustrations have been much imitated in the years since this book was first published. Most of the favourite nursery rhymes are here – and they are given her distinctive treatment.

OTHER BOOKS ILLUSTRATED BY NICOLA BAYLEY
The Patchwork Cat; *The Tyger Voyage*

OH, DEAR!
. . . .

by Rod Campbell (Macmillan, 1989)
Interest level: 2–5/Reading age: 5+

B USTER goes down to the farmyard to fetch the eggs for Grandma. But this proves more complicated than it sounds . . . Lots of practice in word recognition in this jolly lift-the-flap story.

OTHER BOOKS BY ROD CAMPBELL
Dear Zoo; *Noisy Farm*; My Presents; *Buster's Day*

OI! GET OFF OUR TRAIN

by John Burningham (Cape, 1989)
Interest level: 3–6/Reading age: 5+
ANIMALS • ENVIRONMENT

A crowd of animals travels by train across a gradually darkening landscape. But where will their journey end? Burningham's surreal fantasy thoughtfully explores environmental and conservation issues, in a way even younger readers will understand.

OTHER BOOKS BY JOHN BURNINGHAM
Courtney; *Cloudland*; *Granpa*; *Avocado Baby*; *Come Away from the Water, Shirley*; *Mr Gumpy's Outing*; *Mr Gumpy's Motor Car*

ORLANDO THE MARMALADE CAT

by Kathleen Hale (Frederick Warne, 1938)
Interest level: 4–8/Reading age: 6+
ANIMALS

THE appeal of Kathleen Hale's charming picture books featuring an orange cat depends largely on the author's own illustrations, which perfectly complement the gentle humour of the text. The first story in what was to be an enduringly popular series introduces Orlando, his wife Grace and their three kittens; later stories find Orlando travelling abroad and even going to the moon.

OXFORD NURSERY BOOK, THE

Edited by Ian Beck (Oxford University Press, 1995)
Interest level: 1–4/Reading age: 5+
POETRY

THIS charmingly illustrated first anthology includes poems by William Blake, Christina Rossetti and Edward Lear as well as traditional favourites such as 'Little Bo-Peep' and 'Hickory, Dickory, Dock'.

PEEPO!
. . . .
by Janet and Allan Ahlberg (Picture Puffin, 1981)
Interest level: 2–6/Reading age: 5+
BABIES • WAR

THE Ahlbergs' classic picture book follows a baby through a single day, as he wakes up, has his breakfast, sits in his pushchair, goes to the park, has his tea and is eventually put to bed. The ingenious design of the book, in which each page has a hole through which the reader can peep into the next part of the story, is undoubtedly one reason for its tremendous popularity; another is the wonderful detail of Janet Ahlberg's illustrations, which are given added charm and poignancy by the fact that this particular story is set in wartime – inspired, according to Allan Ahlberg, by his own 1940s childhood.

OTHER BOOKS BY JANET AND ALLAN AHLBERG
Burglar Bill; *Each Peach Pear Plum*; *Funnybones*; *The Baby's Catalogue*; *The Ha Ha Bonk Book*; *Ten in a Bed*; *The Jolly Postman*; *The Jolly Christmas Postman*; *The Bear Nobody Wanted*; *Jeremiah in the Dark Woods*

PENGUIN SMALL
. . . .
by Mick Inkpen (Hodder, 1992)
Interest level: 2–5/Reading age: 5+
ANIMALS • FRIENDS

LEFT behind at the North Pole, when the rest of the penguins leave to escape being eaten by polar bears, Penguin Small is befriended by a kindly snowman, with whom he sets off on his travels. As delightfully illustrated as always, Mick Inkpen's charming adventure story is about friendship and overcoming fear.

OTHER BOOKS BY MICK INKPEN
Threadbear; *Nothing*; *Kipper's Toybox*; *Wibbly Pig*; *Jojo's Revenge*

PETER AND THE WOLF
. . . .

by Ian Beck (Picture Corgi, 1995)
Interest level: 4–6/Reading age: 6+
ANIMALS ● MUSIC

P RIZE-WINNING illustrator Ian Beck's retelling of Prokofiev's classic
children's story, in which a resourceful little boy outwits a hungry
wolf. An enjoyable introduction to the instruments of the orchestra.

POSTMAN PAT'S BREEZY DAY
. . . .

by John Cunliffe; illustrated by Celia Berridge (André Deutsch,
1985)
Interest level: 3–6/Reading age: 6+

T HE enduring appeal of John Cunliffe's jaunty postman and his black and
white cat is sometimes hard for adults to understand, but there is no
doubt that – stimulated by repeats of the television series – Pat and his chums
have a faithful following amongst the under-fives. In this fairly typical story,
Pat's task of delivering letters to the inhabitants of Greendale is complicated
by a strong wind, which scatters the letters and blows Pat's cap off his head.

OTHER BOOKS BY JOHN CUNLIFFE
Postman Pat to the Rescue; *Postman Pat's Foggy Day*; *Postman Pat's Rainy
Day*

PRINCESS SMARTYPANTS
. . . .

by Babette Cole (Picture Lions, 1988)
Interest level: 4–7/Reading age: 6+
GENDER STEREOTYPING ● HUMOUR

P RINCESS Smartypants isn't like the conventional idea of a princess at all.
She's independent and very, very clever – especially when it comes to
getting the better of the unsuitable suitors her parents keep inviting to the
castle . . . Babette Cole's wonderfully anarchic illustrations add to the fun of
this role-reversal story.

OTHER BOOKS BY BABETTE COLE
* The Bad Good Manners Book; ** The Smelly Book*; *The Slimy Book*; *Tarzanna*; ** The Trouble with Mum*; ** Mummy Laid an Egg*; *Hurrah for Ethlyn*

RAINBOW FISH TO THE RESCUE!

by Marcus Pfister (North-South Books, 1995)
Interest level: 3–6/Reading age: 5+

RAINBOW Fish feels sorry for his new friend the striped fish, because his scales are dull instead of shiny. But then a hungry shark swims by – and Rainbow Fish learns that friendship is about feelings, not looks.

ROSIE'S BABIES

by Martin Waddell; illustrated by Penny Dale (Walker Books, 1990)
Best Books for Babies Award/Shortlisted for Kate Greenaway Medal
Interest level: 3–6/Reading age: 6+
BABIES • SIBLINGS

As four-year-old Rosie watches her mum putting the baby to bed, she tells her about *her* babies (her toy bear and rabbit), describing what they like to do and how she looks after them – by reading them stories and telling them she loves them. Occupied with the new baby, Rosie's mum finds time to ask Rosie about her babies – and Rosie is happy to answer, until the moment she decides that she wants to talk about herself for a change! Penny Dale's enchanting illustrations of a small girl and her mother capture the spirit of Martin Waddell's sensitive exploration of sibling rivalries. Rosie clearly loves her babies – and her new sibling – but she also needs reassurance that she is special.

ROSIE'S WALK

by Pat Hutchins (Puffin, 1969)
Interest level: 2–4/Reading age: 5+

ILLUSTRATED with the author's distinctive, quirky drawings, this delightfully comic story about a hen who unwittingly leads a predatory fox into one disaster after another has become an established favourite with young readers. The simple, pared-down text makes this a good choice for a first reading book.

OTHER BOOKS BY PAT HUTCHINS
Titch; *Goodnight, Owl!*; *Which Witch is Which?*

RUB-A-DUB-DUB

Compiled by Ernest Henry; illustrated by Joanna Walsh
(Bloomsbury Children's Books, 1997)
Interest level: 0–4/Reading age: 5 +
POETRY

TRADITIONAL verses, action rhymes and counting games – Ernest Henry's collection has something for everyone. Babies and toddlers will love acting out the accompaniment to favourites such as 'The Grand Old Duke of York' and 'Round and Round the Garden', as well as lots of less familiar games.

RUBY AND THE PARCEL BEAR

by Maggie Glen (Hutchinson, 1995)
Interest level: 3–6/Reading age: 6 +
BEARS

RUBY, the spotted teddy bear, knows she is special – after all, she is Susie's favourite toy. But when Albert, a brand-new bear, arrives for Susie's birthday, Ruby starts to wonder if she has been displaced in Susie's affections. According to Albert, only the best kinds of bears come in parcels – so Ruby decides that she, too, will become a parcel bear! Maggie Glen's indomitable heroine wins the day, in a story designed to appeal to teddy bear fans of all ages.

RUFF

by Jane Hissey (Red Fox, 1996)
Interest level: 3–6/Reading age: 6 +

JANE Hissey's gently nostalgic stories about Little Bear, Jolly Tall and others, with their lovingly detailed coloured-pencil illustrations of the assorted soft toys which make up her nursery world, have gained her as much of a following among parents as among children. In this latest story, featuring

Ruff the dog, the toys arrange a series of birthday parties for their new friend, who has never had a birthday before. The story has its moments of quiet humour, but – as with Hissey's previous books – it is the pictures which are the real delight.

SNOWMAN, THE
. . . .
by Raymond Briggs (Hamish Hamilton, 1978)
Interest level: 2–4/no text

A boy builds a snowman in his garden. In the night, the snowman comes to life, and he and the boy explore the house together, before setting off on a magical midnight journey. Told entirely in pictures, this appealing story – which has also been made into an award-winning cartoon – has become a favourite with generations of young children.

OTHER BOOKS BY RAYMOND BRIGGS
Father Christmas; *When the Wind Blows*; *The Man*

STARTING SCHOOL
. . . .
by Janet and Allan Ahlberg (Picture Puffin, 1990)
Interest level: 3–5/Reading age: 5+
SCHOOL

THE first day of school can be an intimidating experience but the Ahlbergs' book makes it seem less like an ordeal and more like fun. A new school also means new friends . . .

OTHER BOOKS BY JANET AND ALLAN AHLBERG
Peepo!; *The Baby's Catalogue*; *Each Peach Pear Plum*; *Funnybones*; *Burglar Bill*; *The Jolly Postman*

STAYING AT SAM'S

by Jenny Hessell; illustrated by Jenny Williams (Picture Lions, 1989)
Interest level: 3–6/Reading age: 5+
FAMILIES • FRIENDS

S TAYING at Sam's is 'like visiting another planet' – according to the young narrator of Jenny Hessell's touching story. For a start, everybody kisses everybody else all the time, and nobody seems to mind if you wander into the bathroom when they're on the loo or in the bath. It's all quite different from home, where everything's a lot quieter and people have their own space. Maybe one day Sam will come and stay – it might make a nice change for him! The subtle differences which make families interesting are seen through the eyes of a perceptive little boy, giving an insight into the lives of two contrasting families.

SUN IS A BRIGHT STAR, THE

by Ken Wilson-Max; illustrated by Sue Hendra (Bloomsbury Children's Books, 1995)
Interest level: 1–4/Reading age: 5+

A LMOST as soon as children can talk, they start wondering about the stars and planets, and what makes them work. This charmingly illustrated book, with its own pull-out mobile of the solar system, will appeal to any young child with a feeling of curiosity about our place in the universe.

SUNSHINE

by Jan Ormerod (Picture Puffin, 1981)
Interest level: 2–4/no text

J AN Ormerod's charming picture story without words has become a classic of its kind. A small girl wakes up in the morning, has her breakfast and gets herself dressed. The whole sequence is conveyed with the humour and sharpness of observation for which this artist has become renowned.

OTHER BOOKS BY JAN ORMEROD
Moonlight; *101 Things to Do with a Baby*

TALE OF PETER RABBIT, THE

by Beatrix Potter (Frederick Warne, 1902)
Interest level: 2–6/Reading age: 6+
ANIMALS

Since its publication almost a century ago, Beatrix Potter's story about a resourceful rabbit, and its companion volumes featuring other animal characters such as Mrs Tiggywinkle the hedgehog and Jemima Puddle-Duck, has achieved international recognition. *Peter Rabbit* alone has been translated into many different languages, each giving its own nuances to the story – 'Pierre Lapin', for example, displays an altogether more Gallic insouciance in his plundering of Mr McGregor's vegetable patch than the stolid English Peter. Although much imitated and occasionally surpassed in terms of anatomical accuracy, Potter's watercolour drawings of Peter and his friends have a delicacy and freshness which make them of lasting appeal to young children. It should, however, be borne in mind that these stories were written for a more robust age, when children were less likely to be upset by thoughts of Mr Rabbit being put in a pie by Mrs McGregor, or the intended fate of Jemima Puddle-Duck at the hands of the sinister Mr Tod.

OTHER STORIES BY BEATRIX POTTER
The Tale of Squirrel Nutkin; *The Tailor of Gloucester*; *The Tale of Benjamin Bunny*; *The Tale of Mrs Tiggywinkle*; *The Tale of Jemima Puddle-Duck*; *The Tale of the Flopsy Bunnies*

THREADBEAR

by Mick Inkpen (Hodder, 1993)
Interest level: 2–5/Reading age: 5+
BEARS

Poor Threadbear's squeaker has never worked properly. What he needs – if Father Christmas can arrange it – is a trip to the land where squeaker trees grow . . . An engagingly imperfect hero is the secret of this book's enormous appeal.

OTHER BOOKS BY MICK INKPEN
*Wibbly Pig; **Penguin Small*; **Nothing*; **Kipper's Toybox*; *Jojo's Revenge*

Through My Window
. . . .

by Tony Bradman; illustrated by Eileen Browne (Mammoth, 1986)
Interest level: 3–5/Reading age: 5+

Jo is ill and has to stay home from school. But there is no need to be bored, because she can see all kinds of interesting things from her window.

OTHER BOOKS BY TONY BRADMAN
*In a Minute; Wait and See; Dilly the Dinosaur

Timothy Goes to School
. . . .

by Rosemary Wells (Picture Puffin, 1981)
Interest level: 3–5/Reading age: 5+
SCHOOL

Timothy is looking forward to his first day at school. But when he meets know-it-all Claude, things don't seem quite so much fun any more. Every time Timothy tries to make friends, Claude thinks of a way of squashing him, until Timothy is just about ready to give up. But then he meets Violet, and suddenly school doesn't seem so unfriendly after all. Rosemary Wells's appealing story will strike a chord with any child who has ever felt left out of things.

Very Hungry Caterpillar, The
. . . .

by Eric Carle (Hamish Hamilton, 1969)
Interest level: 2–5/Reading age: 5+

Eric Carle's boldly colourful paintings and the ingenious design of his classic picture book have made this a firm favourite with generations of young children. An egg hatches into a tiny and very hungry caterpillar. On Monday he eats his way through an apple, on Tuesday he eats through two pears and so on all through the week and – literally – through the book, until the final page, when the caterpillar leaves his cocoon to become a beautiful butterfly. Children love following the caterpillar's progress as he munches his way through an increasingly outlandish list of food, practising their reading, counting and naming skills as they go.

VERY VISIBLE MOUSE, THE

by Anne Merrick; illustrated by Tessa Richardson-Jones
(Bloomsbury Children's Books, 1995)
Interest level: 4–7/Reading age: 5+

Attractive lift-the-flap book about the adventures of Calamity Mouse and her friends who live under the floorboards, in the cupboards and behind the curtains of an old-fashioned house.

WE'RE GOING ON A BEAR HUNT

by Michael Rosen; illustrated by Helen Oxenbury
(Walker Books, 1989)
Interest level: 2–5/Reading age: 5+
BEARS

The rhythmic repetitions and onomatopoeic refrains of Michael Rosen's jaunty tale make this a favourite choice for bedtimes. Helen Oxenbury's lyrical and charming illustrations, showing the different kinds of terrain the family in the story must cross in order to find the bear, are an essential part of the appeal. Young children love following the journey from home to the bear's cave – and then back again – making all the appropriate noises along the way! The final picture, in which the whole family are tucked up safe in bed, leaves the child with a comforting image to offset the scariness of the adventure.

WHAT IS THE MOON?

by Caroline Dunant; illustrated by Liz Loveless (Red Fox, 1993)
Interest level: 3–6/Reading age: 6+

Looking up at the moon makes a little girl ask lots of questions which her mum tries to answer – only to be asked another question! Liz Loveless's boldly atmospheric illustrations give an added appeal to the rhyming text, which is good for reading aloud.

WHEN THE TEDDY BEARS CAME

by Martin Waddell; illustrated by Penny Dale (Walker Books,
1994)
Interest level: 3–7/Reading age: 6+
BABIES

P ENNY Dale's exquisite illustrations perfectly match Martin Waddell's
sensitive text, in this story about a small boy's view of the effect on
the household of a new baby. As more and more visitors come to see the
baby, the number of teddy bears increases, until there is almost no room for
Tom on the sofa. But then Mum gives the baby to Dad to look after, so that
she and Tom can look after the bears! The feelings of a child, anxious about
being displaced in his parents' affections by a new arrival, are conveyed with
great sympathy and warmth. The book's reassuring message, which is that
caring is something everyone can participate in, is equally subtle.

WHERE'S MY TEDDY?

by Jez Alborough (Walker Books, 1992)
Interest level: 2–6/Reading age: 5+
BEARS

E DDY loses his teddy, Freddy, and goes to look for him in the woods.
There he finds a bear that looks just like Freddy, only of gigantic size.
While he is wondering how he is ever going to get this giant Freddy home, he
hears the sound of sobbing. It's a bear who has lost his own teddy and found
Eddy's little Freddy instead. The boy and the bear swop teddies without
further ado and run home to their beds, both very glad to have escaped
unscathed! Delightful pictures and a clear, rhyming text give young readers
lots of incentive to persevere.

WHERE'S SPOT?

by Eric Hill (Heinemann, 1980)
Interest level: 2–4/Reading age: 5+

F IRST in the series of early learning classics, this colourfully illustrated lift-
the-flap book encourages young readers to look for Spot, the mis-
chievous puppy, and to meet all his other friends along the way.

OTHER BOOKS BY ERIC HILL
Spot's First Walk; *Spot's Birthday*; *Spot Goes to School*

WIBBLY PIG
. . . .

by Mick Inkpen (Hodder, 1995)
Interest level: 1–5/Reading age: 5+

MICK Inkpen's appealing picture book captures the adventures of a loveable little pig in his inimitable quirky style.

OTHER BOOKS BY MICK INKPEN
Kipper's Toybox; *Nothing*; *The Blue Balloon*; *Penguin Small*; *Threadbear*; *Jojo's Revenge*

WINTER BEAR, THE
. . . .

by Ruth Craft and Erik Blegvad (Picture Lions, 1974)
Interest level: 3–5/Reading age: 5+

ATTRACTIVE illustrations featuring three children in a winter landscape are the main feature of this appealing picture book, in which a lost teddy bear is rescued from a hedge and taken home to warmth and safety. Clear text and simple rhymes make this a good choice for early readers.

WORRIED ARTHUR
. . . .

by Joan Stimson; illustrated by Jan Lewis (Ladybird, 1994)
Interest level: 3–7/Reading age: 6+
FEARS

ARTHUR the baby penguin is a terrible worrier. He worries about whether he will grow as tall as his father. He worries because his feathers stand on end. Most of all, he worries about Christmas . . . Joan Stimson's humorous story will strike a chord with many parents of over-anxious children. Here, as in the other books in the series, Arthur learns that sometimes it's best to let grown-ups do the worrying.

YEAR IN PERCY'S PARK, A

by Nick Butterworth (Collins, 1995)
Interest level: 3–6/Reading age: 6+

THIS anthology of four stories – 'One Snowy Night', 'The Secret Path', 'The Rescue Party' and 'After the Storm' – about Percy the park-keeper and his animal friends shows the changes which take place in Percy's park over the year. In the first story, Percy rescues some animals from the snow; in the second, he has to find his way out of the park's maze. Each story is accompanied by a large fold-out picture featuring a different aspect of the changing seasons. Younger children will enjoy the delicate line-and-wash illustrations, and the clearly laid-out text is designed to encourage early readers.

OTHER BOOKS BY NICK BUTTERWORTH

Jasper's Beanstalk; *Baby Board Books*; *The Cross Rabbit*

Primary School – Developing Reading Skills

YEAR ONE: 5–6 YEARS

In the first few weeks after starting school, a child has a lot to cope with – making friends and getting used to a full school day, and becoming familiar with a whole range of new experiences. Reading – perhaps the most versatile and useful skill your child will ever learn – has to take its place with all the other essential skills, from adding and subtracting to tying shoelaces, which she will be acquiring during this period.

Many Reception Class teachers like to establish the reading habit as soon as possible by encouraging the children to take a book home with them, in order to continue the reading they have done in class. Most five-year-olds are only too delighted to have a 'grown-up' reading book and a bag or folder with their name on it to carry to and from school every day. In fact, in my experience, most five-year-olds can't wait to learn to read. Whatever other difficulties one encounters at this stage, lack of enthusiasm isn't one of them! And for a child who is used to hearing stories read at home, the transition to hearing stories read by her teacher – and, eventually, to reading for herself – will seem less of a change and more of a natural progression.

So what kind of books are going to help your child to read? Is there any advantage in using a reading scheme rather than relying on 'real' books?

Opinions vary more widely on this question than on almost any other aspect of the reading process. My own view is that, while reading is a lot to do with recognizing shapes of words and matching them with sounds – the building-block idea of learning to read, around which many reading schemes are structured – there is more to it than that. Reading is also about *comprehension* – in other words, using a combination of common sense and inspired guesswork to arrive at a particular meaning. Teaching your child to 'sound' each word as she goes is of course an essential part of learning to read, but it can be terribly laborious. Nothing is more likely to quench a child's enthusiasm for reading than the idea that it is hard work or, worse, that it is boring.

When choosing a book for your child to read at home, it is important to bear in mind what reading is *for*. Children enjoy reading for all the reasons that adults enjoy reading: to learn more about the world, to discover the unexpected, to find out what happens next. Stories with plenty of humour and strong characterization, as well as those which reflect aspects of the child's own life – such as starting school or making friends – are popular with this age group.

But the most important rule when choosing books for young readers is that there are no rules. Young readers – like their grown-up counterparts – have a very wide range of tastes. Some like books about frogs, others will only read books which feature princesses. It doesn't matter in the least what the book is about, as long as it gets them hooked.

For very new readers, a simple text of no more than two or three words per page and with clear, unambiguous illustrations is more useful than one with complicated sentences and too much confusing detail. As the child's reading skills develop, a text mixing more difficult words and phrases with simpler ones with which the child is already familiar helps establish reading confidence.

Some parents adopt a systematic approach to reading practice, setting aside a certain amount of time each day and working through a particular text or series of texts; others prefer a more wide-ranging approach, perhaps mingling simpler stories which the child can read herself with more complex material. Whichever approach you favour, it is important to keep in mind that reading should be fun. It is a skill which, once acquired, will remain with your child for the whole of her life, not just for her school career. So it is essential that she should think of it as a pleasure, not a chore.

YEAR TWO: 6–7 YEARS

By the age of six and a half or seven, most children have acquired basic reading skills and can manage simple texts with short sentences. Some will already be reading quite complex texts, extending their vocabulary with what seems like breathtaking speed. Others find the process considerably more laborious; for these children, learning to read can often seem more like hacking one's way through an impenetrable jungle than striding confidently over the sunlit uplands. It's a boring, unrewarding slog – and let's face it, there are so many more exciting things they want to do with their time, such as climbing trees or making that model rocket they saw on *Blue Peter*.

Don't despair if your child is not a natural reader. As with most of life's skills, there's more than one way of going about it. If your seven-year-old prefers making and doing to reading, then help is at hand. With the wonderful range of books available for budding artists, scientists, chefs, zoologists, botanists and gardeners, there's no reason at all why they should read anything else – as long as you make it clear how much sooner they can get to grips with making that dinosaur mask or paper aeroplane if they can read the instructions themselves.

The same applies to young explorers, ballet dancers, sports fanatics and collectors. This is an age when children often develop a passion for one particular interest. Some of these enthusiasms can last for years, while others fizzle out after a few weeks. But whatever the craze – horses, classic cars or bug-collecting – you can be sure there's a book about it. Any child with an enthusiasm is a child who, sooner or later, is going to want to read.

YEAR THREE: 7–8 YEARS

By the age of eight, children are looking for a lot more sophistication from their stories. The gentle tales of nursery animals and everyday experiences which kept them enthralled at five and six will start to seem a bit tame. This is the age of exploration – of finding out as much as you can about a whole range of other subjects, and other worlds. Stories of adventure and fantasy, of danger and magic, are what seven- and eight-year-olds want to read; challenging stories, which open up all kinds of potential, both linguistically and in terms of ideas.

However fluent a reader your child may have become by the age of eight, it is still helpful to continue the bedtime story habit, if at all possible. Even the most competent reader will find certain vocabulary beyond them at this age, and it would be a pity for your child to miss out on, say, the delights of *Alice in Wonderland* or the *Narnia* stories because her own skills were not up to reading these books for herself. Of course there will be times when your child will prefer reading independently – and it goes without saying that this is not to be discouraged! But it is essential to combine this with a regular bedtime story read by the parent, which can be returned to night after night, and which will give a child a perspective into future reading pleasures.

ACE DRAGON LTD

by Russell Hoban; illustrated by Quentin Blake (Red Fox, 1980)
Interest level: 7–10/Reading age: 7+
DRAGONS

WHEN John meets a dragon on the Underground wearing two pairs of Wellington boots, his adventures have just begun. He finds out all the things that dragons can do (and some of the things they can't). They can fly, and do sky-writing, and even spin gold into straw – a useful skill when you need to find a soft landing in a hurry! Russell Hoban's delightfully humorous tale is perfect for reading aloud, and for young readers to practise their skills. Quentin Blake's lively illustrations add to the fun.

ALFIE TREASURY, THE

by Shirley Hughes (Bodley Head, 1995)
Interest level: 5–8/Reading age: 5+
FAMILIES • SIBLINGS

THE collection includes 'Alfie Gets In First', 'Alfie's Feet', 'Alfie Gives a Hand' and 'An Evening at Alfie's'. Shirley Hughes's endearing little boy and his baby sister, Annie-Rose, are amongst her best-loved creations – as much for the down-to-earth realism with which they are portrayed as for the things they say and do. In the first story, for example, Alfie manages to lock himself inside the family home, with his mother and sister outside. A string of passers-by ranging from the milkman to Mrs MacNally's Maureen try to rescue him, but in the end (to his great self-satisfaction) Alfie opens the door by himself. Shirley Hughes has the gift of making ordinary situations seem interesting and amusing. Her lovingly detailed illustrations of family life have been widely imitated but seldom surpassed. Originally published in the early 1980s, the 'Alfie' stories have become classics.

OTHER BOOKS BY SHIRLEY HUGHES
Helpers; *Dogger*; *Moving Molly*; *Stories by Firelight*

ALGERNON AND OTHER CAUTIONARY TALES

by Hilaire Belloc; illustrated by Quentin Blake (Red Fox, 1991)
Interest level: 6–10/Reading age: 9+
HUMOUR • POETRY

HILAIRE Belloc's splendidly anarchic verses about bad girls and boys and the dreadful fates which befall them – first published in 1907 – are perfectly complemented by Quentin Blake's witty illustrations. Children will revel in the horrid tale of Algernon, Who Played with a Loaded Gun, of Jim, Who Ran Away from his Nurse and was Eaten by a Lion, of Rebecca, Who Slammed Doors for Fun and Perished Miserably and other equally frightful stories. Originally written as a parody of the moralistic tracts of the late-Victorian era, these poems have become essential reading for generations of children, as much for their wonderfully sonorous vocabulary as for their gruesome humour.

ALICE'S ADVENTURES IN WONDERLAND

by Lewis Carroll; illustrated by Sir John Tenniel
(Macmillan, 1866)
Interest level: 5–adult/Reading age: 8+
ADVENTURE • FANTASY • MAGIC • VICTORIANS

FIRST published over a hundred years ago, Lewis Carroll's classic story and its companion volume *Through the Looking Glass* set a standard for children's fiction which has never been surpassed, although they have inspired many imitations. In the famous opening sequence, Alice, a little girl aged about seven, is sitting on a meadow bank with her elder sister, who is reading, when she sees a white rabbit with pink eyes run past, evidently in a great hurry. Alice follows, and falls down a rabbit-hole, which takes her to an extraordinary underground world, where nothing is ever quite what it seems. There she meets a variety of curious characters, ranging from a hookah-smoking caterpillar to a Cheshire Cat, and finds herself growing alternately very small and very large. After an encounter with the Duchess whose baby turns into a pig, and a visit to the Mad Hatter's tea party, Alice arrives at last at the court of the King and Queen of Hearts, where she takes part in a very strange game of croquet. After this, Alice finds herself giving evidence in an even stranger trial, in which the Knave of Hearts stands accused of stealing the tarts made by the irascible Queen. The book ends as Alice wakes from her dream and tells her sister all her adventures.

Alice in Wonderland is one of those books which can shape a child's understanding of the world for ever. The playful humour with which the ideas are conveyed means that even quite complex philosophical concepts of identity and perception can be grasped by young readers. The punning language games with which the book is filled are another delight; as indeed is the character of Alice herself – the paradigm of the resourceful and intelligent heroine. Although there have been many attempts to match them (not least by David Hockney), Tenniel's illustrations are an essential part of the enjoyment of both *Alice* books, perfectly complementing Lewis Carroll's witty and elegant prose.

AMAZING GRACE
. . . .

by Mary Hoffman; illustrated by Caroline Binch
(Frances Lincoln, 1995)
Interest level: 5–8/Reading age: 6+
FAMILIES ● RACIAL STEREOTYPES

G RACE, a little Afro-Caribbean girl growing up in London, loves singing and dancing and playing imaginative games. But sometimes her imagination is checked by other people's *lack* of imagination. Fortunately, her mum and nana show her that you can be anything you want to be if you put your mind to it. Caroline Binch's sensitive illustrations help convey the book's message without stridency.

OTHER BOOKS BY MARY HOFFMAN
* *Grace and Family*

ANGELO
. . . .

by Quentin Blake (Picture Lions, 1970)
Interest level: 5–8/Reading age: 7+

C HARMINGLY illustrated by the author, this story about Angelo, a young acrobat who travels around Italy with his family, and Angelina, the poor little girl he rescues from a life of drudgery, has remained a favourite with young readers since it was first published. Clear, simple text and expressive pictures make this a good choice for reading practice.

ANGUS RIDES THE GOODS TRAIN
· ·

by Alan Durant; illustrated by Chris Riddell (Viking, 1996)
Interest level: 5–8/Reading age: 8+
ENVIRONMENT

A FTER he has gone to bed at night, Angus rides the Goods Train, laden with milk and honey and good things to eat for a country far, far away. On the journey, they pass a forest of withered trees – but there is no water to spare; later, they pass a mother with her sick child, but the train driver refuses to stop. This happens again and again in the course of the journey, with the train driver making excuses each time to avoid helping the needy, until Angus decides he must take charge of the Goods Train himself ... Alan Durant's thought-provoking fable deals with concepts of fairness and sharing that even younger children will understand. Chris Riddell's imaginative and slightly unsettling illustrations sensitively underline the message.

BEAR CALLED PADDINGTON, A
· ·

by Michael Bond (Armada Lions, 1958)
Interest level: 4–8/Reading age: 8+
BEARS

'THE bear puffed out its chest. "I'm a very rare sort of bear," he replied, importantly. "There aren't many of us left where I come from." ' Michael Bond's loveably pedantic character has been a favourite with children since the first book of his adventures was published in 1958, spawning a whole industry of Paddington books, Paddington toys and Paddington collectables. In this original story, he is discovered by Mr and Mrs Brown on Paddington station, as they are about to meet their daughter Judy's train on her return home from boarding school for the holidays. (Details such as this, which establish the Browns as belonging to the affluent middle class of the period, are elided in subsequent stories.) The newly christened Paddington (his own, Peruvian name is much too hard for anyone to understand) is taken back to the Browns' house at 32, Windsor Gardens, to meet Jonathan, Judy's brother, and Mrs Bird, the housekeeper. Once adopted into the household, he has to cope with various new experiences – having a bath, travelling on the Underground and shopping in a department store. On each occasion he leaves chaos in his wake. Paddington belongs to a tradition of fictional bears, beginning with Winnie the Pooh, who combine an appealing cuddliness with a resourceful approach to events.

OTHER BOOKS BY MICHAEL BOND
More About Paddington; *Paddington Goes to Town*; *Paddington Helps Out*

BEAR DANCE, THE

by Chris Riddell (Mammoth, 1990)
Interest level: 5–8/Reading age: 7+
BEARS

K ATYA and her best friend Brown – a big, brown bear – live in a forest where it is always summer. They like climbing trees and paddling in the river – but most of all, they like dancing. They can do lots of different dances, but the one they like the most is the Bear Dance – a 'stomping, shouting, growling, thumping, stamping, jumping-in-the-air' kind of dance! One day, Katya wakes up in her tree-top bed to find that Jack Frost has invaded the forest, and won't go away. It is his forest now, he tells her. But then Katya has the clever idea of asking him to dance with her – because everyone knows that dancing can make you very hot indeed . . . Chris Riddell's attractive illustrations add to the charm of his summer and winter fable.

BIG BABY, THE

by Anthony Browne (Julia McRae, 1993)
Interest level: 8–10/Reading age: 8+
GROWING UP

B ROWNE's cautionary tale about a man who tries so hard to be young that he ends up as a big baby is a picture book, illustrated with the author's distinctively surreal paintings, but its message seems aimed at a much older readership than the one implied by its format. The alarming nature of what happens when youthful Mr Young reverts to babyhood is not glossed over – although, as ever with this author, the element of real threat adds to the fun.

BURGLAR BILL
. . . .

by Janet and Allan Ahlberg (Picture Lions, 1977)
Interest level: 5–8/Reading age: 6+

THE Ahlbergs' witty tale about a burglar whose comfortable existence is disturbed when he inadvertently steals a baby – and is forced to admit that maybe crime doesn't pay – has been a favourite with children since it was first published. Young readers will enjoy the anarchic humour, and will find the use of repetition helpful in gaining reading confidence.

CAPTAIN PUGWASH
. . . .

by John Ryan (Bodley Head, from 1950)
Interest level: 6–9/Reading age: 7+
HUMOUR/PIRATES

JOHN Ryan's appealingly rotund pirate and his crew have been appearing in comic strip and book form since the 1950s, and a number of the stories have been adapted for television. The situations vary but the underlying joke remains the same: Pugwash and the rest of the crew of *The Black Pig* pretend to be brave but are terrified by danger (particularly when it takes the form of Pugwash's old adversary, Cut-throat Jake); only Tom the Cabin Boy is brave enough to confront the enemy. As with *The Adventures of King Rollo*, the appeal of Ryan's hero is that he is a grown-up who behaves like a child, while the only real child in the story – Tom – is the one whose courage and cleverness wins the day.

OTHER BOOKS BY JOHN RYAN
The Quest of the Golden Handshake; *Captain Pugwash and the Huge Reward*

CAT IN THE HAT, THE
. . . .

by Dr Seuss (Collins, 1957)
Interest level: 6–8/Reading age: 6+

THE first of Dr Seuss's Beginner Books, designed to help young readers, was an instant success on its first publication in the United States and Britain, and has remained popular ever since. The combination of zany, rhyming text and appealingly quirky illustrations has proved durable, and generations of children have learned to read using Seuss's enticingly enjoyable system. *The Cat in the Hat* was followed by many others, including the engagingly surreal *Oh, the Places You'll Go!* and *How the Grinch Stole Christmas*, which have become classics in their own right.

OTHER BOOKS BY DR SEUSS
The Sneetches; *The Sleep Book*; *McElligot's Pool*; *I Can Lick 30 Tigers Today!*; *Green Eggs and Ham*

CHARLOTTE'S WEB
. . . .

by E.B. White; illustrated by Garth Williams (Puffin, 1952)
Interest level: 8–10/Reading age: 8+
ANIMALS ● DEATH

FERN is a little girl with an unusual pet – a pig called Wilbur, whom she has looked after since he was a tiny piglet. One day, Wilbur learns that he may be sent to market to be killed and eaten. Just how is he going to escape this terrible fate? Fortunately, Wilbur has a number of friends on the farm, apart from Fern. There is Templeton, the rat – and there is Charlotte. Charlotte is a small grey spider who lives in a corner of the barn doorway. When Charlotte learns what is going to happen to Wilbur, she decides to intervene, by spinning a remarkable web ... E.B. White's classic tale of courage and ingenuity has been a favourite with children for over forty years. Apart from its other pleasures, it offers a clear demonstration of the advantages of being able to read and write!

CHILDREN OF GREEN KNOWE, THE
. . . .

by Lucy M. Boston; illustrated by Peter Boston (Puffin, 1954)
Interest level: 7–10/Reading age: 9+
LONELINESS ● MAGIC

WHEN seven-year-old Tolly arrives at his great-grandmother's house, Green Knowe, it is quite unlike anything he has expected. For a start, the rooms are full of strange and magical things – rocking-horses and dolls' houses and empty birdcages. What is more, the inhabitants of the rooms seem only just to have left them – even though Tolly and his great-grandmother,

Mrs Oldknow, are the house's sole occupants. Mrs Oldknow – who is so old she might be a witch, Tolly thinks – doesn't seem surprised when he tells her he has caught glimpses of Alexander and Toby and Linnet, the children who lived in the house many years ago. But then Mrs Oldknow is no ordinary great-grandmother . . . Lucy M. Boston's haunting story, the first of a series, is one of the most evocative accounts of childhood ever written. Like *The Secret Garden*, which it echoes, it offers a vivid insight into the isolation children can feel, and into the way that loneliness can be dispelled by the power of the imagination.

OTHER BOOKS BY LUCY M. BOSTON
The Chimneys of Green Knowe; *The River at Green Knowe*; *A Stranger at Green Knowe*; *An Enemy at Green Knowe*

CLEVER POLLY AND THE STUPID WOLF

by Catherine Storr; illustrated by Jill Bennett (Faber & Faber, 1955)
Interest level: 8–10/Reading age: 9+
HUMOUR

CATHERINE Storr's witty updating of the Little Red Riding Hood story has entertained young readers for over forty years. The central idea may be simple to the point of banality – the Wolf wants to eat Polly, but Polly does not want to be eaten – but the variations the author achieves on this theme are wonderfully ingenious. Every time the poor Wolf comes up with what he thinks is a foolproof scheme, he is outwitted by Polly. One even starts to feel sorry for him after a while.

OTHER BOOKS BY CATHERINE STORR
Polly and the Wolf Again; *Last Stories of Polly and the Wolf*

CLOUDLAND

by John Burningham (Jonathan Cape, 1996)
Interest level: 4–7/Reading age: 6+
DEATH

ALBERT is walking in the mountains with his parents when he falls over a cliff. His parents think he must be dead, but he is saved in the nick of time by the Cloud Children, who make him lighter than air. With his new-found friends, he floats up into the sky and enjoys some wonderful games – jumping up and down on piles of clouds, making loud noises in thunderstorms and painting pictures with all the colours of the rainbow. But then Albert starts thinking about his own home, and suddenly he knows he wants nothing more than to be back there again . . . Burningham's atmospheric tale combines his familiar eccentric drawings with actual photographs of clouds, to produce another innovative work.

COLLINS TREASURY OF POETRY

Selected by Stephanie Nettell; illustrated by Penny Dann
(Collins, 1995)
Interest level: 5–8/Reading age: 6+
POETRY

Fifty poems by classic children's authors such as Walter de la Mare, Robert Louis Stevenson and A. A. Milne – as well as verse by contemporary poets such as Ted Hughes and Roger McGough – make this a splendid introduction to the pleasures of poetry.

COLM OF THE ISLANDS

by Rosemary Harris; illustrated by Pauline Baynes
(Walker Books, 1989)
Interest level: 8–10/Reading age: 9+
FAIRY TALES

Exquisitely illustrated by *Pauline Baynes, Rosemary Harris's tale about a young turf-cutter on a Hebridean isle, who embarks on a dangerous mission to save his betrothed from the clutches of a giantess, has the feel of a traditional story. While some of the vocabulary may be too difficult for younger readers, older children with a liking for myth and legend will enjoy the story's timeless quality.

COME AWAY FROM THE WATER, SHIRLEY

by John Burningham (Red Fox, 1977)
Interest level: 5–8/Reading age: 5+
PIRATES

B URNINGHAM'S slyly humorous story about a little girl playing on the beach, in which the drearily nagging remarks of her mother are counterpointed by the child's own imagined scenes of pirates and adventure, has become a classic in the twenty years since it first appeared. The author's idiosyncratic pen-and-wash drawings are another delight – switching between Mum and Dad dozing in their deckchairs to Shirley's more colourful fantasies of skulduggery on the high seas.

DAY OF AHMED'S SECRET, THE

by Florence Parry Heide and Judith Heide Gilliland; illustrated by
Ted Lewin (Gollancz, 1990)
Interest level: 5–7/Reading age: 7+

T HE picturesque streets of Cairo provide the background to this touching story, in which Ahmed, a small boy who works all day delivering Calorgas canisters, finally arrives home to share the wonderful secret he has been waiting to tell his family: he can write his name.

DINOSAURS AND ALL THAT RUBBISH

by Michael Foreman (Picture Puffin, 1972)
Interest level: 5–8/Reading age: 5+
DINOSAURS • ENVIRONMENT

F OREMAN'S prescient 'green' fable has become a classic of its kind. A man sees a distant planet and wants to reach it. He puts all his energy, and that of the factories he owns, into building a rocket to reach the stars – with the result that he almost destroys the earth. But then the dinosaurs awaken from their long sleep, and decide to put things right. They break up the motorways and pull down the factories, so that the earth reverts to its natural, unspoiled state. When the man comes back he can't believe they have managed all this without him. He asks for a part of the planet to be returned to him, only to be told that it all belongs to him – and to everyone else.

This is a good book for class discussion of environmental issues, as well as for focusing on wider ideas about what it means to 'own' the planet.

DOGGER
by Shirley Hughes (Random Century, 1977)
Interest level: 5–8/Reading age: 5+
SIBLINGS

DAVE's favourite toy is a well-worn dog called Dogger. One day, Dogger gets lost and Dave is inconsolable. He and his mum and dad and big sister Bella search high and low, but Dogger can't be found. Then the missing toy turns up at the school fête, on a stall selling jumble. The only trouble is, a little girl has just bought him, and refuses to let Dave buy him back. But then big sister Bella comes to the rescue, by offering to swap her new teddy for her brother's long-lost Dogger. Shirley Hughes's story about a little boy's attachment to a special friend will strike a chord with most parents. The story's message about unselfishness is touchingly conveyed.

OTHER BOOKS BY SHIRLEY HUGHES
Helpers; *Moving Molly; *Alfie Gets in First

DON'T DO THAT!
by Tony Ross (Red Fox, 1991)
Interest level: 5–8/Reading age: 5+
HUMOUR

NELLIE has a very pretty nose. In fact, she even wins pretty nose competitions. But Nellie also has a bad habit, which is that she can't stop picking her nose – and one day her finger gets firmly stuck! Everyone tries to help, but nothing works . . . until the very last page. Tony Ross's hilarious illustrations add to the fun of this cautionary tale.

OTHER BOOKS BY TONY ROSS
*I Want My Potty; *Stone Soup; The Shop of Ghosts

EARTH GIANT, THE

by Melvin Burgess (Andersen Press, 1995)
Interest level: 7–10/Reading age: 8+
ADVENTURE • ENVIRONMENT

ONE night, seven-year-old Amy and her brother Peter are woken by a violent storm. Next morning when, at Amy's insistence, the children go to their favourite woods at Barrow Hill, they find that many trees have been torn up by the roots. Buried at the base of one of these, Amy finds the Earth Giant – an enormous woman with earth-coloured skin and wild black hair – who becomes her friend. Amy knows that Giant does not belong to this planet but to a far distant world, to which she must return. She also knows that she is the only person who can help Giant to do this.

Burgess's thoughtful novel – part science fiction, part ecological allegory – considers the relationship between human beings and the natural world, and will appeal to any child with an interest in environmental issues.

EMERALD BLUE

by Anne Marie Linden; illustrated by Katherine Doyle
(Heinemann, 1994)
Interest level: 5–8/Reading age: 6+

ANNE Marie Linden's vivid memories of growing up in her grandparents' house in Barbados provide the text for this wonderfully illustrated book, which celebrates the magic and mystery of childhood and conveys the sense of loss felt by the author as she looks back on an idyllic and now vanished world.

ENORMOUS CROCODILE, THE

by Roald Dahl; illustrated by Quentin Blake (Puffin, 1989)
Interest level: 6–9/Reading age: 6+
ANIMALS

DAHL's tale of a ferocious crocodile who likes nothing better than a juicy child for his lunch, but who is prevented from getting hold of one by the other animals in the jungle, is as gruesomely funny as all his work. Quentin Blake's illustrations are a delight.

OTHER BOOKS BY ROALD DAHL
Matilda; *Charlie and the Chocolate Factory*; *Charlie and the Great Glass Elevator*; *The Witches*; *The BFG*; *Fantastic Mr Fox*

EYE OF THE PHAROAH, THE

by Iain Smyth (Orchard Books, 1995)
Interest level: 8–11/Reading age: 9+

IN this 'pop-up Whodunnit', an ingenious lift-the-flap adventure offers three separate solutions. Young readers are invited to solve the mystery of the stolen jewel, the Eye of the Pharoah, following the clues throughout the book.

EXTRAORDINARY LIGHTEN-ING CONDUCTOR, THE

by Nicola Matthews; illustrated by Rachel Pearce (Bloomsbury Children's Books, 1995)
Interest level: 6–9/Reading age: 7+

WHEN Greg wakes up one morning, he finds something extraordinary has happened: suddenly he's lighter than air and he can't stop himself floating off the ground! At first it's a rather alarming feeling – and it makes getting dressed a bit of a problem – but after a while, Greg discovers that there may be advantages to being a 'lighten-ing conductor' . . . Nicola Matthews's engaging story will appeal to any child who has ever had day-dreams about flying away from it all. Clear, easy-to-read text and attractive illustrations make this a good choice for young readers consolidating their skills.

FAMOUS FIVE, THE

by Enid Blyton (Hodder, from 1942)
Interest level: 8–11/Reading age: 8+
ADVENTURE

ORIGINALLY intended to consist of six books, the *Famous Five* series about a group of children enjoying a variety of adventures eventually ran to twenty-one, of which the last appeared in the early 1960s. The formula in each case is the same: four children – Julian, Dick, Anne and 'George'

(Georgiana) – and Timmy the dog are on holiday together at the seaside, where they invariably encounter a group of villains whose dastardly deeds they expose. Like their companion series *The Secret Seven*, the *Famous Five* books have been enduringly popular with young readers, although perhaps less so with adults.

OTHER BOOKS BY ENID BLYTON
The Secret Seven; *Best Stories for Five-Year-Olds*; *Best Stories for Six-Year-Olds*; *Best Stories for Seven-Year-Olds*; *Best Stories for Eight-Year-Olds*

FATHER CHRISTMAS
. . . .
by Raymond Briggs (Picture Puffin, 1973)
Interest level: 5–8/Reading age: 6+
HUMOUR

B RIGGS's comic-strip account of Father Christmas's preparations for Christmas Eve – his busiest night of the year – has an earthy humour which has appealed to generations of children. Despite the fact that he is depicted as grumpy and all too human, Father Christmas retains enough of his magic to fly, landing his sleigh on some unlikely rooftops – including that of Buckingham Palace.

OTHER BOOKS BY RAYMOND BRIGGS
*The Snowman; *Fungus the Bogeyman*

FINN FAMILY MOOMINTROLL
. . . .
by Tove Jansson (Puffin, 1948)
Interest level: 8–10/Reading age: 8+

T HESE engagingly quirky tales, first published in the author's native Norway, remain very popular with young readers – most recently because they have been animated for television. Moomin, a quaint troll-like figure, lives with his Moominmamma and Moominpapa in peaceful Moomin Valley. Here, he has adventures with his friends Snuffkin and the Snork, and the charming Snork Maiden – adventures which nearly always turn into magic. In this volume, Moomin and his friends find a top hat belonging to a Hobgoblin, which changes anything placed inside it into something completely different. Eggshells turn into clouds, words into small furry creatures and a river into strawberry juice. After this, it is only a matter of time before the Hobgoblin appears, to claim his rightful property . . .

OTHER BOOKS BY TOVE JANSSON
Tales from Moomin Valley; *Moominsummer Madness*

FOUR SEASONS OF BRAMBLY HEDGE, THE

by Jill Barklem (Collins, 1980)
Interest level: 3–8/Reading age: 7+
ANIMALS

THIS collection includes 'Spring Story', 'Summer Story', 'Autumn Story' and 'Winter Story'. First published in 1980 and hugely successful since, Jill Barklem's series of tales about a community of mice living in a hedgerow employs a self-consciously anachronistic style, both in its meticulously detailed illustrations of country life (a mixture of Beatrix Potter and Alison Uttley) and in its content. No one reading them would guess that they were written in the 1980s and not a hundred years before. Rustic pursuits are assiduously followed and the hierarchies of social station upheld, with Lord and Lady Woodmouse presiding at the Old Oak Palace and Dusty Dogwood at the flour mill. Barklem's illustrations are charming and her stories appealing enough, but some parents may feel that she has tried too hard to make these books instant classics. Despite their obvious attraction for very young children, who adore all the intricate detail, there is something rather anodyne about them.

OTHER BOOKS BY JILL BARKLEM
The High Hills; *The Secret Staircase*

FRED

by Posy Simmonds (Picture Puffin, 1987)
Interest level: 6–9/Reading age: 6+
DEATH • PETS

SOPHIE and Nick are sad when their cat, Fred, dies. But that night they hear a strange caterwauling and, when they go to investigate, they find a funeral service in progress, attended by all the cats for miles around. What is more, they discover that Fred, their sleepy pet, led an exciting double life . . .

Renowned as a cartoonist, Posy Simmonds has published a number of books for children, of which this is the first – and one of the most popular with young readers.

OTHER BOOKS BY POSY SIMMONDS
Lulu and the Flying Babies; *The Chocolate Wedding*; *Bouncing Buffalo*

FROG AND TOAD ARE FRIENDS

by Arnold Lobel (Mammoth, from 1970)
Interest level: 5–8/Reading age: 5+
FRIENDS

ARNOLD Lobel's popular characters have helped children in the United States and Britain to learn to read for over twenty-five years, using a mixture of simple text, engaging pictures and humour. In each story, one of four in each book, competent and practical Frog helps his somewhat less practical friend Toad with a particular project – doing the garden, spring cleaning or baking cookies. The result is not always what either friend expects – but there are plenty of amusing moments for young readers.

OTHER BOOKS BY ARNOLD LOBEL
Frog and Toad Together; *Days with Frog and Toad*; *Frog and Toad All Year*

FUNNYBONES

by Janet and Allan Ahlberg (Picture Lions, 1980)
Interest level: 5–7/Reading age: 5+

'ON a dark dark hill there was a dark dark town. In the dark dark town there was a dark dark street . . .' So begins the Ahlbergs' comical story about a most unlikely trio of characters – Big Skeleton, Little Skeleton and Dog Skeleton. As the opening sentence indicates, rhythm and repetition are used to engage young readers' interest, and serve to create a text that is good for reading practice.

OTHER BOOKS BY JANET AND ALLAN AHLBERG
*Peepo!; **Each Peach Pear Plum*; *The Jolly Postman*; **Burglar Bill*; **Jeremiah in the Dark Woods*

GARDEN, THE

by Dyan Sheldon; illustrated by Gary Blythe (Hutchinson, 1993)
Interest level: 6–8/Reading age: 6+
ENVIRONMENT

WHEN Jenny finds a strangely shaped stone in her garden, it sets in motion a train of thought which leads all the way back into the past. For the stone is a flint arrowhead, as used by the Indian braves who once roamed the country where Jenny now lives. That night, Jenny asks if she can sleep in her tent in the garden – and it is then that she has a wonderful dream . . . Previously renowned for their award-winning picture book *The Whale's Song*, Dyan Sheldon and Gary Blythe have produced a no less thoughtful story here, focusing on a fascinating era of American history.

OTHER BOOKS BY DYAN SHELDON
*The Whale's Song

GARGLING WITH JELLY

by Brian Patten (Puffin, 1989)
Interest level: 6–9/Reading age: 6+
HUMOUR • POETRY

GIANTS, goblins, mermaids, vampires and cartoon characters all tumble out of this marvellously inventive collection of verses by Brian Patten, which sets out to show that poetry doesn't have to be boring. It's great for reading aloud, too.

GIVE YOURSELF A HUG

by Grace Nichols (Puffin, 1996)
Interest level: 8–10/Reading age: 8+
POETRY

LIVELY and evocative verse from one of the foremost Black British children's poets, with lots of rhythm and rhyme to get hands clapping and feet tapping.

OTHER BOOKS BY GRACE NICHOLS
Poetry Jump Up (anthology); *No Hickory, No Dickory, No Dock (with John Agard)

GOBBOLINO THE WITCH'S CAT
. . . .

by Ursula Moray Williams (Puffin, 1988)
Interest level: 5–8/Reading age: 7+
MAGIC • WITCHES

G OBBOLINO the witch's cat would much rather be an ordinary cat. But will he ever attain his heart's desire and find a new home? Lots of magical fun, in a story that is perfect for reading aloud.

OTHER BOOKS BY URSULA MORAY WILLIAMS
Further Adventures of Gobbolino

GORILLA
. . . .

by Anthony Browne (Random Century, 1983)
Interest level: 7–10/Reading age: 8+
ANIMALS • LONELINESS

B ROWNE's distinctive, lovingly detailed graphic style and thought-provoking treatment of difficult themes is seen at its best in this story about a lonely little girl who finds happiness through an unusual friendship. Neglected by her father, who is always 'too busy' to spend time with her, Hannah is forced to take refuge in her own imaginative play. This is dramatized, in Browne's sensitively rendered account, by the toy gorilla who comes to life when Hannah is asleep, and who (suitably disguised in her father's hat and coat) takes her to the zoo to meet his fellow primates. As with most of Browne's stories, this one ends with a reconciliation between Hannah and her father, but not before it has made some important points about the relationship between parent and child. The ideas are conveyed in a simple, clear language which presents few problems for young readers. The use of colour and imagery subtly underlines the message.

OTHER BOOKS BY ANTHONY BROWNE
Bear Hunt; **Willy the Wimp*; **Piggybook*; **Zoo*; **The Big Baby*

GRACE AND FAMILY

. . . .

by Mary Hoffman; illustrated by Caroline Binch
(Frances Lincoln, 1995)
Interest level: 6–8/Reading age: 7+
FAMILIES • SIBLINGS

THIS sequel to Mary Hoffman's award-winning *Amazing Grace*, about a little Afro-Caribbean girl growing up in Britain, follows Grace on a journey to stay with her father and his other family in Africa. When Grace arrives in the Gambia, where her father now lives, she is at first jealous of his new wife, Jatou, refusing to have anything to do with her. But gradually Jatou's kindness wins her over, and Grace is able to see that extended families have their advantages – even if they do not always resemble the families in storybooks!

Caroline Binch's sensitive illustrations enhance the impact of this story, whose underlying message, celebrating the diversity of families and the unexpectedness of life, is firmly – although never stridently – stated. The book's heroine, Grace, is an attractively real little girl, with whose volatile moods and occasional uncertainties many children will identify. This is a book which challenges stereotypes, but which does so with subtlety and eloquence.

GRANDFATHER'S PENCIL
AND THE ROOM OF STORIES

. . . .

by Michael Foreman (Red Fox, 1993)
Interest level: 4–8/Reading age: 7+

IN Foreman's enchanting picture book, exquisitely illustrated with the author's distinctive watercolour paintings, a pencil writes its own story, beginning with its memories of being part of a tall tree, and following the process through until it becomes one of a box full of other pencils, in a shop, waiting to be bought as a present for a small boy. Other objects – the piece of paper on which the pencil is writing, the table, the door and the floorboards in the room – tell their stories in turn. Many years later, the boy who owned the pencil tells the story he heard – or dreamed – that night to his grandson. As thoughtful and sensitive as Foreman's other work, this is a story which provokes a whole series of questions about the world we live in, and the everyday objects we take for granted.

GREAT BIG ENORMOUS TURNIP, THE

by Alexei Tolstoy; illustrated by Helen Oxenbury
(Heinemann, 1968)
Interest level: 5–8/Reading age: 5+

A N old man grows a turnip which is so big he cannot pull it up. So he asks
his wife to help – but she cannot do it either. So they ask their
granddaughter . . . Tolstoy's classic tale is wittily complemented by Helen
Oxenbury's illustrations.

HAPPY FAMILIES

by Allan Ahlberg; various illustrators (Puffin, from 1980)
Interest level: 4–7/Reading age: 5+
FAMILIES

A LLAN Ahlberg's attractive series of books for young readers combines a
clear text, using frequent repetitions of certain words to help build up
vocabulary and reading confidence, with lively illustrations. The theme in
each case is a particular family, focusing on a different individual in each story.
'Mrs Plug the Plumber' (illustrated by Joe Wright) mixes role reversal with
light-hearted adventure; 'Mrs Wobble the Waitress' (illustrated by *Janet
Ahlberg) is more traditional in its portrayal of gender roles; while 'Mr and Mrs
Hay the Horse' (illustrated by *Colin McNaughton) depicts a very unusual job
indeed – that of pantomime horse!

HAUNTED HOUSE

by Jan Pienkowski (Reed, 1979)
Interest level: 5–8/Reading age: 5+
GHOSTS

J AN Pienkowski's fantastically grotesque illustrations, combined with
some wonderful paper-engineering, make this a classic of pop-up fun.
In this house, something nasty is *bound* to pop out of the wardrobe or from
under the bed – or even out of the loo!

OTHER BOOKS BY JAN PIENKOWSKI
Nursery Board Books; *Meg and Mog* (with Helen Nicoll)

HAVE YOU SEEN WHO'S JUST MOVED IN NEXT DOOR TO US?
. . . .

by Colin McNaughton (Walker Books, 1991)
Interest level: 5–8/Reading age: 7+
HUMOUR ● MONSTERS

THE author's wonderfully wacky illustrations are the perfect complement to this catalogue of ghoulies, ghosties and Things That Go Bump in the Night, all of which, it seems, inhabit the same street. Children will enjoy the detail in every picture – whether it is of Dracula's house, King Kong's house – or even that of the really weird people who have just moved in . . . who of course are the only 'normal' family in the street.

HEARD IT IN THE PLAYGROUND
. . . .

by Allan Ahlberg (Puffin, 1991)
Interest level: 5–8/Reading age: 6+
POETRY

A sequel to the equally hilarious *Please Mrs Butler*, this brilliantly funny collection of rhymes sung, chanted and overheard in school playgrounds everywhere will bring back nostalgic memories for anyone over eight.

OTHER BOOKS BY ALLAN AHLBERG
Please Mrs Butler; **Peepo!*; **Each Peach Pear Plum*; **The Baby's Catalogue*; **Jeremiah in the Dark Woods*; **Funnybones*; **Happy Families*; **Burglar Bill*

HODGEHEG, THE
. . . .

by Dick King-Smith (Puffin, 1989)
Interest level: 6–8/Reading age: 7+
ANIMALS

MAX is a hedgehog who decides to become a 'hodgeheg' and find a safe crossing for the other hedgehogs across a dangerous road. A good choice for young readers, with a likeable hero and clear, simple language.

OTHER BOOKS BY DICK KING-SMITH
*Sophie's Snail; **The Sheep-Pig*

HUE BOY
. . . .

by Rita Phillips Mitchell; illustrated by Caroline Binch (Gollancz, 1992)
Smarties Prize
Interest level: 5–8/Reading age: 8 +

Hue Boy is the smallest boy in his class at school, and the smallest boy of his age in the village. His mother tries everything to make him grow – from feeding him her special pumpkin soup to sending him to the local faith healer. Everyone offers advice, but none of it can make Hue Boy get any taller – until the day his dad comes home from sea, and suddenly Hue Boy finds he doesn't care so much about being tall … Caroline Binch's sensitive illustrations of the central character and his Caribbean surroundings make this engaging story all the more appealing.

HUNTER, THE
. . . .

by Paul Geraghty (Red Fox, 1996)
Interest level: 4–7/Reading age: 7 +
ANIMALS ● ENVIRONMENT

Walking with her grandfather in the African bush, Jamina longs to see a herd of elephants, like the ones Grandfather can recall seeing when he was a boy. But the hunters have killed many of the elephants for their tusks, and the rest are too frightened of humans to show themselves. Then Jamina gets separated from her grandfather, and finds herself lost in the bush. Trying to get back to her village, she stumbles across a baby elephant whose mother has been killed by hunters, and together they make their way home. Renowned for his wildlife illustrations, Paul Geraghty has written a moving and sensitive plea for conserving the world's endangered species.

I DIN DO NUTTIN
. . . .

by John Agard (Red Fox, 1993)
Interest level: 8–10/Reading age: 8 +
POETRY

Poems which take a child's-eye view of everyday experiences, by an award-winning Guyanese poet.

OTHER BOOKS BY JOHN AGARD
Laughter is an Egg; * *No Hickory, No Dickory, No Dock* (with Grace Nichols)

I DON'T WANT TO!

by Bel Mooney; illustrated by Margaret Chamberlain
(Mammoth, 1990)
Interest level: 5–8/Reading age: 6+

First of a highly popular series about Kitty, a little girl who knows her own mind about a lot of things, such as whether she likes vegetables, or wants to share her toys, or go to bed – or does she? Margaret Chamberlain's lively drawings add to the humour of these familiar, real-life situations.

OTHER BOOKS BY BEL MOONEY
I Know!; *I'm Scared!*; *It's Not Fair!*; *But You Promised!*

IMAGINARY MENAGERIE, AN

by Roger McGough; illustrated by Tony Blundell (Puffin, 1990)
Interest level: 8–10/Reading age: 8+
POETRY

Roger McGough's poetry is renowned for its laconic wit and clever wordplay – and both are very much in evidence in this collection of humorous poems about animals, featuring such weird and wonderful juxtapositions as an anaconda riding a Honda and a budgerigar smoking a cigar.

OTHER BOOKS BY ROGER MCGOUGH
* Sky in the Pie; *Lucky*; *Helen Highwater*; *Nailing the Shadow*; *Pillow Talk*

IT'S YOUR TURN, ROGER!

by Susanna Gretz (Red Fox, 1985)
Smarties Prize
Interest level: 5–8/Reading age: 6+
HUMOUR

Roger the pig is fed up with having to do his share of the chores. So one evening at suppertime, he decides to find himself a new family, where he won't be expected to help set the table. He goes to each of the families in his block of flats – but finds that, not only is the food not to his taste, but he doesn't like being treated as a guest after all! Susanna Gretz's lively illustrations add to the humour of this story – one of a popular series.

IVOR THE ENGINE

by Oliver Postgate; illustrated by Peter Firmin
(Picture Lions, 1960)
Interest level: 5–8/Reading age: 7+
TRAINS

THE first in this much-loved series about a little steam engine and his friends is set, like the other stories, in rural Wales. One evening after he has been working all day delivering coal and goods up and down the line of the Merioneth and Llantisilly Rail Traction Company, Ivor hears the Grumbly and District Choral Society practising in the Congregational Hall, and wishes that he, too, could join in the singing . . . First published in the 1960s, these stories reflect a vanished society of collieries and small communities – but remain as popular as ever with young readers.

OTHER BOOKS BY OLIVER POSTGATE
Ivor's Birthday; Ivor and the Elephant; Ivor and the Dragon

JO-JO'S JOURNEY

by Grahame Baker-Smith (Bodley Head, 1994)
Interest level: 8–11/Reading age: 8+

WRITTEN and illustrated by the author, this comic-strip format science fiction tale follows the adventures of Jo-Jo, boy space-crusader and collector of rare plants and animals, as he flees from the Darkships of the evil Madame Amentia. Crash-landing on Earth, he is befriended by Daisy, the skateboard queen, whom he saves from the gang of thugs who have been terrorizing her, before making his escape once more as the Darkships arrive.

An unusual format and exciting story give this book at least as much appeal as the computer games from which it takes many of its images.

JOLLY POSTMAN, THE

by Janet and Allan Ahlberg (Heinemann, 1986)
Interest level: 5–8/Reading age: 6+

THE innovative format of this picture book – in which actual letters, complete with envelopes, are incorporated into the text – is one reason for its enduring popularity with young children; another is its use of rhymes and repetition, which help to make reading fun, and new words easy to remember. The Jolly Postman delivers his sackful of letters to a range of favourite nursery characters, from the Three Bears to Cinderella, and the story ends with a birthday tea at Goldilocks's cottage, to which all the characters are invited.

ALSO BY JANET AND ALLAN AHLBERG
The Jolly Christmas Postman; **Peepo!*; **The Baby's Catalogue*; **Burglar Bill*; **Funnybones*; **Starting School*; **Each Peach Pear Plum*

JOSIE SMITH

by Magdalen Nabb (Collins, 1989)
Interest level: 6–8/Reading age: 6+
FAMILIES

FIRST of a series about a little girl dealing with various real-life events and problems. The stories convey a child's-eye view with sensitivity and humour, and the language is challenging enough without being too difficult for independent readers.

OTHER BOOKS BY MAGDALEN NABB
Josie Smith at School; *Josie Smith at the Seaside*; *Josie Smith in Hospital*; *Josie Smith at Christmas*

JUST SO STORIES

by Rudyard Kipling (Puffin, 1902)
Interest level: 7–11/Reading age: 10+
ANIMALS

GENERATIONS of children have loved these humorous tales and poems, and have pored over the author's intricate black-and-white illustrations for clues as to their meaning. The stories each feature a different animal character, giving far-fetched explanations as to how each acquired its chief characteristic. This is generally a physical feature – as in 'How the Camel Got His Hump', 'How the Leopard Got His Spots' and so on; but one of the most amusing stories, 'The Cat That Walked by Himself', explains the peculiar independence of cats in relation to human beings. Kipling wrote the stories for his own children, and they were published while he was recovering from the shock of his daughter Josephine's death. Their blend of whimsical humour and extravagant language has made them of enduring appeal, and the author's jocular habit of addressing the reader ('O Best Beloved') makes them ideal for reading aloud.

OTHER BOOKS BY RUDYARD KIPLING
* *The Jungle Book*; *Rewards and Fairies*; *Kim*

KATIE MORAG'S ISLAND STORIES
. . . .
by Mairi Hedderwick (Bodley Head, 1995)
Interest level: 5–8/Reading age: 6+
FAMILIES

THE collection includes 'Katie Morag Delivers the Mail', 'Katie Morag and the Two Grandmothers', 'Katie Morag and the Tiresome Ted', and 'Katie Morag and the Big Boy Cousins'.

Illustrated with the author's evocative pen-and-wash sketches, these stories about a little girl who lives on a remote Scottish island are filled with fascinating detail about rural life in all its harshness and beauty. Katie Morag's parents run the post office on the island of Struay. They work very hard and don't often have much time to spare for their energetic little daughter. Fortunately, Katie Morag has her grandmother to turn to when she needs help with the occasional setback – such as coping with a new baby sister or sorting out her rough boy cousins. Despite having no television, video or computer, she is never at a loss for something to do.

LAZY DAISY
. . . .

by Rob Lewis (Red Fox, 1996)
Interest level: 3–6/Reading age: 6+
PETS

D AISY the ship's cat is supposed to catch rats – but she is far too fond of snoozing in the sun. Then the Captain delivers an ultimatum – either Daisy must step up her rat-catching or her days on board the ship are numbered. Poor Daisy does her best to outwit the cunning rats, but just ends up looking foolish. Then one night there is a terrible storm – and Daisy is at last able to show what she is made of . . . Rob Lewis's gently humorous story is illustrated with authentic-looking nautical images, and Daisy herself is an appealing heroine.

LITTLE GREY RABBIT'S STORYBOOK
. . . .

by Alison Uttley; illustrated by Margaret Tempest (Collins, from 1929)
Interest level: 3–7/Reading age: 7+
ANIMALS

T HIS collection includes 'Little Grey Rabbit's Party', 'Wise Owl's Story', 'Little Grey Rabbit's Washing Day', 'Moldy Warp the Mole', 'Fuzzypeg Goes to School' and 'Little Grey Rabbit's Christmas'.

Alison Uttley wrote the first Little Grey Rabbit story for her son over sixty years ago, and the stories have remained favourites with young children ever since. Her three main characters, Hare, Squirrel and Little Grey Rabbit herself, live in a cottage in the woods, where they fulfil the roles assigned to them (Hare is boastful but cowardly, Squirrel vain and Little Grey Rabbit sensible and wise) and mark the passage of the seasons with appropriately rural pursuits. As with Uttley's other popular series, *The Adventures of Sam Pig*, one of the delights of these stories is the detail with which they record now-vanished country rituals and nature lore. Many of these details were drawn from the author's own childhood experience of growing up on a farm, as described in her autobiography, *The Country Child* (1931).

MARY POPPINS
. . . .

by P.L. Travers; illustrated by Mary Shepard (Collins, 1934)
Interest level: 8–10/Reading age: 8+
MAGIC

THE continuing popularity of P.L. Travers's story may be largely attributed to the 1964 Disney film, although to aficionados the latter hardly does justice to the book's quirky humour. Blown by the east wind, Mary Poppins arrives as governess to the unruly Banks children, Jane and Michael, and within a matter of hours has transformed their lives with her inimitable mixture of bossiness and magic. With her assistance, they find themselves able to step inside the drawings of a pavement artist, float up to the ceiling filled with Laughing Gas, and travel to all kinds of interesting places. While some critics have disliked the book's reliance on an authoritarian nanny figure, most young readers enjoy the anarchic fun, and the way quite ordinary events – a tea-party, a visit to the park – are made to seem magical and extraordinary.

METEORITE SPOON
. . . .

by Philip Ridley; illustrated by Chris Riddell (Puffin, 1995)
Interest level: 8–11/Reading age: 8+

FILLY and Fergal's parents are always arguing, and one day they have a violent row. It is then that the children discover the alternative world of Honeymoonia, which they reach with the aid of the magic meteorite spoon. There, they meet a couple just like their parents – except that they never, ever argue . . . Philip Ridley has established himself as one of the foremost writers of fantasy for the under-twelves, with a series of hauntingly surreal books which often confront disturbing issues (such as parental violence) in an offbeat and thought-provoking way. Chris Riddell's wonderfully quirky illustrations are the perfect visual equivalent.

OTHER BOOKS BY PHILIP RIDLEY
Krindlekrax; **Mercedes Ice*

MINI BEASTIES

by Michael Rosen (Puffin, 1993)
Interest level: 5–8/Reading age: 6+
ANIMALS • POETRY

Poems about all kinds of crawling, creeping, flying beasties, to delight any child with a love of language and a fondness for humour.

OTHER BOOKS BY MICHAEL ROSEN
We're Going on a Bear Hunt

MISS FANSHAWE AND THE GREAT DRAGON ADVENTURE

by Sue Scullard (Picturemac, 1986)
Interest level: 6–8/Reading age: 7+
DRAGONS

Intrepid Victorian explorer Harriet Fanshawe journeys to Patagonia in search of a magical dragon's egg. Follow her journey into the volcano and out again, enjoying Sue Scullard's intricate illustrations of everything from tropical jungles to Renaissance cities.

OTHER BOOKS BY SUE SCULLARD
The Flyaway Pantaloons

MOVING MOLLY

by Shirley Hughes (Random Century, 1978)
Interest level: 5–8/Reading age: 5+
MOVING HOUSE

Molly is at first very pleased about moving from the flat where she has been living with her family to a bigger house in the country. But when her big brother and sister are away at school she has no one to talk to. It's then that she decides to explore the garden of the empty house next door, which becomes her own special hiding-place. She can't help being disappointed when people eventually move into the house – but then she discovers that there are some children of her own age to play with . . . Shirley Hughes's charmingly illustrated story focuses on the anxieties as well as the excitement of moving, and will help to allay the fears children often feel about change and displacement.

MS WIZ SPELLS TROUBLE
. . . .

by Terence Blacker (Young Piper, 1988)
Interest level: 7–10/Reading age: 7+
HUMOUR • WITCHES

LIFE is never the same after Ms Wiz walks into St Barnabas's School. With her long black hair, her black nail-varnish and her china cat called Hecate, she's the strangest teacher Class 3 has ever had – and also the cleverest! When Ms Wiz is around, the weirdest things keep happening, but school is never, ever, boring . . . In this, the first of Terence Blacker's popular series about a witch-turned-teacher, Ms Wiz brings order to an unruly classroom.

OTHER BOOKS BY TERENCE BLACKER
In Stitches with Ms Wiz; *You're Nicked, Ms Wiz*; *In Control, Ms Wiz?*; *Time Flies for Ms Wiz*

MUMMY LAID AN EGG
. . . .

by Babette Cole (Red Fox, 1993)
Interest level: 5–8/Reading age: 7+
BABIES • HUMOUR

IN Babette Cole's refreshingly amusing approach to a traditionally awkward subject, two children explain the Facts of Life to their parents, after the latter have tried to fob them off with fanciful stories about babies being found under stones and in greenhouses. The children's explanation – complete with drawings of 'the Great Egg Race' – is accurate enough, without being anatomically specific, and should help broach the subject of how babies are made, without embarrassment for adult or child.

MY MUM IS MAGIC!

by Hannah Roche; illustrated by Chris Fisher (De Agostini, 1996)
Interest level: 3–6/Reading age: 6+
SCIENCE

JAMIE's mum can do a very special kind of magic, which involves separating yolks of eggs from whites, whisking them in a bowl, adding sugar and putting the mixture in the oven, where it turns into some delicious meringues. Hannah Roche's appealingly straightforward approach to the 'magic' of science is aimed at very young children, encouraging them (with parental help) to make their own magic in the kitchen.

OTHER BOOKS BY HANNAH ROCHE
My Dad's a Wizard!

NO HICKORY, NO DICKORY, NO DOCK

by John Agard and Grace Nichols (Puffin, 1992)
Interest level: 5–8/Reading age: 6+
POETRY

CARIBBEAN nursery rhymes which combine chanting, singing and rhyming – but definitely no hickory, dickory or dock! Great for reading aloud and for joining in.

NOT NOW, BERNARD

by David McKee (Andersen Press, 1980)
Interest level: 5–8/Reading age: 5+
MONSTERS

BERNARD's parents are too busy to talk to him and so he goes into the garden where he finds a monster. Instead of ignoring Bernard, the monster gobbles him up – but then it is the monster's turn to be ignored . . . David McKee's witty illustrations offer a silent commentary on the pared-down text, conveying more clearly than words what it feels like to have no one pay any attention to you, even when you're behaving like a monster.

OTHER BOOKS BY DAVID MCKEE
The Adventures of King Rollo; *Tusk Tusk*; *Elmer

NOTHING
. . . .

by Mick Inkpen (Hodder, 1995)
Interest level: 5–7/Reading age: 6+

S ENSITIVELY illustrated by the author, this thought-provoking story is about a soft toy left behind when a family moves house, who embarks on a quest to find out who he is. Battered and shapeless, he seems to belong to no particular species; worst of all, it is so long since anybody has played with him that he can't remember what or who he is supposed to be. Assisted by a friendly cat, he makes his way back to the family with whom he used to live – and is eventually recognized by the grandfather as the toy cat he used to play with when he was a baby.

OTHER BOOKS BY MICK INKPEN
The Blue Balloon; *Jojo's Revenge*; **Kipper*; **Jasper's Beanstalk* (with Nick Butterworth); **Penguin Small*; **Threadbear*

OLD POSSUM'S BOOK OF PRACTICAL CATS
. . . .

by T.S. Eliot; illustrated by Nicolas Bentley (Faber & Faber, 1939)
Interest level: 6–9/Reading age: 7+
ANIMALS ● PETS ● POETRY

M ACAVITY, Mr Mistoffelees, Mungojerrie and Rumpelteazer – these and other feline characters make up the cast of T.S. Eliot's endearingly quirky collection of poems, written for the children of various friends, including Tom Faber, his publisher's son. Despite its enormous success, the 1981 Andrew Lloyd Webber musical based on the poems does not convey the charm of the original.

OLIVER'S VEGETABLES
. . . .

by Vivian French; illustrated by Alison Bartlett (Hodder, 1995)
Interest level: 5–8/Reading age: 5+

A LISON Bartlett's striking illustrations give an added impact to this amusing tale about a boy who will only eat chips – until the day he goes to stay with his grandparents and learns that there are other vegetables he enjoys . . . A story which will strike a chord with any parent who has ever despaired of getting their child to eat healthy food.

ONE HUNDRED AND ONE DALMATIANS

by Dodie Smith (Puffin 1956)
Interest level: 8–10/Reading age: 8 +
ADVENTURE • PETS

B OTH the Disney cartoon and the more recent film have done much to prolong the popularity of Dodie Smith's canine adventure story, in which the Dalmatian dogs Pogo and Missis go in search of their litter of puppies, stolen by the monstrous Cruella de Vil to make a spotted fur coat. Enlisted in this quest are a large number of other dogs, who form a secret fraternity across the nation, communicating (naturally enough) by barking.

OUTSIDE OVER THERE
. . . .

by Maurice Sendak (Picture Puffin, 1981)
Interest level: 7–10/Reading age: 7 +

D ESCRIBED by its author as the concluding part of a trilogy on the theme of make-believe, which includes *Where the Wild Things Are and *In the Night Kitchen, this haunting retelling of a Grimm tale, in which a baby is stolen by goblins who leave a changeling made of ice in its stead, is considerably more disturbing than the other two books. Sendak's illustrations, which mingle an almost photographic realism with dreamlike fantasy, are full of haunting images (a child flying through the air; a baby turning into a goblin and vice versa) but could be unsettling for very young readers, for whom the book may be too frightening.

PAPER BAG PRINCESS, THE
. . . .

by Robert N. Munsch; illustrated by Michael Martchenko
(Annick Press, 1980)
Interest level: 5–9/Reading age: 6 +
GENDER STEREOTYPING • HUMOUR

M UNSCH'S amusing tale about a resourceful princess, who takes to wearing a paper bag when her clothes are burnt by a dragon's fiery breath, has become a classic of role-reversal stories. Princess Elizabeth sets off on a quest to rescue her prince and outwit the dragon who has carried him off. She succeeds in the latter, but changes her mind about marrying prissy Prince Ronald when he tells her to come back when she is dressed like a 'real princess'.

A good book for class discussion of gender stereotypes which is also a lot of fun.

PATCHWORK CAT, THE

by William Mayne; illustrated by Nicola Bayley (Jonathan Cape, 1981)
Interest level: 5–8/Reading age: 5+
ANIMALS ● PETS

TABBY the cat loves her patchwork quilt almost as much as she loves her friend the milkman. When Tabby's owners put the quilt out with the rubbish, Tabby decides to go in search of it, and finds herself spending a terrifying night alone in the rubbish dump. In the morning, when she tries to make her way home, she gets lost – but then the friendly milkman comes to the rescue, and Tabby travels home in style. Nicola Bayley's exquisitely detailed illustrations perfectly complement this charming story, which has become a favourite with adults and children alike.

PIPPI LONGSTOCKING

by Astrid Lindgren (Puffin, 1945)
Interest level: 8–10/Reading age: 8+

PIPPI Longstocking, heroine of Astrid Lindgren's series about a red-headed nine-year-old who lives in a cottage with only her friends, a horse and a monkey for company, has been a popular success since it first appeared in Sweden over fifty years ago. As well as being self-sufficient, Pippi is also very strong: she can lift a horse in her arms, and easily resists arrest when two policemen come to take her to the local children's home. Pippi's anarchic tendencies are displayed to the full the day she attends school – for the first and only time – much to the delight of her more law-abiding friends, Tommy and Annika.

OTHER BOOKS BY ASTRID LINDGREN
Pippi Goes Abroad; *Pippi in the South Seas*

RED HERRING MYSTERY, THE
. . . .

by Paul Adshead (Child's Play, 1996)
Interest level: 8–12/Reading age: 8+

WHEN Detective Gregory Sullivan is invited to Sir Reginald and Lady Magdella Bannister's fancy-dress party, to celebrate their cat winning the Cat of the Year Show, he already suspects that something fishy may be about to happen – especially when he remembers that the trophy is the fabulous Red Herring Ruby. Could it be that one of the guests is going to steal it? When the ruby goes missing, Gregory has his work cut out to track it down – which he does by following the fishy clues hidden in the pictures on every page. Young detectives will enjoy pitting their wits against Gregory's – and against the burglar's – and will find the solution by no means as obvious as it seems. Plenty of red herrings are mixed up with the clues, and the answer to the puzzle is hidden behind a sealed page to prevent peeking.

REVOLTING RHYMES
. . . .

by Roald Dahl (Puffin, 1989)
Interest level: 8–11/Reading age: 8+
HUMOUR ● POETRY

THE inimitable Roald Dahl in characteristically revolting form, with a collection of humorous verse about scorpions, ant-eaters, crocodiles, pigs and other suitably unsavoury beasts.

OTHER BOOKS BY ROALD DAHL
Dirty Beasts; *Matilda; *The Witches; **Charlie and the Chocolate Factory*; *Charlie and the Great Glass Elevator*; **The B.F.G.*; *Fantastic Mr Fox*; *The Minpins*; **The Enormous Crocodile*; *Esio Trot*

RUPERT BEAR
. . . .

by Mary Tourtel and Alfred Bestall (*Daily Express*, from 1920)
Interest level: 5–8/Reading age: 6+
BEARS

FOLLOWING his first appearance as a comic strip in the *Daily Express* in 1920, Rupert and his pals Algy, Bill and Edward became an established feature of English childhood, appearing in annual form (and latterly on a whole range of merchandise from T-shirts to lunchboxes). The stories, which generally involve Rupert in some kind of magical adventure, are told in verse and prose; their old-fashioned quality – enhanced by the illustrations – is part of their charm.

SEVENTH DOOR, THE

by Norman Leach; illustrated by Patricia Ludlow (Child's Play, 1996)

Interest level: 6–9/Reading age: 8+

FAIRY TALES

B EAUTIFULLY illustrated with Patricia Ludlow's delicate watercolour paintings, this original fairy tale tells the story of Carrots-and-Cream – youngest of seven daughters – who is taken from her parents' cottage in the woods to the king's palace, where she tries to find out what has happened to her sisters, all of whom have been spirited away by their sinister royal suitor. With the bunch of keys she has been given by the king, Carrots-and-Cream tries all the doors in the palace, and finds herself in a variety of wonderful rooms, each of a different colour. Here, she tries to find clues to her sisters' disappearance – but it is not until the seventh and last room that she discovers the truth . . . Based on the *Bluebeard* story – but with a happier ending – Norman Leach's tale will delight any child with a liking for mystery and magic.

SHEEP-PIG, THE

by Dick King-Smith (Puffin, 1983)

Interest level: 8–10/Reading age: 8+

ANIMALS

B ABE, the piglet, has an unusual ambition – to herd sheep! With the assistance of his good friend Fly the sheepdog, Babe soon learns all he needs to know – but will he be able to fulfil his heart's desire and compete in the local sheepdog trials? Dick King-Smith's entertaining story, which was filmed in 1996, shows how you can be anything you want, if you try hard enough!

OTHER BOOKS BY DICK KING-SMITH

Tumbleweed; *Saddlebottom*; *The Water Horse*; **The Hodgeheg*; **Sophie's Snail*

SKY IN THE PIE

. . . .

by Roger McGough (Puffin, 1989)
Interest level: 8–10/Reading age: 8+
HUMOUR ● POETRY

'WAITER, there's a sky in my pie!' More humorous verse from the master of the surreal tongue-twist.

OTHER BOOKS BY ROGER MCGOUGH
*An Imaginary Menagerie; *Lucky*; *Helen Highwater*; *Nailing the Shadow*; *Pillow Talk*

SMELLY BOOK, THE

. . . .

by Babette Cole (Picture Lions, 1987)
Interest level: 5–9/Reading age: 6+
HUMOUR

ONCE again, Babette Cole has surpassed herself with horrid rhymes about nasty things – illustrated in her own inimitably revolting style. This book chronicles the joys of smelly things, from over-ripe cheeses to stinky socks, and will delight any child with a similarly anarchic sense of humour.

SNOW SPIDER, THE

. . . .

by Jenny Nimmo (Magnet, 1986)
Smarties Prize
Interest level: 8–10/Reading age: 9+
ADVENTURE ● DEATH ● MAGIC

ON his ninth birthday, Gwyn receives some unusual presents from his grandmother: a piece of seaweed, a scarf, a tin whistle, a brooch and a little broken horse. These will help him find out if he is a magician, she tells him. But Gwyn's pleasure in his birthday is marred by the memory of what happened that night four years ago, when his sister Bethan walked out into the storm and never returned. Surely, if he is really a magician, he can make a spell to bring her back? So, with the aid of his five gifts – and the Snow Spider who comes to him out of the wind – Gwyn starts to weave his magic, and finds himself drawn into some very strange events indeed . . . Jenny Nimmo's lyrical and exciting story, the first in a trilogy (the others are *Emlyn's Moon* and *The Chestnut Soldier*) about a boy who knows he is different, incorporates supernatural elements and echoes of Welsh legend into a convincingly real tale.

OTHER BOOKS BY JENNY NIMMO
Emlyn's Moon; *The Chestnut Soldier*

READ-ONS
*The Weirdstone of Brisingamen, by Alan Garner; **The Owl Service*, by Alan Garner

SOPHIE'S SNAIL
. . . .
by Dick King-Smith (Walker Books, 1988)
Interest level: 5–8/Reading age: 6+
ANIMALS • PETS

FIRST of a series featuring Dick King-Smith's endearing heroine, this story describes four-year-old Sophie's first attempt at looking after a pet – which happens to be a snail! Other books in the series introduce us to Sophie's family, including her twin brothers and Great-Great-Aunt Alice from Scotland, as well as a menagerie of different wildlife, pets and farm animals – all described with the author's customary warmth and humour.

OTHER BOOKS BY DICK KING-SMITH
The Hodgeheg ; **The Sheep-Pig*

STINKERBELL
. . . .
by J. J. Murhall; illustrated by Tony Blundell (Bloomsbury Children's Books, 1996)
Interest level: 6–9/Reading age: 7+
FAIRIES • HUMOUR

STINKERBELL is no common-or-garden fairy – in fact, the only bit of the garden she feels at home in is the dustbin! With her magic going wrong all over the place and the other fairies looking down on her because she's so dirty and smelly, she longs for a way to prove herself worthy of her wings. And then, one day, she overhears Mr and Mrs Gob, the ghastly goblins, plotting to kidnap the royal baby – and realizes that only she can foil their plan . . . Stinkerbell is a heroine with whom every less-than-tidy child will identify. The clear text and lively pictures are an added incentive to reading.

STONE SOUP
by Tony Ross (Collins, 1987)
Interest level: 5–8/Reading age: 6+

WHEN the Bad, Bad Wolf threatens to eat Mother Hen and steal all her goodies, she placates him with the offer of Stone Soup – the most special soup he's ever tasted. But first she has to find the right kind of stone. And, while he's waiting for the soup to cook, Bad, Bad Wolf can help out with the chores . . . Ross's lively illustrations give an engagingly quirky look to this classic tale of cleverness outwitting stupidity. The Bad, Bad Wolf gets his come-uppance – but not before he (and the reader) has learned how to make Stone Soup!

OTHER BOOKS BY TONY ROSS
I Want My Potty; I Want to Be

STORIES FROM CLASSICAL BALLET
by Belinda Hollyer; with performance notes by Irina Baronova; illustrated by Sophy Williams (Macmillan, 1995)
Interest level: 8–11/Reading age: 8+
BALLET

STORIES from eight classical ballets are retold in this beautifully illustrated book, with an introduction and notes on each ballet by the great Russian ballerina, Irina Baronova.

TATTERCOATS
by Margaret Greaves; illustrated by Margaret Chamberlain (Frances Lincoln, 1990)
Interest level: 5–7/Reading age: 5+

BANISHED to the kitchens by her gloomy grandfather the king, Tattercoats spends her days with her good friend the goose-boy. But then one day, a handsome prince comes to the castle in search of a bride, and love brings about a magical transformation. Margaret Chamberlain's lively illustrations perfectly complement this rags-to-riches story.

THOMAS THE TANK ENGINE
. . . .

by the Rev. W. Awdry; illustrated by C. Reginald Dalby
(Edward Ward, 1946)
Interest level: 3–8/Reading age: 7+
TRAINS

WHEN the Reverend Awdry published the first of his stories about a little steam engine and his friends, he can have had little idea of the extraordinary popularity they were to enjoy, with a whole industry of pop-up books, TV animations, videos and other merchandise developing out of his rather modest concept. Thomas and his trucks, Annie and Clarabel, and his fellow engines, James, Henry, Percy and the rest, have become as familiar to millions of children worldwide as the characters of Beatrix Potter. Younger children may prefer the redesigned books, with illustrations based on the popular television series, but for aficionados the original, miniature volumes, with period drawings by Reginald Dalby, capture the gentle humour of the text far more precisely. In this, the first of many similar tales, Thomas, a rather anxious and fussy little engine, is patronized by bigger, grander engines such as Gordon, but in the end he is given his own branch line by the Fat Controller.

OTHER BOOKS IN THE SERIES
James the Red Engine; *Tank Engine Thomas Again*; *Henry the Green Engine*; *Gordon the Big Engine*; *Percy the Small Engine*

THREE LITTLE WOLVES AND THE BIG BAD PIG, THE
. . . .

by Eugene Trivizas; illustrated by Helen Oxenbury
(Mammoth, 1993)
Interest level: 5–8/Reading age: 6+
ANIMALS

A wonderfully comic retelling of the familiar story of the Three Little Pigs, in which the pig as the baddie is eventually outwitted by three little wolves. Helen Oxenbury's delightful illustrations add to the humour of a story with a real twist in the tail!

TIGER-SKIN RUG, THE

by Gerald Rose (Picture Puffin, 1979)
Interest level: 5–8/Reading age: 6+
ANIMALS

A N old, thin tiger watches the Rajah's family enjoying a banquet and longs to join them – but how? Disguised as a moth-eaten tiger-skin rug, he sneaks into the palace, only to find that his presence is not appreciated. But that night, a gang of robbers breaks in, and the tiger finds it isn't so bad being a tiger after all.

TINTIN

by Hergé (Georges Remi) (Methuen, from 1930)
Interest level: 8–12/Reading age: 8+
ADVENTURE

TINTIN, the hero of Hergé's hugely popular comic-strip adventures, first published in the early 1930s and since adapted for television and film, is a teenage reporter more often to be found moonlighting as an amateur detective, on the trail of a startling range of international villains from forgers (*The Black Island*) to anarchists (*King Ottokar's Sceptre*). He is assisted by his trusty sidekicks, Snowy, a small white dog, and Captain Haddock, a retired sea captain given to colourful expletives, 'Blistering barnacles' being one of his favourites. Other characters who recur throughout the twenty-odd books include the foolishly pedantic detectives Thomson and Thompson (Dupont et Dupond in the original French), Professor Calculus the eccentric inventor and the opera singer Bianca Castafiore – one of the few female characters in the series, who is, somewhat inevitably, a figure of fun. Although some of the social attitudes expressed are very much of their time, the *Tintin* books are distinguished overall by a liveliness of plot and an exuberant humour which is conveyed both in the dialogue and in the superbly detailed and colourful illustrations. For any child who is bored by reading, the comic-strip format, here and in the *Asterix books, offers an attractive – but by no means undemanding – alternative. Interestingly, the vocabulary in both series is often quite difficult, while the storylines – in the *Tintin* books especially – can be mind-bogglingly complicated. Children, apparently, are not deterred. The series includes. *The Blue Lotus, The Cigars of the Pharoahs, The Black*

Island, King Ottokar's Sceptre, The Crab with the Golden Claws, The Shooting Star, Destination Moon and others titles.

TROUBLE WITH MUM, THE

. . . .

by Babette Cole (Mammoth, 1986)
Interest level: 6–9/Reading age: 6+
HUMOUR • WITCHES

T HE trouble with Mum is she isn't like other mums – for a start, she's a witch. No wonder the other parents look askance at her at the school gates. But one day the school catches fire, and suddenly Mum's magic skills don't seem so embarrassing after all . . . Babette Cole's witty illustrations make this – the first in a series – one of her funniest creations.

OTHER BOOKS BY BABETTE COLE
The Trouble with Dad; *The Trouble with Uncle*; **Princess Smartypants*; *Hurrah for Ethlyn*; **The Bad Good Manners Book*; **Mummy Laid an Egg*; **The Smelly Book*; *The Slimy Book*; *Tarzanna*!

TWO NAUGHTY ANGELS: DOWN TO EARTH

. . . .

by Mary Hooper; illustrated by Lesley Harker (Bloomsbury Children's Books, 1995)
Interest level: 6–9/Reading age: 7+

W HEN two small angels called Angie and Gaby fall through a mirror and find themselves back on earth – as pupils at St Winifred's School – the stage is set for some very strange goings-on indeed. Just how do they explain (truthfully, of course) how they got there – or why they don't have any clothes apart from the long white nightdresses they stand up in? Fortunately Macy, one of the other girls at the school, and her friend Julia decide to take the newcomers under their wing. But before long they discover that there's more to the angelic-looking pair than meets the eye . . . Mary Hooper's delightful story makes the most of its potential for out-of-this-world jokes. Lesley Harker's illustrations are also great fun.

OTHER BOOKS IN THE SERIES
The Ghoul at School

TYGER VOYAGE, THE

by Richard Adams; illustrated by Nicola Bayley (Picturemac, 1976)
Interest level: 5–8/Reading age: 8 +
ANIMALS ● FANTASY

A DAMS's engaging tale about a family of tigers who embark on a voyage of discovery pays tongue-in-cheek homage to the adventure stories of *H.G. Wells and *Sir Arthur Conan Doyle and is enhanced by Nicola Bayley's richly detailed illustrations, in which tigers, Victorian backgrounds and exotic settings combine to great advantage.

VELVETEEN RABBIT, THE

by Margery Williams (Mammoth, 1922)
Interest level: 6–9/Reading age: 7 +
ANIMALS ● MAGIC

M ARGERY Williams's touching story about a velveteen rabbit who longs to be real will appeal to any child who has ever wished the same about a favourite toy. The story's magical ending is wonderfully done.

WALKER BOOK OF BEAR STORIES, THE

(Walker Books, 1995)
Interest level: 5–8/Reading age: 5 +
BEARS

T HE collection includes * *We're Going on a Bear Hunt* by Michael Rosen and Helen Oxenbury; *Goldilocks and the Three Bears* illustrated by Charlotte Voake; *Midnight Teddies* by Dana Kubick; * *When the Teddy Bears Came* by Martin Waddell and Penny Dale; *Let's Go Home, Little Bear* by Martin Waddell and Barbara Firth. Some of the best stories about bears around are to be found in this anthology, showing what a range of different approaches and styles of illustration the subject has attracted. Here are bears of all kinds – from the friendly nursery variety to the more scary (but still appealing) kind you find in the forest.

WAR AND PEAS
. . . .

by Michael Foreman (Picture Puffin, 1974)
Interest level: 5–7/Reading age: 5+
WAR

FOREMAN'S classic fable about what happens when the citizens of a poor
country take up arms against a neighbouring kingdom ruled by greed is
illustrated with the author's distinctive paintings. Mountains are made out of
cakes and trifles and cannon-balls turn into peas, as King Lion and his army
overcome their selfish adversaries. This thought-provoking story raises issues
to do with poverty and wealth and selfishness and fairness which even young
children will have no difficulty grasping.

Foreman has become renowned for his sensitive watercolour illustrations
and the resolutely anti-war and egalitarian message of his books.

OTHER BOOKS BY MICHAEL FOREMAN
Dinosaurs and All That Rubbish; *War Boy*; *Michael Foreman's World of
Fairy Tales*; *Jack's Fantastic Voyage*; *War Game*; and as illustrator, *A Child's
Garden of Verses* by Robert Louis Stevenson

WHALE'S SONG, THE
. . . .

by Dyan Sheldon; illustrated by Gary Blythe (Red Fox, 1990)
Kate Greenaway Award
Interest level: 5–8/Reading age: 6+
ANIMALS ● ENVIRONMENT

LILY's grandmother tells her of the whales' singing, and one unforgettable
night she hears it for herself . . . Dyan Sheldon's award-winning tale
conveys a sense of awe at the wonders of nature – a quality perfectly captured
by Gary Blythe's marvellous illustrations.

OTHER BOOKS BY DYAN SHELDON
The Garden

WHEN WE WERE VERY YOUNG
. . . .
by A. A. Milne; illustrated by E. H. Shepard (Methuen, 1924)
Interest level: 3–8/Reading age: 7+
POETRY

IN the seventy-odd years since it was first published, Milne's collection of verses for children, together with its companion volume *Now We Are Six*, has become an indelible part of English culture. Most of the poems have dated very little – even the much-parodied 'Buckingham Palace' reflects an experience most of us have had at one time or another, of being taken to watch the Changing of the Guard – and in any case, it hardly matters. Everyone has his or her own favourite. 'Disobedience', with its eminently chantable refrain, 'James James Morrison Morrison Weatherby George Dupree', is hard to resist, as is the no less hypnotic rhythm of 'The King's Breakfast'. That Milne was an accomplished poet, in addition to his skills as a storyteller and wit, is evident from poems such as the mock-heroic 'Teddy Bear', whose rhyming couplets have the effortless feel of all good writing.

WHERE THE WILD THINGS ARE
. . . .
by Maurice Sendak (Picture Lions, 1963)
Interest level: 5–8/Reading age: 5+
FEARS • MONSTERS

MAX's wild behaviour when he is wearing his wolf suit results in his being sent to bed without his supper. That night in his room a forest grows, and Max finds himself transported to the home of the Wild Things – engagingly grotesque monsters who like nothing better than roaring and ranting. Max is crowned King of the Wild Things – but even kings get lonely. So he sails back to his own room, to find his supper waiting for him.

Sendak's magical fantasy has delighted generations of young readers with its combination of surreal images and evocative text, which can be chanted like a magic spell. Apart from the exuberant delights of its celebration of 'wildness', the book is a good one for calming children's fears of monsters and the dark. One of the most renowned illustrators of children's literature, Sendak has worked with a range of other writers, including Else Minarik (*Little Bear* books), but it is for his own stories – especially his fantastic trilogy (*Where the Wild Things Are*, *In the Night Kitchen* and *Outside Over There*) that he is justifiably celebrated.

OTHER BOOKS BY MAURICE SENDAK
Chicken Soup with Rice; *Hector Protector*; *Higglety Pigglety Pop!*; *The Sign on Rosie's Door*; **In the Night Kitchen*; *Seven Little Monsters*; **Outside Over There*; *Dear Millie*

WHERE'S WALLY?

by Martin Handford (Walker Books, 1987)
Interest level: 8–10/Reading age: 8+

First of a still-growing series that has become a minor cult, this distinctive puzzle-book features the unmistakeable Wally with his bobble-hat and glasses. Children can spend hours trying to find Wally in each densely populated illustration – an exercise which, however pointless it might seem to an adult, will sharpen their perceptive skills.

WILLY THE WIMP

by Anthony Browne (Walker Books, 1984)
Interest level: 6–9/Reading age: 6+
BULLYING

Willy the Gorilla gets picked on because he is small – but then he decides to get his own back on the bullies and prove to himself he's not a wimp . . . Anthony Browne's likeable hero features in a series of books about his adventures, which will strike a chord with any child who has ever been teased about being too little.

OTHER BOOKS BY ANTHONY BROWNE
*Willy the Wizard; **Zoo*; **Piggybook*; **The Big Baby*

WILLY THE WIZARD

by Anthony Browne (Red Fox, 1996)
Interest level: 6–9/Reading age: 7+
FOOTBALL

Latest in Anthony Browne's much-loved series about a timid young gorilla finds Willy longing to be part of the football team, along with all his bigger, sportier friends. But how will he ever be able to join, without a proper pair of football boots? Then, one night as he is passing the deserted pie factory, he sees a stranger wearing old-fashioned football kit kicking a ball around. With the aid of the funny-looking boots the stranger gives him, Willy is good enough to join the team. He even gets picked to play in the big match on Saturday. Disaster strikes when Willy finds, on reaching the football ground, that he has forgotten his magic boots. But then he finds that he can play as well – if not better – without them. Illustrated with the author's humorous pictures, this story will appeal to anyone who has ever wanted to join a team, but been afraid they might not have what it takes.

WINNIE-THE-POOH

by A.A. Milne; illustrated by E.H. Shepard (Methuen, 1926)
Interest level: 4–adult/Reading age: 8+
BEARS

S INCE his first appearance over seventy years ago, Winnie-the-Pooh – Pooh Bear to his friends – has delighted young readers (and those not so young) with his adventures. Instantly recognizable as a symbol of childhood, the story of Winnie-the-Pooh has been translated into every language including Latin, and spin-off books, toys and games outsell its contemporary rivals. The enduring appeal of Pooh is not hard to understand. The characters – Pooh himself, and his friends Piglet, Eeyore, Kanga, Roo and Tigger – are vividly realized, and the woodland settings epitomize both the freedom and safety of childhood. More than this, the wit and humour of the narrative appeal to both children and adults, so that reading the stories aloud is always a delight. In the first book, we meet Pooh (briefly referred to as 'Edward Bear') as he comes downstairs 'bump, bump, bump, on the back of his head' with his young friend, Christopher Robin. After this initial encounter, establishing him as a familiar nursery teddy bear, we see him in a different capacity – as a forest-dwelling bear, living 'all by himself under the name of Sanders'. From then on, the scene is set for a series of adventures and occasional near-disasters, which Pooh survives with his customary cheerful stoicism – assisted by his good friend, Piglet, and copious amounts of honey. In the first episode, Pooh's attempts to reach a bee's nest at the top of a tree, with the aid of a balloon and a great deal of wishful thinking, are brought to an abrupt end:

'Christopher Robin, you must shoot the balloon with your gun. Have you got your gun?'

'Of course I have,' you said. 'But if I do that, it will spoil the balloon,' you said.
'But if you *don't*,' said Pooh, 'I shall have to let go, and that would spoil *me*.'

No summary of the stories adequately conveys their charm. This is one of those books which can be read time and time again, and which reveals fresh pleasures on each re-reading.

OTHER BOOKS BY A.A. MILNE
The House at Pooh Corner; *When We Were Very Young*; *Now We Are Six*

WORST WITCH, THE

by Jill Murphy (Puffin, 1974)
Interest level: 8–10/Reading age: 8+
HUMOUR • WITCHES

M ILDRED Hubble is a pupil at Miss Cackle's Academy for Witches, where she tries very hard to remember everything she is taught – about how to control her broomstick, for example, or how to make a really good spell. In this, the first of a series, Mildred gets into hot water when she turns one of her fellow pupils into a pig – and then can't remember how to turn her back again . . . The large, clear print and lively illustrations make this a good choice for independent readers.

OTHER BOOKS BY JILL MURPHY
The Worst Witch Strikes Again; *A Bad Spell for the Worst Witch*

WOW! I'M A WHALE!

by Tony Bradman (Bloomsbury Children's Books, 1996)
Interest level: 6–9/Reading age: 7+
ANIMALS

E VER wondered what it would be like to be the largest creature on earth? In Tony Bradman's entertaining story – one of the *Swoppers* series – Nathan gets a chance to find out! With the assistance of his friend, Drew the Dolphin, he discovers the hidden treasure under the sea and saves the day – before returning to his own familiar shape . . . Young readers in search of adventure will enjoy getting to grips with this larger-than-life tale.

Zoo in the Attic, The
. . . .

by Hilary McKay; illustrated by Tony Kenyon (Gollancz, 1995)
Interest level: 8–10/Reading age: 8+
ANIMALS

Wʜᴇɴ Danny receives a goldfish instead of the sheepdog he wants for his birthday, he decides to create his own zoo – in the attic! This of course leads to trouble . . . One of a series of amusing adventures about the Paradise House gang from the Smarties Prize-winning author.

Junior School – Consolidating Reading Skills

YEAR FOUR: 8–9 YEARS

Adventure, humour, fantasy, magic, monsters, mystery, space exploration . . . It's never a problem finding something to interest eight- to nine-year-olds – the only challenge is keeping up with their apparently insatiable need for intellectual stimulation. This is an age when ideas often run ahead of the child's ability to express them, resulting in frustration for both child and parent. The books your child can now read easily may be discarded as too babyish, while the more complex and rewarding stories she craves may seem too difficult.

Many publishers have responded to this perceived gap between reading and comprehension age by producing series of books aimed specifically at young readers, which contain just enough new material to provide a challenge while helping to consolidate what is already familiar. The text in these stories is often broken up by line drawings or, in some cases, strip cartoons, providing a transition between picture books and what my son used to refer to as 'chapter' books. They are generally fairly easy to read, without being boring, and can be polished off at a sitting. This in itself is satisfying, and helps build reading confidence.

In addition to consolidating established skills, it is important to provide incentives for your child to read more widely. These may come through schoolwork – perhaps as part of a class project – or from outside stimuli, such as a visit to the theatre or to a museum. This is an age when children start to become interested in history, and in other cultures. They begin to question the world around them, demanding information about everything from rainforests to radioactivity, from the Knights of the Round Table to the Hubble telescope.

YEAR FIVE: 9–10 YEARS

Information books are one way of coping with a child's need to know; another is to make sure she is reading the right kind of fiction. Increasingly, stories for children deal with a range of ideas and issues which would at one time have seemed unthinkable. There are novels about death and divorce and novels about coming to terms with being different; novels with historical settings and novels set in the future. For this age group, the sky really *is* the limit.

Unlike children of past generations, most modern children are exposed from an early age to a very wide variety of different stimuli, mainly from the television and computers. They are bombarded with information – not all of it appropriate to their level of understanding – on every conceivable subject. So it is hardly surprising that, around this age, many children seem to lose interest in reading, preferring more instantly accessible forms of entertainment, such as playing computer games or watching videos. Compared with the delights of Nintendo or *Neighbours*, settling down with a good book seems too much like hard work.

So what do you do, if your child won't read? Is there anything you *can* do, apart from getting rid of the television and banning Super-Mario?

Well, the first thing to remember is that for many children, being anti-reading is only a stage, and is often connected with growing independence and self-assertiveness. 'I *hate* reading' can be a way of saying 'I want to be left alone', or 'I want to make up my own mind about what I do with my time'. It may be difficult for parents to sympathize, but switching off the television and insisting your child reads a book instead is more likely to increase her resistance than otherwise. Reading is something you have to *want* to do.

A more positive approach to the problem is to take advantage of the reading incentives offered by television and films. Scarcely a week goes by without a television dramatization of a children's classic – distinguished examples from the 1990s include *The Lion, the Witch and the Wardrobe*, *The Box of Delights* and *The Borrowers* – while a glance around any bookshop will show a huge range of TV tie-ins, from novels to 'make and do' books. Films – even the non-literary kind – are another way of awakening children's interest in books. For a couple of years, my son's reading was dominated by books about Ninja Turtles and other superheroes – but at least it kept him reading.

For the computer addict, there is an increasing number of interactive games and stories available on CD-ROM, often with the text included as part of the package. OK – so it's not the same as turning the pages of a book, but at least it involves the same kind of mechanisms. The key word here is 'interactivity' – the relationship that's being created between your child's brain and the text. Writing your own story on the computer or making decisions about what direction a story should take are very different activities from merely sitting passively in front of the television.

And because publishers are all too aware of the fascination computers and computer games hold for children, a lot of books have started appearing on the market which take advantage of this fact. These are not only factual books about computers, but fiction which incorporates some of the aspects of computer technology children find so attractive – such as multiple-choice endings, colourful graphics and comic-strip format. Not that the latter is new by any means – as the publishers of the very popular *Tintin* and *Asterix* books would doubtless agree!

YEAR SIX: 10–11 YEARS

The final year of primary school, with SATs tests and Key Stage 2 attainment scores to contend with – not to mention the prospect of secondary school – can be an overwhelming one for many children. Suddenly, their reading and writing skills are foregrounded, as they and their parents begin the gruelling task of visiting and selecting schools for the following year. They may even start to bring home more work from school, as teachers try to prepare them for the levels of homework they will have to deal with in Year Seven. Some children may be working towards entrance examinations for private schools – and this, in addition to their ordinary schoolwork, may seem like an additional burden.

It is hardly surprising that some children react against school at this time, resisting encouragement from teachers and parents alike, and alternating between saying that primary school is 'boring' and saying that they never want to leave. Teachers I have spoken to have said that they find this a difficult year, with so much of it taken up by the transfer to secondary school. They have the unenviable task of keeping children involved in current work and developing existing skills as far as possible, while knowing that the focus of interest for both children and parents has already shifted elsewhere.

Reading is of course crucial to this whole year. Not only is it essential to the child's achievement across a range of subjects, all of which will be taught at a level appropriate to the child's age and abilities, but it is also, for many education authorities, the yardstick by which a child's overall attainment is measured. In the London area, Reading Tests, with their concomitant bands ranging from 1 to 3, have been in use for a number of years.

Even for those children moving from a state primary school into the private sector, reading scores can make all the difference to whether a child is offered a place at a particular school or not. In addition, where the school's selection procedure involves an interview, your child may well be asked what books she likes, or what she has read recently. Without making it too obvious that she has been coached to say the right thing, it's a good idea to talk this over with your child beforehand. Children – like adults – sometimes freeze in interviews. Going over a brief list of favourite books may be just the thing she needs to get her to relax.

If your child has enjoyed a book she usually has good reasons for it – so get her to say why. This will be helpful not just in a hypothetical interview, but when she comes to do practical criticism in Year Seven. Some primary schools encourage the development of critical skills from quite an early stage, by getting children to write weekly book reports. By the age of ten or eleven, a child should be able to talk about character, plot and even style with some confidence. Given that a lot of fiction written for the eleven-plus age group is as sophisticated in terms of plot and characterization as some adult fiction, there is generally plenty to talk about.

This is an age when – despite the stresses and strains of secondary transfer – many children become voracious readers, with the stamina to tackle complex and lengthy texts.

AESOP'S FABLES

Retold by Jacqueline Morley; illustrated by Giovanni Caselli
(Macdonald Young Books, 1995)
Interest level: 9–11/Reading age: 9 +
ANIMALS

CHILDREN's literature is nothing if not eclectic – and the continuing popularity of these moral tales, supposedly dating from the sixth century BC, is a case in point. First printed in an English version by Caxton, the tales were later adapted in a characteristically Gallic form by La Fontaine. Their wit and universal nature has made them part of Western cultural tradition, so that even someone who has not read the story of 'The Fox and the Grapes' can understand what is meant by the expression 'sour grapes'. In this version, Jacqueline Morley's clear retelling and Giovanni Caselli's fine illustrations enhance the pleasure of the original.

ALCHYMIST'S CAT, THE

by Robin Jarvis (Simon & Schuster, 1991)
Interest level: 11–15/Reading age: 11 +
ADVENTURE • ANIMALS • FANTASY • MAGIC • TUDORS & STUARTS

WHEN young orphan Will Godwin travels to London to seek his uncle, his life takes a frighteningly unexpected turn. After witnessing the murder of his travelling companion, he is taken in by the eccentric apothecary, Doctor Spittle, who forces him to become his servant in return for sheltering him from the mob. Will soon discovers that there is more to Doctor Spittle than meets the eye. For the irascible apothecary also dabbles in black magic, in his quest for the Philosopher's Stone which will turn base metal into gold – a quest in which Will becomes his helpless accomplice. The only element of comfort in the boy's miserable existence is when he stumbles across a family of new-born kittens and their mother in a nearby churchyard, and brings them home to rear. Unknown to Will, the kittens have powers of their own – which the wicked Doctor Spittle attempts to harness . . .

Robin Jarvis's ingenious novel – the first in a highly popular series – excitingly conveys the atmosphere of seventeenth-century London, both through the eyes of his young hero and through those of Will's feline friends. Rich in historical incident – the book is set in 1664, on the eve of the Plague and the Great Fire – and filled with authentically gruesome details about black magic, this is a book that will appeal to any young reader with a vivid imagination and a liking for history.

OTHER BOOKS BY ROBIN JARVIS

The *Deptford Histories: The Oaken Throne Thomas*; The **Deptford Mice* trilogy: *The Dark Portal*; *The Crystal Prison*; *The Final Reckoning*; The **Whitby* series: *The Whitby Witches*; *A Warlock in Whitby*

ANGEL FOR MAY, AN

by Melvin Burgess (Puffin, 1992)
Interest level: 11–14/Reading age: 11+/Key Stage: 3
ADVENTURE ● DIVORCE ● MENTAL ILLNESS ● WAR

TAM lives with his divorced mother in the Yorkshire town of Cawldale. Still angry with his parents for ending their marriage, he spends a lot of time on his own, especially in the ruined farmhouse called Thowt-It, high on the hill overlooking the town. It is there that he encounters Rosey, a down-and-out woman whom he has seen wandering around Cawldale with her dog, Winnie. Tam is repelled by Rosey's dirty and unkempt appearance, but is also fascinated by her. Through her, he is transported back in time to the Second World War, when Cawldale looked very different from the way Tam has known it, and Thowt-It was a prosperous-looking farm, not a blackened ruin. During his sojourn in the past, Tam meets May, a girl his own age who is different from all the other children. Considered mentally retarded, she is in fact a survivor of a terrible childhood, whom Tam is able to help with his kindness towards her. But then Tam has to return to his own time, and finds he has some explaining to do as to exactly where and with whom he has been . . .

Burgess's novel incorporates ideas about time and history, as well as concerns about the way people now and in the past regarded mental illness, into a plausible and compelling story. Tam is a likeable hero, with whose hurt and confusion many children of separated parents will identify. His befriending of May and Rosey – who turn out to be one and the same person – gives him a perspective on his own unhappiness, and helps him to deal with it.

OTHER BOOKS BY MELVIN BURGESS
*The Baby and Fly Pie; **The Earth Giant*

READ-ONS
*The Stone Menagerie, by Anne Fine

ANNE OF GREEN GABLES

by L.M. Montgomery (Puffin, 1908)
Interest level: 10–12/Reading age: 10+
ADVENTURE • VICTORIANS

M ONTGOMERY'S classic novel about a plucky orphan girl has been a
favourite with young readers since it first appeared. Sent by mistake to
Green Gables, a farm in Canada whose elderly owners have advertised for a
boy to help them with the farmwork, eleven-year-old Anne Shirley proves
herself a match for anyone. With her red hair and feisty attitude, Anne was the
prototype for a whole range of fearless and independent heroines in
children's literature. The book's success prompted a number of sequels,
which never quite live up to the appeal of the original.

OTHER BOOKS BY L. M. MONTGOMERY
Anne of Avonlea; *Anne of the Island*; *Anne's House of Dreams*; *Anne of
Windy Poplars*; *Anne of Ingleside*

ASTERIX

by René Goscinny; illustrated by Albert Uderzo (Hodder Dargaud,
from 1959)
Interest level: 9–13/Reading age: 11+/Key Stage: 2
HUMOUR • HISTORY • ROMANS

G OSCINNY and Uderzo's brilliant comic series about a diminutive Gallic
hero and his dim-witted but loveable sidekick Obelix is more popular
than ever, after being successfully adapted for film and television and even
given its own theme park near Paris. The first story, *Asterix the Gaul*, in which
Asterix, Obelix and the rest of the 'village of indomitable Gauls' use the
superhuman strength derived from a magic potion made by the druid Getafix
to defeat the Roman invaders, sets the tone of the following thirty or so
books. Asterix and his friends do battle with a variety of adversaries, from the
British (where they accidentally invent afternoon tea) to the Goths; they visit
the Olympic Games, meet Cleopatra and Julius Caesar and generally create
havoc wherever they go. The stories can of course be read in their original
French, and provide an enjoyable introduction to the language. The English
translation works well, however, and retains the witty place and character
names: Cacofonix the bard, Dogmatix the dog, Unhygienix the fishmonger

and so on. No less enjoyable are the illustrations, which combine a robustly comic approach to character with wonderfully detailed backgrounds, whether of Roman cities or 'barbarian' villages. As with the *Tintin* series, the comic-strip format proves enduringly popular with young readers.

BABYSITTERS' CLUB, THE
. . . .

by Anne M. Martin (Scholastic, 1995)
Interest level: 11–14/Reading age: 11+

THIS popular American series aimed at girls concerns the adventures of the various members of the eponymous club. These range from the day-to-day exigencies of coping with neighbours' troublesome toddlers to much spookier goings-on – as seen, for example, in the Mystery Special story, *Babysitters' Haunted House*. While these and other series books (such as *Point Horror* and the *Sweet Valley* series) are not great literature, they often bridge a gap between, say, children's adventure stories of the *Famous Five* variety and more demanding fiction.

BACK HOME
. . . .

by Michelle Magorian (Puffin, 1985)
Interest level: 11–15/Reading age: 11+/Key Stage: 3
FAMILIES • GROWING UP • WAR

IT is 1945, and the Second World War is over. All across Europe, people are picking up the pieces of their lives – and none more so than twelve-year-old Rusty Dickinson, returning home to England after spending five years as an evacuee in America. After so long away from her real family, Rusty finds it hard to adjust. Life in austerity Britain seems a far cry from the affluence she has enjoyed as a member of an American household – to say nothing of the greater independence she had there. To add insult to injury, Rusty's mother, Peggy, doesn't seem all that pleased to have her back. May be she should have stayed 'back home' in America after all? Michelle Magorian's sensitive account of the strains of growing up in two different cultures has all the more impact because of its post-war setting. For any child who wants to know what civilian life during and just after the war was like, this book offers some invaluable insights.

OTHER BOOKS BY MICHELLE MAGORIAN
* *Goodnight, Mr Tom*

BALLET SHOES
. . . .
by Noel Streatfield (Puffin, 1936)
Interest level: 9–12/Reading age: 9+
ADVENTURE ● BALLET

DESPITE its title, Streatfield's classic is not just a story for balletomanes, but one of the first children's career novels, exploring the attractions – and drawbacks – of life on the stage. Pauline, Petrova and Posy are adopted by Great-Uncle Matthew (a.k.a. GUM) and sent to the Children's Academy of Dancing and Stage Training. Here, they develop their respective careers: Pauline eventually goes to Hollywood, Posy becomes a ballet dancer and Petrova forsakes the performing arts altogether in order to learn to fly.

BATH RAT, THE
. . . .
by Sian Lewis (Andersen Press, 1995)
Interest level: 9–13/Reading age: 9+
ANIMALS ● ENVIRONMENT ● PETS

EVERAT the rat – or plain Rat as he prefers to be known – is an escapee from the Martingale Institute, a scientific research laboratory where, until recently, he led a pampered existence. But a few words from Doc, a visiting sewer rat, have left Rat feeling disillusioned about his life. He is not the star he has thought himself to be, but a deluded creature who has bartered his freedom for an easy life . . . Lewis's previous books have dealt with environmental concerns, as this thoughtful novel for younger teenagers does. Animal rights are also touched on – although the question of animal experimentation is avoided.

OTHER NOVELS BY SIAN LEWIS
Plug. Project Kite

READ-ONS
* *Watership Down*, by Richard Adams

BFG, THE
....

by Roald Dahl; illustrated by Quentin Blake (Puffin, 1982)
Interest level: 9–11/Reading age: 9+
ADVENTURE ● HUMOUR

O NE night Sophie is plucked out of her bed by a giant. She is afraid that he is going to eat her – but it turns out that she is in luck. For unlike his terrifying neighbours, man-eating giants who like nothing better than 'guzzling and swallomping little childers', this is a Big Friendly Giant – and he is definitely on Sophie's side . . . Even at its most boisterously gruesome, there is an affable side to Dahl's humour which is much in evidence here. Of all his books, *The BFG* is probably the funniest, and certainly one of the best.

OTHER BOOKS BY ROALD DAHL
Charlie and the Chocolate Factory; *Charlie and the Great Glass Elevator*; *The Witches*; *Matilda*; *James and the Giant Peach*; *The Enormous Crocodile*; *The Minpins*; *Fantastic Mr Fox*

BIG BAZOOHLEY, THE
....

by Peter Carey; illustrated by Abira Ali (Faber & Faber, 1995)
Interest level: 9–11/Reading age: 9+
ADVENTURE ● FANTASY

O NE winter's night in the middle of a blizzard, nine-year-old Sam Kellow arrives with his parents in Toronto, in search of what Sam's father, a professional gambler, calls the 'Big Bazoohley' – the big win which will transform their lives. Sam's mother, Vanessa, is an artist who specializes in painting miniatures. It is one of these which she hopes to sell to Mr de Vere, an eccentric millionaire who lives in an underground mansion hidden behind the door to a janitor's room on Bloor Street subway station. When this plan misfires, Sam realizes that it is up to him to rescue the family fortunes. But it is not until the night he is inadvertently locked out of the family's hotel room that he finds a way of doing so. For the hotel is full of other families, waiting to compete in the 'Perfecto Kiddo' competition to find the child with the most perfect manners. Sam decides that if anyone is going to win the $10,000 prize money, it has to be him . . .

In this, his first novel for children, Peter Carey displays the same surreal sense of humour which distinguishes his adult fiction. Sam is a likeable and resourceful hero, who wins the day by being himself – which is, of course, the underlying moral of this entertaining fable.

BIGGLES

by Captain W. E. Johns (Red Fox, from 1932)
Interest level: 11–13/Reading age; 11+
ADVENTURE

H EROIC First World War flying ace Major James Bigglesworth – a.k.a. Biggles – was the creation of Captain W. E. Johns, whose stories about Biggles and his pals Algy and Ginger appeared between the early 1930s and the 1970s, attracting a devoted following amongst young readers and aspiring aviators. Although they have been frequently castigated for their jingoistic and xenophobic attitudes, the stories have remained in print – doubtless because they are also very exciting.

OTHER BOOKS BY W. E. JOHNS
Biggles in France; *Biggles Learns to Fly*; *Biggles Flies West*; *Biggles and Co*; *Biggles – Flying Detective*

BLACK BEAUTY

by Anna Sewell (Puffin, 1877)
Interest level: 9–11/Reading age: 10+
ADVENTURE ● ANIMALS ● HORSES

A RGUABLY the most famous animal story ever written, Sewell's novel tells the story of the eponymous horse, from his days as the pride of Squire Gordon's stable to his treatment at the hands of a cruel cab-owner, and subsequent rescue. The book has been filmed several times, and remains popular with young animal lovers today for its imaginative portrayal of the sufferings of a beautiful, sentient creature.

Black Ships before Troy
. . . .

by Rosemary Sutcliff; illustrated by Alan Lee
(Frances Lincoln, 1993)
Interest level: 10–13/Reading age: 10+

D ISTINGUISHED writer of children's historical fiction, Rosemary Sutcliff's
retelling of Homer's *Iliad* captures the excitement and vividness of the
original, while making the story more accessible to younger readers. Alan
Lee's dramatic illustrations enhance the effect.

OTHER BOOKS BY ROSEMARY SUTCLIFF
* *The Eagle of the Ninth*; *The Mark of the Horse Lord*; *The Shining Company*;
Warrior Scarlet; *The Silver Branch*; *The Lantern Bearers*; *Frontier Wolf*;
Outcast; *Blood Feud*; *Dawn Wind*

Blitzcat
. . . .

by Robert Westall (Macmillan, 1989)
Smarties Prize
Interest level: 11–13/Reading age: 11+/Key Stage: 3
ADVENTURE ● ANIMALS ● WAR

S ET in wartime Coventry, Westall's gripping adventure story is unusual in
featuring as its central character a cat, but is otherwise a straightforward
and very realistic account of what life was like for civilians in wartime. The
Blitzcat – or Lord Gort as she is called – is an ordinary cat who gets caught up in
extraordinary events, in the course of her quest for her original owner, an RAF
pilot involved in cross-Channel bombing raids. Blitzcat's journey takes her into
some dangerous places, but she always emerges unscathed, inadvertently
acting as guide and good-luck talisman to the people she encounters.

Blubber
. . . .

by Judy Blume (Macmillan, 1981)
Interest level: 9–11/Reading age: 9+
BULLYING

E VERYBODY teases Linda about being fat – especially Jill. Then one day the
tables are turned and Jill finds out exactly how miserable it feels to be
bullied . . . Judy Blume's story sensitively explores the all-too-common

phenomenon of bullying, showing it from both the victim's and the perpetrator's angle.

OTHER BOOKS BY JUDY BLUME
Otherwise Known as Sheila the Great; *Freckle Juice*; *Fudge-a-mania*

BORROWERS, THE
. . . .
by Mary Norton; illustrated by Pauline Baynes (Puffin, 1952)
Interest level: 9–12/Reading age: 9+
FANTASY • LONELINESS

FIRST and best of the *Borrowers* series, about a family of tiny people who live under the floorboards of an old house otherwise inhabited only by a bedridden old lady, her ferocious housekeeper, Mrs Driver, and the gardener, Crampfurl. Fourteen-year-old Arriety and her parents Pod and Homily have lived under the grandfather clock in the hall for as long as Arriety can remember, subsisting on what Pod can 'borrow' from the great house above – everything from scraps of food to the materials from which their underground home is built. Their peaceful but also rather limited existence is disturbed when Arriety, who has accompanied her father on her first 'borrowing' expedition, encounters another child – the old lady's ten-year-old great-nephew, who is staying in the house. Despite the disparity in their respective sizes, the two become friends – a relationship brought to an abrupt end when Mrs Driver spies on the boy during his midnight visits to the little family. The story ends with the Borrowers forced to leave the house for the wide world beyond it – a situation explored in the first of several sequels, *The Borrowers Afield*.

OTHER BOOKS BY MARY NORTON
The Borrowers Afloat; *The Borrowers Aloft*; *Bednobs and Broomsticks*

READ-ONS
The Mennyms series, by Sylvia Waugh

BOX OF DELIGHTS, THE
. . . .

by John Masefield (Heinemann, 1935)
Interest level: 9–12/Reading age: 9 +
ADVENTURE ● FANTASY ● MAGIC

M ASEFIELD'S classic tale, the self-contained sequel to * The Midnight Folk, is one of the most exciting and atmospheric stories ever written for children. Like C.S. Lewis's * The Lion, the Witch and the Wardrobe, it has all the ingredients of the perfect adventure: a group of children snowed in over Christmas in a remote, rambling house, with adults conveniently absent and a heady mixture of mystery, danger and magic in the air. The book (which has been well dramatized for television) opens with young Kay Harker returning home for the Christmas holidays and meeting some very suspicious-looking clergymen on the train. Just as Kay realizes that the 'clergymen' have picked his pocket, he runs into the mysterious Punch-and-Judy man, Cole Hawlings, who entrusts him with the magical Box of Delights. With this device, which bestows time-travelling, shape-shifting and telekinetic powers on its possessor, Kay is able to eavesdrop on the dastardly schemes of sorcerer Abner Brown and his gang of ruffians, who are determined to get their hands on the Box of Delights for their own evil ends . . . Although some of the period details may be puzzling to contemporary readers (there is reference to a villain 'getting the rope', for example), the set-piece scenes of magical transformation, in which Kay meets mythological figures such as Herne the Hunter and witnesses the siege of Troy, are spell-binding. As with the *Narnia* stories – and, indeed, most children's books published more than a decade ago – young readers simply filter out the bits they don't understand and get on with enjoying the rest.

BUG MULDOON
. . . .

by Paul Shipton (Oxford University Press, 1995)
Interest level: 9–13/Reading age: 9 +
HUMOUR

'T HE name's Muldoon – Bug Muldoon . . .' The expectations aroused by the arresting opening to Paul Shipton's very funny spoof of the classic private-eye genre are amply fulfilled by the rest of the story, in which the eponymous Bug, a tough, wise-cracking detective who just happens to be a beetle, has to solve the mystery of the disappearing earwig and, in doing so, uncovers a conspiracy between the ants and the wasps to take over the garden . . . Nature study will never seem the same again.

BUTTY BOY, THE

by Jill Paton Walsh; illustrated by Juliette Palmer (Puffin, 1975)
Interest level: 9–11/Reading age: 9+
ADVENTURE • VICTORIANS

WHEN Harriet – who prefers to be called Harry – moves with her parents to the countryside near Shipton, she is at first disappointed to find that it is not near the sea. But then she discovers the canal, and her two new friends, Ned the 'butty boy' and his sister, Bess, and a series of wonderful adventures begins . . . Jill Paton Walsh's charming story about life on a canal barge in the 1880s conveys the strenuous hardship but also the warmth of Ned's and Bess's family life.

OTHER BOOKS BY JILL PATON WALSH
The Dolphin Crossing; *A Parcel of Patterns*; *Fireweed*; *A Chance Child*

READ-ONS
The Peppermint Pig, by Nina Bawden

CAN YOU SUE YOUR PARENTS FOR MALPRACTICE?

by Paula Danziger (Mammoth, 1986)
Interest level: 11–13/Reading age: 11+
FAMILIES • GROWING UP

BEING an adolescent is always hard – especially when you've got the kind of problems Lauren's got. As if it wasn't bad enough having a big sister who's much prettier than she is, and a little sister who drives her mad, her parents just don't seem to care . . . Paula Danziger's witty tale of teenage angst will strike a chord with many children – and parents – currently experiencing this turbulent stage.

OTHER BOOKS BY PAULA DANZIGER
The Divorce Express

CARRIE'S WAR
. . . .

by Nina Bawden (Puffin, 1973)
Interest level: 9–11/Reading age: 10+
ADVENTURE ● WAR

Bawden's gripping novel – based on her own experience as an evacuee during the Second World War – describes its young heroine's evacuation, with her brother, to wartime Wales, where she is taken in by the overbearing religious zealot Councillor Samuel Evans and his downtrodden sister. Things go from bad to worse when Carrie takes it upon herself to try to patch up the rift between Councillor Evans and his relatives at a nearby farm. Utterly convincing in its portrayal of a child's view of the world, this is Bawden at her most realistic and compelling.

OTHER BOOKS BY NINA BAWDEN
The Peppermint Pig; *Keeping Henry*; *The Outside Child*; *Humbug*; *The Real Plato Jones*; *The White Horse Gang*; *The Secret Passage*

READ-ONS
The Machine Gunners, by Robert Westall; *Goodnight, Mr Tom*, by Michelle Magorian; *Fireweed*, by Jill Paton Walsh; *Stonestruck*, by Helen Cresswell

CHARLIE AND THE CHOCOLATE FACTORY
. . . .

by Roald Dahl (Puffin, 1964)
Interest level: 9–11/Reading age: 9+
ADVENTURE ● HUMOUR

Dahl's famous story, about a small boy who wins a day out at a magical chocolate factory run by the millionaire confectioner Willy Wonka, has been a favourite with children since it was first published in the 1960s, for its anarchic humour and its cast of splendidly grotesque characters, including the odious Veruca Salt, a spoilt little rich girl, gum-chewing Violet Beauregard, the television-addicted Mike Teavee, the monstrously fat Augustus Gloop and the eccentric Mr Wonka himself. As with most of Dahl's books, there isn't much of a plot – not that it matters because the main thing is the book's slapstick humour. The five children who have won one of Willy Wonka's Golden Tickets to the chocolate factory undergo a series of tests, which only nice, unspoiled Charlie Bucket passes with flying colours. The bad children are all appropriately punished (greedy Augustus falls into the chocolate river, Violet turns blue and Veruca is incinerated in the nut-roasting machine) but Charlie lives to enjoy another adventure in the book's sequel, *Charlie and the Great Glass Elevator.*

OTHER BOOKS BY ROALD DAHL
*Matilda; *The Witches; *The BFG

COMPUTER NUT, THE
. . . .
by Betsey Byars (Red Fox, 1984)
Interest level: 9–11/Reading age: 9+
COMPUTERS

W HEN Kate's art teacher asks the class to do a self-portrait for their homework, Kate decides to do hers on her dad's computer. But while she is putting the finishing touches to her 'Portrait of a Computer Nut', a very strange message flashes up on the screen – from someone calling himself BB9. BB9 claims to be an alien, who has tapped into her computer from outer space. Kate's first reaction is that it must be a joke. After all, aliens don't exist – or *do* they? An ideal read for young computer nuts everywhere.

OTHER BOOKS BY BETSEY BYARS
The TV Kid; McMummy; Bingo Brown; The Cybil War

CRACK A STORY
. . . .
by Susan Price (Faber & Faber, 1990)
Interest level: 9–11/Reading age: 11+
FAIRY TALES

A perfect little nut tree grows, just like any ordinary tree, with supple branches and trunk. But this tree's leaves are made from bronze, and on its branches grow nuts made from every substance. There are nuts of sherbet in glass shells, nuts of moonstone in shells of silver, rock-salt in gold, and even poison in a shell of steel. In the nut tree lives a carnelian squirrel, who spends her time running from limb to limb, cracking the shells and eating the nuts. For every nut she cracks, she tells a different story . . . A unique and captivating compilation of traditional and original fairy stories, which will enchant younger readers and help to recapture the interest of older ones. For as we are told at the very end of the book, 'when no nuts grow, and there are none to crack, and no stories to tell, then it must be that the world will end.'

OTHER BOOKS BY SUSAN PRICE

* *The Ghost Drum* trilogy; *Ghosts at Large*; *In a Nutshell*; *Sticks and Stones*

CRAZY SHOE SHUFFLE, THE
. . . .

by Gillian Cross (Methuen, 1995)
Interest level: 9–11/Reading age: 9+
GROWING UP • HUMOUR

L EE's day at school begins badly when his football is confiscated by grumpy Mr Merton. Then he falls foul of stern Mrs Puddock, the headmistress. Even nice Miss Cherry finds fault with him. Worst of all, he has to stay behind and tidy up the school cloakroom, sorting out all the jumbled-up shoes. On his way home, Lee meets a strange old woman and finds that some very odd things start happening. Next day, there is no sign of the three teachers – but three new pupils have arrived at school in their place. Weedy Geoffrey bears an uncanny resemblance to Mr Merton, bossy Valerie is the spitting image of Mrs Puddock and goody-goody Marigold is so like Miss Cherry that Lee can't believe he's the only one who's noticed . . .

Gillian Cross's comic tale has an underlying message about the way people can become trapped in roles they would like to break out of. Children love the idea of teachers getting their come-uppance – but should also appreciate the moral.

CRIMSON FAIRY BOOK, THE
. . . .

edited by Andrew Lang (Longmans, 1903)
Interest level: 9–11/Reading age: 9+
FAIRY TALES

O NE of a highly successful series of twelve launched in 1890 with *The Red Fairy Book*, this and its companion volumes (*Blue, Green, Yellow, Pink, Grey, Violet, Brown, Orange, Olive* and *Lilac*) introduced many young readers to the delights of fairy tales from around the world, and set a standard for imaginative retelling of traditional tales which has never been surpassed. Tales from Perrault, the Arabian Nights and the Brothers Grimm are mingled with English folk tales and legends from other cultures, to provide an inspiring and exciting mix, in which most children will find something to enthrall them.

DAYDREAMER, THE

by Ian McEwan; illustrated by Anthony Brown
(Jonathan Cape, 1995)
Interest level: 9–11/Reading age: 10 +
FANTASY

TEN-YEAR-OLD Peter Fortune is a daydreamer whose fantasies sometimes get him into trouble. At home and at school he is often accused of time-wasting, when he is in fact engaged in a whole range of exciting pursuits – from sliding down mountains to saving his younger sister from a pack of hungry wolves. Sometimes Peter's daydreams can be frightening – like the time his sister's dolls, led by the sinister figure of the Bad Doll, decide to take over Peter's room. Others have a magical quality. Peter changes places with the family cat, and finds out what being an animal is *really* like; he also becomes a baby for a day.

Ian McEwan, better known for his adult fiction, envisages the world of a child's imagination with great sensitivity, and with an accuracy of observation which any parent of an imaginative child will appreciate.

DEMON HEADMASTER, THE

by Gillian Cross (Puffin, 1982)
Interest level: 9–12/Reading age: 10 +
FANTASY • HORROR • SCHOOL

WHEN orphan Dinah Glass goes to live with the Hunter family she gets sent to the school already attended by the Hunter boys, Harvey and Lloyd. It is not long before she starts to notice that there is something not right about her new school. Instead of the children running about enjoying themselves in the playground, they just stand in circles chanting their times tables. Dinah finds out why when she meets the school's sinister Headmaster, who uses his hypnotic powers to control his pupils. Can Dinah and her friends resist the evil power of the Headmaster and his prefects – or will he succeed in his dastardly plan to take over the world? Exciting, funny and very readable, this is Gillian Cross at her best.

OTHER BOOKS BY GILLIAN CROSS
The Revenge of the Demon Headmaster; *The Prime Minister's Brain*; *The Great Elephant Chase*; *Wolf*; *Twin and Super-Twin*; *The Crazy Shoe Shuffle*

DEPTFORD MICE TRILOGY, THE

by Robin Jarvis (Simon & Schuster, 1989)
Interest level: 11–14/Reading age: 11 +
ADVENTURE ● ANIMALS ● FANTASY ● MAGIC

I N the sewers of Deptford lives a community of mice whose lives are ruled by terror of a dark presence, known to them only as Jupiter, Lord of All. But then one day, an innocent little mouse named Albert sets in motion a terrifying train of events culminating in sorcery, murder and mayhem . . . Robin Jarvis's gripping saga combines its more far-fetched elements with realistic details of London life. A must for any young reader with a liking for fantasy, magic and adventure and plenty of reading stamina.

OTHER BOOKS BY ROBIN JARVIS
The Alchymist's Cat (Book I of the *Deptford Mice* Trilogy); *The Whitby series

DOWN WITH SKOOL!

by Geoffrey Willans; illustrated by Ronald Searle (Pavilion, 1953)
Interest level: 10–13/Reading age: 10 +
HUMOUR ● SCHOOL

G EOFFREY Willans's wickedly funny satire of school life has been much imitated (notably by Colin and Jacqui Hawkins in *School*), but no other book has quite matched its mixture of irreverent humour and zany fantasy – like *Stalky & Co* crossed with *Monty Python's Flying Circus*. This, the first of four books (the others are *How to be Topp*, *Back in the Jug Agane* and *Whizz for Atoms*), features the inimitable Nigel Molesworth (surely a precursor of Adrian Mole?), who gives us the low-down on 'kanes, lat. french, geog. hist, algy, geom, headmasters, skool dogs, skool sossages, my bro molesworth 2 and MASTERS everywhere . . .' A gem.

EMIL AND THE DETECTIVES
. . . .

by Erich Kastner (Red Fox, 1929)
Interest level: 9–11/Reading age: 9 +
ADVENTURE

WHEN ten-year-old Emil Tischbein, the son of a poor widow, is sent by his mother from their home in Neustadt to Berlin, he is entrusted with some money for his keep, which Emil is supposed to give to his grandparents. On the train, however, the money is stolen and Emil – for reasons of his own – decides not to go to the police. Instead, he sets out to track down the thief himself – and in doing so, enlists the aid of a whole gang of children . . . Kastner's funny and entertaining tale set a fashion for 'child detective' stories (others include Enid Blyton's *Famous Five* series) and has remained very popular with young readers.

EXILES, THE
. . . .

by Hilary McKay (Collins, 1991)
Guardian Children's Fiction Award
Interest level: 9–11/Reading age: 9 +
ADVENTURE • FAMILIES • SIBLINGS

PACKED off to stay with their grandmother during the summer holidays while their parents get on with some home improvements, Ruth, Naomi, Rachel and Phoebe are horrified to find that they are expected to *work* for their keep, digging 'Big Grandma's' garden and doing her household chores. Worse than that, there aren't even any books for the girls to read – and (doubtless because they have grown up without a television) all four are voracious readers. So, when the work is finished for the day, the youthful exiles are obliged to make their own entertainment – which they do to hilarious effect in Hilary McKay's engaging story.

OTHER BOOKS BY HILARY MCKAY
The Exiles at Home

FAIRY TALES
. . . .

Various collections
Interest level: 7–adult

F AIRY tales have been around as long as story-telling itself, and are interwoven with the narrative traditions of most cultures. Shakespeare incorporated elements of fairy tale and folk myth into many of his plays, as Spenser did into his epic poem *The Faerie Queene*; but it was not until the seventeenth century that collections of fairy stories began to appear in Europe, becoming increasingly fashionable in the early 1700s, with the publication of Antoine Galland's translation of *The Arabian Nights*. This was followed by other collections, including *Charles Perrault's *Contes* in 1729. Between 1823 and 1826, the first translations of stories by Jacob and *Wilhelm Grimm appeared in England; to be followed, in the 1840s, by those of *Hans Christian Andersen. By the end of the nineteenth century, fairy tales had become an established part of children's literature. In 1889, *Andrew Lang published the first of his *Fairy Books*, containing stories from around the world, to be followed by eleven further volumes. Other notable collections include W.B. Yeats's *Irish Fairy Tales* (1892); *The Arthur Rackham Fairy Book* (1933), with illustrations by the author, and *Fairy Tales from the British Isles* (1960), retold by *Amabel Williams-Ellis and illustrated by *Pauline Baynes. In 1974, those distinguished anthropologists of childhood, *Iona and Peter Opie, published their study of fairy tales (*The Classic Fairy Tales*) which included many of the most famous stories. *The Faber Book of Favourite Fairy Tales* (1988), edited by Sara and Stephen Corrin and illustrated by Juan Wijngaard, is one of the best recent collections.

FAMILY FROM ONE-END STREET, THE
. . . .

by Eve Garnett (Puffin, 1937)
Carnegie Medal
Interest level: 9–11/Reading age: 10+
FAMILIES

G ARNETT'S comic novel was much admired when it first appeared for its attempt to portray a working-class family, at a time when few children's books even mentioned such class distinctions. The story concerns Mr and Mrs Ruggles and their seven children, and focuses largely on the trials and tribulations of Kate, the clever daughter, in her efforts to better herself by gaining a scholarship to the local Grammar School, in spite of the fact that her father, a dustman, is too poor to afford the expensive uniform. Although the book's depiction of this and other realities of working-class life was ground-breaking at the time, its account has since been criticized as patronizing. Whatever the truth of this, the book's influence on children's fiction has been considerable, if only in establishing a precedent for subsequent writing about real-life subjects.

FANTORA FAMILY FILES, THE

by Adele Geras; illustrated by Tony Ross (Puffin, 1988)
Interest level: 9–12/Reading age: 9+
FAMILIES ● HUMOUR ● VAMPIRES

A grandmother who can predict the future, an aunt who is a vegetarian vampire . . . the Fantora family is no ordinary family, it appears. Their hilarious adventures, as recorded by Ozymandias the cat, are for young readers who enjoy a touch of black comedy, along the lines of *The Addams Family*.

OTHER BOOKS BY ADELE GERAS
My Grandmother's Stories; *A Lane to the Land of the Dead*; *The Tower Room*

FATSO IN THE RED SUIT

by Matthew Sweeney; illustrated by David Austen
(Faber & Faber, 1995)
Interest level: 10–13/Reading age: 10+
POETRY

THE title poem in Matthew Sweeney's lively collection is about a boy who writes a special letter to Santa asking for his dad to come home for Christmas, and finds that wishes sometimes do come true.

FIVE CHILDREN AND IT
. . . .

by E. Nesbit; illustrated by H.R. Millar (Puffin Classics, 1902)
Interest level: 8–11/Reading age: 8+
ADVENTURE • FAMILIES • MAGIC • SIBLINGS • VICTORIANS

THE first in a series of stories about the magical adventures of a family of children, *Five Children and It* has remained a favourite with young readers since its publication over ninety years ago. Robert, Anthea, Jane, Cyril and the Baby (a.k.a. the Lamb) are spending the summer with their mother – and the assorted servants without whom no upper-middle-class household of the era would have been complete – in a cottage in the Kentish countryside. Here, in a nearby gravel pit, the children encounter the Psammead, a small furry creature with eyes on stalks which turns out to be a kind of fairy. The Psammead has the power to grant wishes, and the rest of this highly entertaining book is concerned with the children's attempts to make the most of this magical opportunity. In one episode, they experience a version of the King Midas story, when their wish for inexhaustible riches turns out to be a dubious blessing; other wishes, such as a rashly expressed desire to be 'beautiful as the day', are equally fraught with complexities. The story's underlying message is that one ought to be very careful about making wishes, because sometimes one gets exactly what one wishes for. Nesbit conveys all this with the minimum of moralizing and with a great deal of delightful humour. Her children come across as real children, with all their idiosyncrasies and occasional imperfections. Some (adult) readers are uncomfortable with the fact that most of the households Nesbit describes include cooks and nannies (similar objections can be made to *A.A. Milne); attentive readers will observe that the servants in this and the other books in the series play a far more important role in the story and are more differentiated as characters than the children's parents. Most young readers, in my experience, are well able to put such matters into perspective.

OTHER BOOKS IN THE SAME SERIES BY E. NESBIT
The Story of the Amulet; *The Phoenix and the Carpet*

FLAT STANLEY
. . . .
by Jeff Brown (Mammoth, 1964)
Interest level: 9–11/Reading age: 9+
DISABILITY

JEFF Brown's engaging story about a boy who ends up only half an inch thick after being squashed flat by a notice-board – and then finds himself able to squeeze into all kinds of tight situations – has appealed to young readers' sense of the absurd ever since it was first published over thirty years ago. Stanley's fantastic adventures, which include letting his younger brother 'fly' him like a kite and slipping through a grating to recover his mother's ring, culminate in the scene where he foils a gang of art thieves by posing as a painting on the wall of the gallery! Underlying the fun is a serious message about how we treat people who are 'different'.

OTHER BOOKS BY JEFF BROWN
Stanley and the Magic Lamp; *Stanley in Space*; *Stanley's Christmas Adventure*; *Invisible Stanley*

GHOST DRUM, THE
. . . .
by Susan Price (Faber & Faber, 1987)
Carnegie Medal, 1987
Interest level: 9–12/Reading age: 9+
ADVENTURE • FANTASY • GHOSTS • MAGIC • WITCHES

IN a land ruled by a cruel and despotic Czar, a young prince is kept in captivity in a windowless tower, dreaming of the day when he will find out what the world is really like, and a young girl, Chingis, learns the arts of shape-shifting and magic, instructed by her witch-mother. When the time comes for the older witch to die, she leaves Chingis her spells and her magic drum, from which she can find out everything she needs to know. With the help of the drum, Chingis rescues Prince Safa from his tower – only to find that she has made a powerful enemy in his wicked aunt, Margaretta, and an even more fearsome adversary in the evil wizard, Kuzma . . . The first book in Susan Price's Carnegie Medal-winning trilogy, set in an imaginary Eastern European country, is a wonderfully compelling read, full of richly evocative detail and haunting images.

OTHER BOOKS BY SUSAN PRICE
The Ghost Song; *The Ghost Dance*; **Crack a Story*

GHOST OF THOMAS KEMPE, THE

by Penelope Lively (Mammoth, 1973)
Carnegie Medal
Interest level: 9–11/Reading age: 9 + /Key Stage 2
GHOSTS • TUDORS & STUARTS • VICTORIANS

W HEN ten-year-old James Harrison and his family move into picturesque
Elizabethan East End Cottage, in the sleepy Oxfordshire village of
Ledsham, they are unprepared for the havoc that is to follow. For the cottage
has a resident poltergeist – one Thomas Kempe Esquire, who manifests
himself as an extremely noisy and destructive spirit indeed. Unfortunately,
neither James's parents nor his older sister believe in ghosts, so James is the
one who gets the blame every time Thomas plays one of his pranks. Things
finally come to a head when the ghost starts leaving messages around the
village pointing to James as the perpetrator – and he realizes that the only way
of dealing with the unwelcome guest at East End Cottage is by hiring an
exorcist . . . Penelope Lively's award-winning story conveys its young hero's
predicament with sympathy and humour, showing that the worst thing about
James's encounter with the paranormal is not the spooky goings-on themselves but the fact that no one else believes a word he is saying.

OTHER BOOKS BY PENELOPE LIVELY
The Revenge of Samuel Stokes; *Uninvited Ghosts*; *The House in Norham
Gardens*; *A Stitch in Time*

READ-ONS
My Friend Walter, by Michael Morpurgo; *The Haunting*, by Margaret Mahy

GOODNIGHT, MR TOM

by Michelle Magorian (Puffin, 1988)
Guardian Children's Fiction Award
Interest level: 11–14/Reading age: 11 +
ADVENTURE • WAR

W HEN evacuee Willie Beech, a solitary and difficult child, is billeted with
elderly and irascible Tom Oakley, the situation looks bleak for them
both. But then, against the odds, a relationship begins to form, based on
mutual trust and affection. This inoffensive friendship is disrupted when
Willie is recalled to London, and decides to disappear – leaving Tom with a

stark choice between losing him for ever or going in search of him . . . Moving and powerful, Michelle Magorian's wartime drama conveys a sense of the rootlessness and uncertainty of civilian life at the time, and offers a hauntingly real account of a child's experience.

OTHER BOOKS BY MICHELLE MAGORIAN
*Back Home

GOOSEBUMPS SERIES
· · · · · · · · · · · · · · · · · ·
by R.L. Stine (Scholastic, 1996)
Interest level: 9–11/Reading age: 9 +
HORROR

POPULAR series of horror and ghost stories, aimed at a younger readership than that of *Point Horror* (also published by Scholastic). Plenty of spooks, shrieks and shivers, but otherwise fairly undemanding stuff.

GREAT ELEPHANT CHASE, THE
· ·
by Gillian Cross (Puffin, 1992)
Smarties Prize/Whitbread Prize
Interest level: 11–14/Reading age: 11 +
ADVENTURE ● ANIMALS ● VICTORIANS

SET in America at the end of the nineteenth century, Cross's prize-winning novel follows its two protagonists, fifteen-year-old Tad and thirteen-year-old Cissie, on a journey across the States. Tad is escaping his miserable upbringing in a small Pennsylvania mining town; Cissie has lost her father and sister in a railway accident. Cissie's late father was a travelling showman, with a sideline in patent medicines; when he dies, she is left with nothing but a box of worthless elixir – and an elephant named Khush. But then the villainous Mr Jackson claims that Khush belongs to him, and Cissie has to resort to desperate measures to keep what she believes is rightfully hers. She enlists Tad's help in a daring plan to steal Khush from under Mr Jackson's nose and take him by river to Nebraska, where she hopes they will be safe. What follows is a series of adventures and near-disasters which will keep young readers avidly turning the pages.

OTHER BOOKS BY GILLIAN CROSS
The Dark behind the Curtain; **The Demon Headmaster*; *On the Edge*; *The Prime Minister's Brain*; *Twin and Super-Twin*; *Wolf; *Chartbreak*; **The Crazy Shoe Shuffle*

HAPPY PRINCE, THE
. . . .

by Oscar Wilde (Puffin, 1888)
Interest level: 9–12/Reading age: 9+
FAIRY TALES

POET, playwright, essayist, raconteur – Wilde was among the most versatile of writers, and these nine stories show a more playful side to his gifts. Although originally written for the author's two young sons, they are as highly polished as anything he wrote, combining elements from fairy tale, myth and allegory, and incorporating some of his most lyrical prose. In one of the best-known stories, 'The Selfish Giant', an ogre prevents the children of the town from playing in his garden, until his heart is touched by a very special child. In 'The Remarkable Rocket', a vain and foolish firework deludes himself into believing that he is the most important being in the world, before expiring in a shower of sparks. As with the stories of *Walter de la Mare, there is a rich and sometimes overwrought quality to these works, betraying Wilde's allegiance to the Symbolist tradition.

HAUNTING, THE
. . . .

by Margaret Mahy (Mammoth, 1982)
Carnegie Medal
Interest level: 9–13/Reading age: 9+
FAMILIES ● FANTASY ● GHOSTS ● MAGIC

BARNEY is used to seeing and hearing things that other people can't see and hear, but when he starts receiving visitations from Great-Uncle Cole – who may or may not be a magician – he feels things have gone far enough. But who can he turn to? His sisters, Tabitha and Troy, are no help; Tabitha is wrapped up in the novel she is writing, and Troy spends most of her time aloof from the rest of the family. Even Claire, Barney's adored stepmother, can't hope to understand what he is going through. But then, on a visit to his great-grandmother, Barney learns that he, too, may be a magician – and finds himself able to confront his strange destiny with greater confidence.

Mahy makes the fantastic world of a child's imagination seem real and believable, showing how people can learn to confront their fears – even when these seem beyond control. The terrifying aspects of magic and the supernatural are not played down, but are seen as elements which can be tamed and used for benign purposes – like the imagination itself, in fact.

OTHER BOOKS BY MARGARET MAHY
Underrunners; **A Lion in the Meadow*; **The Other Side of Silence*

READ-ONS
*The Secret World of Polly Flint, by Helen Cresswell

HEIDI
. . . .
by Johanna Spyri (Puffin Modern Classics, 1881)
Interest level: 9–11/Reading age: 10+
FRIENDS

SPYRI's classic novel about a little girl growing up in the Swiss Alps has enjoyed widespread popularity since it first appeared, and has been filmed several times and adapted for television. Heidi, a five-year-old orphan, is taken to stay with her grandfather in his isolated mountain hut. Here, she becomes friends with Peter, a young goatherd, and with Peter's blind grandmother. When she is eight years old, she is removed from her grandfather's care by her officious cousin, Dete, and sent to stay with a family in Frankfurt, whose daughter, Clara, is a cripple. After a period of bitter unhappiness, Heidi is allowed to return to the mountains, where Clara comes to visit her. In a final, near-miraculous episode that is typical of the Christian mysticism pervading the whole book, Clara learns to walk.

HOMECOMING
. . . .
by Cynthia Voigt (Lions, 1981)
Interest level: 11–15/Reading age: 11+
ADVENTURE ● FAMILIES ● HOMELESSNESS ● SIBLINGS

FOUR children – Dicey, James, Maybeth and Sammy Tillerman – are abandoned by their mother in a car park in Connecticut, on their way to visit an aunt they have never seen. Even though they are still many miles from where they have to go, thirteen-year-old Dicey decides that they will try and get to Bridgeport (where their aunt lives) on foot. They accordingly set out, using the map that Dicey has bought to find the way. After several days, during which they eke out their money by scavenging and doing odd jobs, they reach their aunt's house – only to find that she has died, and that their middle-aged Cousin Eunice is living there. When living with Eunice – a pious churchgoing type – doesn't work out, the children decide to take to the road once more – this time heading for their grandmother's place in Massachusetts. After further adventures, including falling in with a travelling circus and narrowly escaping from a psychopathic farmer, they arrive at their grandmother's house, where they are met with a less than warm welcome from the irascible old lady. Eventually, after misunderstandings on both sides have been overcome, their grandmother offers them a home – and a respite from their wanderings.

One of a series of books about the Tillerman family, this is a powerful and often harrowing drama, which never pulls its punches about the dangers to which children can be exposed through the carelessness or malice of adults. Despite its grittily realistic emphasis, the book's message is an upbeat one, perhaps because it also stresses how resourceful and intelligent children can be in a crisis.

OTHER BOOKS BY CYNTHIA VOIGT
Dicey's Song; *Jackeroo*; *On Fortune's Wheel*

READ-ONS
* *The Kingdom by the Sea*, by Robert Westall

INDIAN IN THE CUPBOARD, THE
. . . .

by Lynne Reid Banks (Collins, 1988)
Interest level: 9–12/Reading age: 9 +
ADVENTURE ● MAGIC

WHEN Omri puts his toy Indian in the old bathroom cabinet and turns the key, he finds himself drawn into a world of 'real-life' Wild West adventure as exciting as it is occasionally dangerous . . . Lynne Reid Banks's ingeniously inventive story was the first in a series of four, designed to enthrall young readers with a taste for adventure – and magic.

OTHER BOOKS BY LYNNE REID BANKS
Return of the Indian; *The Secret of the Indian*; *Mystery of the Cupboard*

IRON MAN, THE

by Ted Hughes; illustrated by Andrew Davidson (Faber & Faber, 1968)

Interest level: 9–11/Reading age: 9+

ENVIRONMENT

HUGHES's visionary fable about an Iron Man who appears from nowhere to consume whole junkyards full of scrap-metal – and who then engages in a contest of strength with a giant 'space-bat-angel-dragon' which threatens the world – has become a classic of children's fiction, both for its environmental and its anti-war message. A companion volume, *The Iron Woman*, appeared in 1994.

OTHER BOOKS BY TED HUGHES

The Dreamfighter; *Tales of the Early World*; *Moonwhales

JENNINGS GOES TO SCHOOL

by Anthony Buckeridge (Macmillan, from 1950)

Interest level: 9–11/Reading age: 9+

SCHOOL

ALTHOUGH inevitably somewhat dated, Buckeridge's comic stories about Jennings and his best friend Darbishire and their escapades at Linbury Court Preparatory School have had a devoted following since they first appeared and are in the tradition of the (even more popular) *Just William* stories by Richmal Crompton.

OTHER BOOKS BY ANTHONY BUCKERIDGE

Thanks to Jennings; *Jennings in Particular*; *Especially Jennings*

JUNGLE BOOK, THE

by Rudyard Kipling (Puffin, 1894)

Interest level: 9–13/Reading age: 12+

ADVENTURE ● ANIMALS

ONE of the most powerful and exciting stories ever written for children, Kipling's famous tale (which will be known to most children in the Disney cartoon version) is set in India, and concerns a young Indian boy,

Mowgli, who is brought up by wolves after his own parents have been attacked by a tiger – the fearsome Shere Khan. When the tiger tries to claim Mowgli as his rightful prey, he is driven off by the wolves, but vows his revenge. Instructed by Akela, the Leader of the Wolf-pack, with the assistance of Baloo the bear and Bagheera, the black panther, Mowgli learns the Law of the Jungle, and becomes adept at fending for himself. Some years later, when the villainous Shere Khan attempts to overthrow Akela and assume the leadership of the pack himself, Mowgli leads a successful counter-attack against him, before returning to live in his own village.

JUST WILLIAM

by Richmal Crompton; illustrated by Thomas Henry
(Macmillan, from 1922)
Interest level: 9–13/Reading age: 11 +
ADVENTURE • HUMOUR

R ICHMAL Crompton's incorrigibly unruly schoolboy, with his perpetually dirty face and his falling-down socks, was the hero of over forty books published between 1922 and 1970. In these, William Brown, an eleven-year-old boy, lives with his parents, his eighteen-year-old brother Robert and his sister, Ethel – who is much pursued by the local young men – in an otherwise peaceful village in the Home Counties. Here, William and his gang of friends, the Outlaws, pursue various devious schemes for making money and avoiding unpleasant realities such as homework and household chores – with generally devastating results for all concerned. Apart from the official Outlaws – Ginger, Douglas and Henry – there is also a self-appointed member of the gang. This is Violet Elizabeth Bott, who, with her curls and her lisp, is an unforgettable – and unavoidable – presence in William's life. Some of the finest comic moments in the stories arise from the conflict between William's scornful resentment at Violet's intrusion into his plans, and Violet's sweetly determined refusal to be rebuffed. As with the stories of *P.G. Wodehouse, much of the humour in the *William* books is ironic, depending on the discrepancy between the hero's perception of things and reality. William's frequent misunderstanding of events in the adult world is one of the reasons why the books remain so attractive to both adult and child readers – since both, in one way or another, can share the joke.

OTHER BOOKS BY RICHMAL CROMPTON

More William; *William Again*; *William – the Fourth*; *William – the Conqueror*; *William – the Outlaw*; *William – in Trouble*; *William – the Good*

KINGDOM BY THE SEA, THE

by Robert Westall (Mammoth, 1990)
Guardian Children's Fiction Award
Interest level: 11–13/Reading age: 11+/Key Stage: 3
ADVENTURE • DEATH • WAR

WHEN twelve-year-old Harry Baguley loses his parents and younger sister in an air raid, he is left without anyone in the world – except Don, a lost dog he finds on a beach near his home in Northumberland, and which he adopts as his own. Together, Harry and Don embark on a series of adventures, in which they are always one step ahead of the authorities, whom Harry fears will send him to an orphanage – or worse, to live with Aunt Elsie. Finding that he can survive by scavenging, Harry makes a home for himself in an abandoned pillbox on the beach, and is later befriended by a kindly soldier who feeds him sandwiches from the barracks canteen. But before long Harry is on the run again . . . Westall's exciting and moving story about a child caught up in the horror and confusion of wartime is amongst his most impressive. An ideal choice for any thoughtful young reader with an interest in the period.

OTHER BOOKS BY ROBERT WESTALL
The Machine Gunners; *Blitzcat*; *A Time of Fire*

READ-ONS
Fireweed, by Jill Paton Walsh; *Goodnight, Mr Tom*, by Michelle Magorian

LAST THESAURUS, THE

Paul Muldoon; illustrated by Rodney Rigby (Faber & Faber, 1995)
Interest level: 10–12/Reading age: 10+
POETRY

PAUL Muldoon's amusing poetic fantasy, which is set on a planet inhabited by dinosaurs, describes what happens when Bert and Brunhilde Brontosaurus encounter the Last Thesaurus – a dinosaur who sounds as if he has swallowed a dictionary.

LION, THE WITCH AND THE WARDROBE, THE

. . . .

by C.S. Lewis (Lions, 1950)
Interest level: 8–11/Reading age: 9+
ADVENTURE • FAMILIES • FANTASY • MAGIC

C.S. Lewis's *Chronicles of Narnia* – of which this was the first written – have acquired a wide following in the forty years since the books were originally published. Lewis, a quirky and irascible Oxford don who was also a renowned poet and theologian, seems an unlikely candidate for a popular children's writer, and indeed, some of his writing for children has an uncomfortably moralistic tone. The Christian symbolism in the *Narnia* stories may strike some adult readers as heavy-handed; children seem untroubled by it, preferring to concentrate on the more exciting and colourful aspects of the work.

The Lion, the Witch and the Wardrobe opens with the arrival of four children – Peter, Susan, Lucy and Edmund – at a country house belonging to an elderly professor, where they have been evacuated during the Blitz. The house is rambling and half-deserted, and the children decide to amuse themselves one wet day with a game of hide-and-seek. The scene in which Lucy, the youngest of the four, hides in the wardrobe in one of the empty rooms, and finds that it is the door into the strange and magical land of Narnia, is one of the most famous in all children's literature. In her first visit to Narnia, Lucy encounters the faun, Mr Tumnus, who tells her that the whole country is under a spell cast by the White Witch, which means that it is 'always winter and never Christmas'. The White Witch, it later emerges, maintains control over her subjects through a network of informers, into which she recruits Edmund, Lucy's brother. Edmund joins the Witch in her castle, while the rest of the children align themselves with Aslan, the heroic lion, who represents the forces of Good as opposed to those of Evil.

The book ends with a battle between the two sides, in which all four children (including the treacherous Edmund) prove themselves worthy of Aslan's leadership. As a result of this battle – the first of several such encounters in the *Chronicles of Narnia* – the wicked White Witch is overthrown, and summer returns to the land.

As even a brief summary indicates, Lewis's book is a highly poetic and symbolic work, full of striking imagery and vividly imagined incidents. The characters of the children are strongly differentiated – resourceful Lucy, sly Edmund, sensible Susan and brave Peter – and there is plenty of exciting action as well as suspense to alleviate the philosophizing. Lewis's greatest achievement in these books is the creation of a complete world, with its own laws and customs and its distinctive topography.

OTHER BOOKS BY C.S. LEWIS (IN SEQUENTIAL ORDER)
The Magician's Nephew; *The Horse and His Boy*; *Prince Caspian*; *The Voyage of the* Dawn Treader; *The Silver Chair*; *The Last Battle*

LITTLE PRINCESS, A
....

by Frances Hodgson Burnett (Puffin, 1905)
Interest level: 10–12/Reading age: 10 +

W HEN eleven-year-old Sara Crewe is sent by her father from their home in India to boarding school in England, she has little idea of the reversals which are soon to overtake her. For her father's death leaves her a penniless outcast, forced to work as a servant to the school's cruel head-mistress, Miss Minchin, in return for her board and lodging. But then Sara discovers that there is more to being a 'little princess' than having money – and that sometimes goodness can triumph over adversity . . . Frances Hodgson Burnett's classic Cinderella story remains enduringly popular, and has been filmed several times, most recently in 1996.

OTHER BOOKS BY FRANCES HODGSON BURNETT
* *The Secret Garden*; *Little Lord Fauntleroy*

READ-ONS
* *Back Home*, by Michelle Magorian; * *Anne of Green Gables*, by L.M. Montgomery

MACHINE GUNNERS, THE
....

by Robert Westall (Macmillan, 1975)
Carnegie Medal
Interest level: 11–15/Reading age: 11 + /Key Stage: 3
ADVENTURE ● WAR

F OURTEEN-YEAR-OLD Chas McGill stumbles across a crashed German bomber in the woods near his home, with the pilot's body still inside it. His first thought is to report his find to the authorities, but then he sees the machine-gun – and knows he has to have it for his collection of war souvenirs. Enlisting the help of his friends, 'Cemetery' Jones, the undertaker's son, and tomboyish Audrey Parton, he retrieves the gun, only to find himself embroiled in more trouble. The police – and the Home Guard – are on the look-out for the missing weapon, and Chas knows he has to hide it or risk the consequences. So, with the help of his gang, he decides to build a fortress. And it is then that his troubles really start . . . Westall's books are sparely and movingly written, with a sensitive awareness of the way that children cope with death, pain and loss, and convincingly evoke the wartime period with a wealth of authentic detail.

OTHER BOOKS BY ROBERT WESTALL
Full Fathom Five; *Blitzcat*; *The Kingdom by the Sea*; *A Time of Fire*

READ-ONS
The Dolphin Crossing, by Jill Paton Welsh; *The Silver Sword*, by Ian Serraillier; *Carrie's War*, by Nina Bawden

MADAME DOUBTFIRE
. . . .
by Anne Fine (Puffin, 1987)
*Shortlisted for the Observer Teenage Fiction Prize
and the Guardian Children's Fiction Award*
Interest level: 10–14/Reading age: 10+
DIVORCE • FAMILIES

CAUGHT in the crossfire of their divorced parents' continual sniping, Lydia, Christopher and Nadia long for the day when the adults will see sense – and perhaps start *behaving* like adults. So when their mother, Miranda, refuses to let Daniel, their father, look after them when she is at work, preferring to advertise for a childminder instead, they are at first indignant. But when the new childminder – the exotic Madame Doubtfire – arrives, the children begin to see that the situation might have its advantages. In fact, it's almost like having their father around again . . . Anne Fine's wickedly funny story dramatizes the painful realities of divorce with unflinching accuracy. The novel was filmed in 1995, as *Mrs Doubtfire*, with Robin Williams in the title role.

OTHER BOOKS BY ANNE FINE
Bill's New Frock; *Goggle Eyes*; *Flour Babies*; *The Stone Menagerie*; *Book of the Banshee*

READ-ONS
The Divorce Express, by Paula Danziger

MATILDA
. . . .

by Roald Dahl; illustrated by Quentin Blake (Puffin, 1988)
Interest level: 9–11/Reading age: 9+
HUMOUR

MATILDA is an exceptional child – at the age of five, she can do complicated mathematical problems in her head, and she has read Dickens, Kipling and Hemingway. Far from appreciating her cleverness, her stupid and materialistic parents are embarrassed by their brilliant daughter, and are only too glad to have her taken off their hands by Miss Honey, her kind and sensitive form teacher. Miss Honey encourages Matilda to develop her prodigious gifts, despite the opposition she encounters from Miss Trunchbull, the sadistic headmistress of the school, who terrorizes the children with her threats of physical violence. During one such classroom confrontation, Matilda discovers that, in addition to her other abilities, she has an extraordinary power over objects, which she can move around using sheer will-power. With this skill at her disposal, she terrifies Miss Trunchbull into submission, and – after her good-for-nothing parents have cleared off – begins a happy new life under the guardianship of Miss Honey. As with many of Roald Dahl's stories for children, the emphasis is on revenge – camouflaged here as knock-about comedy. In this instance, as elsewhere in his fiction, the revenge is that of the weaker against the stronger – that is, of children against adults; the latter depicted as such monstrous grotesques that it is difficult (for an adult at least) to take them seriously. Other aspects of Dahl's style, such as his tacit encouragement of nasty practical jokes (in one of the book's milder episodes, Matilda pours super-glue into her father's hat), tend to be more worrying to adult readers than to children – perhaps for obvious reasons.

OTHER BOOKS BY ROALD DAHL
Charlie and the Chocolate Factory; *The BFG*; *The Witches*; *George's Marvellous Medicine*

MENNYMS, THE
. . . .
by Sylvia Waugh (Julia McRae, 1993)
Interest level: 9–12/Reading age: 9+
FANTASY

THE Mennyms have lived at 5, Brocklehurst Grove for many years. They are a quiet family, who keep themselves to themselves, sometimes venturing out, but only when they can be sure of not being seen. Apart from bedridden Sir Magnus and his wife Tulip, there are Joshua and Vinetta, and their five children, Appleby, Soobie, Poopie, Wimpey and Googles. The oddity of their names is not the only thing which makes them different from other families. For the Mennyms are not human beings at all, but life-size dolls, made out of cloth and kapok, whose lives are a mixture of 'real' and 'pretend' events. They neither eat nor drink – although they enjoy having tea parties – but in most other respects they lead perfectly ordinary lives. This peaceful existence is disrupted when a letter arrives at Brocklehurst Grove from a certain Albert Pond, a cousin of their landlord, whom they have never seen, announcing his intention of paying them a visit . . .

Sylvia Waugh's delightful novel mingles fantasy and reality in much the same way as her characters do. The Mennyms, like the Borrowers, may not be altogether human but they are loveable, and their predicaments are made to seem entirely real. Any child who enjoys pretending, or who owns a doll's-house, will love this intricately worked out story.

OTHER BOOKS BY SYLVIA WAUGH
Mennyms in the Wilderness

READ-ONS:
*The Borrowers, by Mary Norton

MERCEDES ICE
. . . .
by Philip Ridley; illustrated by Chris Riddell
(Viking Penguin, 1989)
Interest level: 9–12/Reading age: 10+

CHARACTERISTICALLY surreal story – with eerily humorous illustrations – about a little boy who becomes Prince of Shadow Point, a decaying tower block filled with rats and spiders. Peopled with Ridley's usual cast of loveable grotesques – ranging from the enormously fat Rosie Ice, Mercedes's mother, to the diminutive Hilda Sparkle and her resourceful daughter Hickory, the book offers a nightmarish vision of inner-city life which is redeemed only by the obligatory happy ending.

OTHER BOOKS BY PHILIP RIDLEY

Meteorite Spoon; *Krindlekrax*

MIDNIGHT FOLK, THE
. . . .

by John Masefield (Mammoth, 1927)
Interest level: 9–11/Reading age: 9 +
ADVENTURE • FANTASY • LONELINESS • MAGIC

M ASEFIELD'S classic fantasy for children chronicles the adventures of Kay Harker, an orphan brought up by his guardian Sir Theopompus and an even nastier governess, Miss Sylvia Daisy Pouncer, who turns out to be a witch. With the assistance of Nibbins the cat and the midnight folk – an assortment of toys and animals – Kay tracks down the treasure hidden by his great-grandfather, which is also being sought by the villainous Abner Brown. Whimsical and extravagant in tone, the book has dated less well than its sequel, *The Box of Delights*, which also features Kay as the central character.

READ-ONS

The Lion, the Witch and the Wardrobe, by C.S. Lewis

MIDNIGHT IS A PLACE
. . . .

by Joan Aiken (Red Fox, 1974)
Interest level: 10–13/Reading age: 10 +
ADVENTURE • FANTASY

S HUT away in gloomy Midnight Court, his guardian's mansion, Lucas feels alone and unhappy. Hated by the townspeople, many of whom work in appalling conditions in one of his guardian Sir Randolph's carpet factories, he has no one he can turn to – not even his tutor, Mr Oakapple. Then, one day, someone else comes to stay at Midnight Court, and Lucas's life undergoes a dramatic – and frightening – change . . . Joan Aiken's historical fantasy skilfully mixes fact and fiction in a wonderfully Gothic narrative, which will grip the imagination of young readers.

OTHER BOOKS BY JOAN AIKEN

The Wolves of Willoughby Chase; *Blackhearts in Battersea*; *Night Birds on Nantucket*; *Arabel*

MIRROR IMAGE GHOST, THE
. . . .

by Catherine Storr (Faber & Faber, 1994)
Interest level: 10–12/Reading age: 10+
GHOSTS ● WAR

WHEN eleven-year-old Lisa sees the ghost of a young girl in her mother's bedroom mirror she is unable to tell anyone else about it. Her mother, Fanny, is preoccupied with her recent marriage to Lisa's stepfather, Laurent; her grandparents seem reluctant to talk about ghosts – or indeed, about anything to do with the past – and Lisa hates her new step-sister and step-brother, Alice and Pierre. So her dilemma is all the greater when she realizes, from something Fanny has said, that the girl in the mirror is none other than Lisa's great-aunt Elsbet, who died in a Nazi concentration camp when she was a child. Is there any way that Lisa can warn her of her terrible fate, and avert the catastrophe? Catherine Storr's novel explores its themes with sensitivity, showing how its central character's interaction with the past helps her to deal more effectively with the present.

OTHER BOOKS BY CATHERINE STORR

Polly and the Stupid Wolf series

READ-ONS

A Stitch in Time, by Penelope Lively; *The Children of Green Knowe*, by Lucy M. Boston

MOUSE AND HIS CHILD, THE
. . . .

by Russell Hoban (Puffin, 1967)
Interest level: 9–11/Reading age: 9+

IN a toyshop lives a mouse and his child; clockwork figures which, when wound up, begin to dance. The dancing mice are bought by a family, but are accidentally broken and thrown away. It is then that they begin a quest to find a home and family where they can be safe . . . Hoban's poetic fable about the precariousness of human life established his reputation as one of the most original and thought-provoking writers for children and adults.

OTHER BOOKS BY RUSSELL HOBAN
Frances stories; *The Trokeville Way*; *Ace Dragon Ltd*

MY FRIEND WALTER
. . . .

by Michael Morpurgo (Mammoth, 1988)
Interest level: 10–13/Reading age: 10 +
GHOSTS ● TUDORS & STUARTS

WHEN eleven-year-old Bess Throckmorton goes on a class trip to the Tower of London, she has little idea of how much it will change her life. For while she is having a look around the Bloody Tower, she finds herself confronted with the ghost of Sir Walter Raleigh – and not only that, but he claims they are related. When the time comes for Bess to rejoin her classmates, Sir Walter is reluctant to let her go. Since she cannot stay, he decides to come with her – and it is then that Bess's troubles really start . . . Morpurgo's lively mixture of historical fact and contemporary detail will attract any child with an interest in this period of English history. Learning about the Tudors and Stuarts will never be the same.

OTHER BOOKS BY MICHAEL MORPURGO
Why the Whales Came; *The War of Jenkins' Ear*

READ-ONS
The Ghost of Thomas Kempe, by Penelope Lively

MY GRANDMOTHER'S STORIES
. . . .

by Adele Geras; illustrated by Jael Jordan (Mammoth, 1995)
Interest level: 8–10/Reading age: 9 +
FAMILIES

EACH room and its contents trigger a grandmother's imagination and memories and she tells her granddaughter a story relating to them. Many of the stories in the collection are linked to Central European Jewish tradition, and give a wonderfully vivid portrait of a vanished culture.

OTHER BOOKS BY ADELE GERAS
The Fantora Family Files; *A Lane to the Land of the Dead*

NAPPER'S LUCK
. . . .
by Martin Waddell (Puffin, 1993)
Interest level: 9–11/Reading age: 9+
FOOTBALL

NAPPER McCann plays football for his local team, Warne County Colts, who are tipped to win the League championship. But the season starts badly when the team's goalkeeper is injured in the first match – and that is only the beginning of their troubles . . . The question is, has Napper's luck run out – or can he save the day? One of a highly enjoyable series aimed at young football fanatics.

OTHER BOOKS IN THE SERIES
Napper Goes for Goal; *Napper Strikes Again*; *Napper's Big Match*

NOTHING TO BE AFRAID OF
. . . .
by Jan Mark (Puffin, 1980)
Highly commended for Carnegie Medal
Interest level: 10–12/Reading age: 10+
HORROR

JAN Mark's collection of spooky tales for younger readers is enjoyably scarey without ever becoming too worrying, dramatizing the kind of fears and fantasies everyone has had at one time or another.

OTHER BOOKS BY JAN MARK
The Hillingdon Fox; *Thunder and Lightnings*; *The Dead Letter Box*

READ-ONS
A Bundle of Nerves, by Joan Aiken; *The Stones of Muncaster Cathedral*, by Robert Westall

OTHER SIDE OF SILENCE, THE
. . . .
by Margaret Mahy (Hamish Hamilton, 1995)
Interest level: 12–16/Reading age: 12+
FAMILIES • LONELINESS • MENTAL ILLNESS

TWELVE-YEAR-OLD Hero has taken refuge from her argumentative family, by refusing to speak. The trouble is that none of the other members of her family understands why. Her mother, Annie – author of a bestselling book on child-rearing – is too busy going to conferences, leaving the running of the home to her husband, Mike. Mike is preoccupied with the demands of the household; the other siblings – bright, opinionated Ginevra, studious Athol and lively, talkative Sap – are much too concerned with their own lives to bother with Hero's problems. Then Hero encounters Miss Credence, an eccentric recluse who offers her a gardening job. At first excited by the independence this gives her, Hero eagerly agrees to the proposal, but as time goes by she begins to regret her decision. For Miss Credence has a shameful secret: many years before, she gave birth to an illegitimate child whose existence she has kept hidden from the outside world. When Hero accidentally discovers this, she finds herself in terrible danger – from which her only escape is to resort to speech again.

Mahy's novel, which is set in her native New Zealand, deals thoughtfully and often humorously with the stresses and strains of family life which can affect many adolescents, as well as uncovering the darker side of parent–child relationships.

OTHER BOOKS BY MARGARET MAHY

A Lion in the Meadow; *The Haunting*; *The Changeover*; *The Tricksters*; *Aliens in the Family*; *The Greatest Show off Earth*; *Underrunners*; *Dangerous Spaces*

OTHERWISE KNOWN AS SHEILA THE GREAT

by Judy Blume (Macmillan, 1980)
Interest level: 9–11/Reading age: 9 +
FEARS • FRIENDS

SHEILA is afraid of a lot of things – dogs, thunderstorms, swimming – but is too scared to admit it. Then her new friend, Mouse, takes a hand and suddenly the world doesn't seem like such a frightening place . . . Funny and touching, Judy Blume's story is about getting to grips with some common anxieties. Her books have an American setting, but the issues they deal with are universal ones – to do with growing up, family life and coping with feelings.

OTHER BOOKS BY JUDY BLUME

Tales of a Fourth Grade Nothing; *Superfudge*; *Fudge-a-mania*; *Freckle Juice*; *Blubber*

OWL SERVICE, THE
....

by Alan Garner (Collins, 1967)
Carnegie Medal/Guardian Children's Fiction Award
Interest level: 11–13/Reading age: 11+
FANTASY ● GROWING UP

S ET on a farm in rural Wales, Garner's lyrical story about a group of adolescents who find themselves unwittingly re-enacting a tragic story from the past was acclaimed on its publication as a milestone in writing for young readers. The novel incorporates episodes from the Mabinogion legend, in which a man makes himself a beautiful bride out of flowers and is then destroyed by her – as a result of which the flower-woman is turned into an owl.

OTHER BOOKS BY ALAN GARNER
* The Weirdstone of Brisingamen; *Elidor*; *The Moon of Gomrath*; *The Stone Book*

READ-ONS
* The Dark is Rising trilogy, by Susan Cooper

PEACOCK PIE
....

by Walter de la Mare; illustrated by Edward Ardizzone (Faber & Faber, 1913)
Interest level: 9–12/Reading age: 9+
POETRY

W ALTER de la Mare's poems for children are widely regarded as amongst his finest work. Full of mystery and imagination, they offer glimpses into the supernatural, and a variety of moods, from the sinister to the elegiac. Some of the verses – notably the title poem – have the hauntingly rhythmic quality of nursery rhymes. These are poems which linger in the mind, long after the first reading. Any child with a taste for the romantic and the unexpected will find much to enjoy.

PEPPERMINT PIG, THE
. . . .

by Nina Bawden (Puffin, 1975)
Guardian Children's Fiction Award
Interest level: 11–14/Reading age: 11 + /Key Stage: 3
FAMILIES • VICTORIANS

F ORCED to leave their prosperous London home after their father has been wrongfully suspected of theft, the Greengrass children, Polly, Theo, Lily and George, establish themselves in a Norfolk market town. At first they miss their old life, but there are compensations to living in the country – such as being able to keep a pig as a pet . . . Nina Bawden's perceptive and moving story conveys the atmosphere of the Edwardian era with great charm, without ever resorting to sentimentality. *Jill Paton Walsh described it as 'a perfect, small masterpiece'.

OTHER BOOKS BY NINA BAWDEN
*Carrie's War; Rebel on a Rock; The Secret Passage; The White Horse Gang

READ-ONS
*The Railway Children, by E. Nesbit

PETER PAN
. . . .

by J.M. Barrie (World's Classics, 1904)
Interest level: 9–12/Reading age: 10 +
ADVENTURE • FAIRIES • FANTASY • GROWING UP
• MAGIC • PIRATES

F IRST produced as a play in 1904 and later published in a novel version entitled *Peter and Wendy*, Barrie's celebrated story about a boy who refuses to grow up, preferring to spend his time in Never-Never Land, a fantastical country peopled by mermaids, Red Indians and a band of pirates led by the fearsome Captain Hook, has gripped children's imaginations from the start. Central to both the play and the novel is the relationship – often closer to that of son and mother than brother and sister – of Peter and Wendy Darling, eldest of the Darling children, who, led by the audacious Peter and Tinkerbell the fairy, leave the family's home in London for the wilder shores of Never-Never Land. Here, Wendy becomes surrogate mother to the Lost Boys, a group of children who have lost their mothers, while Peter plots his revenge against Hook and the pirates. Although, inevitably, some of the work's social attitudes have dated, it still retains its power to enthrall more than eighty years after its first appearance, with new productions of the play appearing every Christmas and the recent Steven Spielberg film (*Hook*, 1991) attracting fresh audiences.

PHANTOM TOLLBOOTH, THE

by Norton Juster (Collins, 1962)
Interest level: 9–12/Reading age: 9 +
ADVENTURE • FANTASY

MILO is bored with just about everything. When he's at school, he longs to be at home, and when he's at home he longs to be somewhere else. That is, until the day he unwraps a mysterious package containing the Phantom Tollbooth, and journeys through it to a land where anything can happen. For this is the Kingdom of Wisdom, off the coast of the Sea of Knowledge and bordered by the Mountains of Ignorance and the Foothills of Confusion. With the assistance of his friend the Watchdog, Milo must travel through a whole range of interesting places, from Dictionopolis, whose citizens all speak in dictionary definitions, to the no less learned city of Digitopolis, which is run according to the laws of mathematics. On the way he encounters a whole host of fascinating types, such as the untrustworthy Humbug and the pedantic Spelling Bee, the sinister Doctor Dischord and the beautiful princesses Rhyme and Reason. By the end of his journey, Milo has discovered that the world is actually a very interesting place, and that the more you know, the more interesting it becomes. Norton Juster's witty fable about the pleasures of learning is as relevant today as it was when it was published over thirty years ago.

READ-ONS

Alice in Wonderland and *Through the Looking-glass*, by Lewis Carroll

PHOENIX AND THE CARPET, THE

by E. Nesbit (Puffin, 1904)
Interest level: 9–11/Reading age: 9 +
ADVENTURE • MAGIC

IN this sequel to *Five Children and It* (which can be read as a self-contained novel), Robert, Anthea, Jane and Cyril discover a mysterious egg rolled up inside their newly acquired nursery carpet; the egg rolls into the fire and a Phoenix hatches out of it. This mythical bird, who has just woken out of a 2,000-year sleep, explains that the carpet in which he arrived is a flying carpet, with the power to transport the children anywhere they wish to go . . . The ensuing adventures are as hilarious – and occasionally alarming – as anything in Nesbit's fiction, but the story's main charm lies in its determinedly unsentimental portrayal of its four young protagonists.

OTHER BOOKS BY E. NESBIT
The Story of the Treasure Seekers; *The Story of the Amulet*; *The Railway Children*

READ-ONS
The Lion, the Witch and the Wardrobe (and sequels), by C.S. Lewis

PROPER LITTLE NOORYEFF
. . . .

by Jean Ure (Corgi, 1992)
Interest level: 9–11/Reading age: 9 +
GENDER STEREOTYPING

JAMIE knows his friends will laugh at him if they find out he's going to take part in a ballet – after all, it isn't the sort of thing boys do, is it? But he's determined to go through with it. The show must go on . . . Jean Ure's wryly humorous novel takes a long, hard look at the way society expects males to behave, and the importance of resisting peer group pressure to conform.

OTHER BOOKS BY JEAN URE
Watchers at the Shrine; *Plague 99*

READ-ONS
The Turbulent Term of Tyke Tiler, by Gene Kemp

THE RAILWAY CHILDREN
. . . .

by E. Nesbit (Methuen, 1906)
Interest level: 9–12/Reading age: 9 +
ADVENTURE ● FAMILIES ● SIBLINGS ● VICTORIANS

E. Nesbit's classic story about a family of three children – 'Bobby' (Roberta), Peter and Phyllis – whose lives change for ever when their father is wrongfully arrested and they are obliged to leave their prosperous London suburb for the country, remains perennially popular more than eighty years after it was first published. This is largely due to the engaging realism with which Bobby and her siblings are portrayed, and to the liveliness of Nesbit's writing. Undeterred by the hardship they face in their new life, the children settle into their new home – a cottage near a railway cutting. They make friends with Perks, the station master, and become familiar with the day-to-day life of the railway. Various adventures involving the railway befall them – the most dramatic being when Bobby's quick thinking prevents an accident – as a result of which the children are befriended by an elderly gentleman, whom they wave to every day when his train is passing. It transpires that the old gentleman is actually a highly placed civil servant, who is instrumental in arranging the release from prison of the children's father.

OTHER BOOKS BY E. NESBIT

The Phoenix and the Carpet; *The Wouldbegoods*; *The Story of the Treasure Seekers*; *Five Children and It*

READ-ONS

The Peppermint Pig, by Nina Bawden

REDWALL
. . . .

by Brian Jacques (Red Fox, 1986)
Interest level: 11–13/Reading age: 11+
ANIMALS ● FANTASY

FIRST in a highly popular series, Brian Jacques's fantasy saga focuses around a community of mice in the medieval abbey of Redwall, whose preparations for a special feast are disrupted by the news that the evil, one-eyed rat Cluny is advancing on the abbey with his battle-scarred mob . . . In this and subsequent books, Jacques creates a compellingly plausible world of empire-building rodents and their peace-loving adversaries, which will appeal to any child with a taste for fantastic adventure.

OTHER BOOKS BY BRIAN JACQUES

The Bellmaker; *Mariel of Redwall*; *Martin the Warrior*; *Mattimeo*; *Mossflower*; *Outcast of Redwall*

READ-ONS

*The *Deptford Mice* trilogy, by Robin Jarvis

ROLL OF THUNDER, HEAR MY CRY

by Mildred D. Taylor (Puffin, 1976)
Newbery Medal
Interest level: 11–14/Reading age: 11 +
FAMILIES • RACIAL STEREOTYPING

M ILDRED D. Taylor's prize-winning novel is set in the Deep South during the 1930s and is narrated by nine-year-old Cassie Logan, whose family own land purchased during the reconstruction period which followed the Civil War – land which they are determined to keep, despite attempts by a neighbouring landowner, Harlan Granger, to intimidate them into selling. For the Logan family are black and Granger is white – with all the power his position as a local dignitary gives him. When Cassie's mother, Mary – a teacher at the Great Faith Elementary School attended by Cassie and her brothers – attempts to tell her pupils about slavery, Granger has her suspended. Together with his vicious cronies, the Wallaces and the Simmses, he is also behind the spate of violent attacks on black people in the region by the fearsome 'Night Men' of the Ku Klux Klan.

Taylor's powerful novel conveys the turbulent mood of this period in American history, showing how, despite all the odds that were stacked against them, families such as the Logans managed to live their lives. This book offers a sympathetic portrayal of one black family's struggle against prejudice, in a society still crippled by the legacy of slavery.

OTHER BOOKS BY MILDRED D. TAYLOR
Let the Circle be Unbroken; *The Road to Memphis*

READ-ONS
To Kill a Mocking-bird, by Harper Lee

ROSE AND THE RING, THE

by William Makepeace Thackeray (Puffin, 1885)
Interest level: 9–11/Reading age: 10 +
FAIRY TALES

T HACKERAY's lively spoof of the classic fairy tale was subtitled 'A Fire-side Pantomine for Great or Small Children' and there are elements of pantomime in its use of names (Countess Gruffanuff; Count Kutsoff Hedsoff) and in the plot, which hinges around a magic rose and a ring, with the power to make their owners seem beautiful and charming to anyone who beholds them. The misfortunes of the genuinely beautiful and charming Princess Rosalba and Prince Giglio are contrasted with the good fortune of the plain and stupid Prince Bulbo and Princess Angelica; later, in true pantomime style, the roles are reversed and goodness triumphs.

SCHOOL
. . . .
by Colin and Jacqui Hawkins (Collins, 1994)
Interest level: 9–12/Reading age: 9+
HUMOUR ● SCHOOL

Toadies and Creeps, Bullies and Teacher's Pets . . . Colin and Jacqui Hawkinses illustrated guide to the perils of school has them all – together with different types of teachers to watch out for, the horrors of homework and other unpleasant topics. An updated version of Geoffrey Willans and Ronald Searle's classic *Down with Skool!*, the Hawkinses' book is distinguished by their usual revolting humour (lots of references to zits, snot and lumpy custard) and by their engagingly horrible drawings. A must for any child (and adult) with a sense of humour.

SECRET, THE
. . . .
by Ruth Thomas (Puffin, 1990)
Interest level: 9–11/Reading age: 9+

When Nicky and Roy's mum fails to come home after a weekend away, they are too frightened to inform the authorities. Instead they try to cope on their own, determined to get their mum to return of her own accord . . . Award-winning author Ruth Thomas, a former teacher, has made a name for herself in recent years as a writer of powerfully realistic fiction for younger readers, which deals with a whole range of issues in a sensitive and thoughtful way.

OTHER BOOKS BY RUTH THOMAS
The Runaways; *Guilty*; *The Hideaway*; *The New Boy*; *The Class That Went Wild*

SECRET GARDEN, THE

by Frances Hodgson Burnett (Methuen, 1911)
Interest level: 9–11/Reading age: 9+
FRIENDS ● LONELINESS ● VICTORIANS

WHEN her parents die in a cholera epidemic in India, ten-year-old Mary Lennox is sent to live with her uncle, the reclusive Archibald Craven, at his rambling mansion on the edge of the Yorkshire moors. Neglected from her earliest years, Mary has grown up a difficult and unattractive child, whose stiffness of manner conceals her insecurity. Befriended by Martha, one of the servants at Misselthwaite Manor, she begins to come out of her shell – especially when, at Martha's insistence, she starts to explore the grounds of the manor, and discovers that there is an abandoned garden in which nobody has set foot since the death of the mistress of the house ten years before . . . Frances Hodgson Burnett's classic story about an unhappy child who discovers how to be happy – and how to make others happy – remains as relevant for our times as it was for contemporary readers. Beautifully written and moving, it will appeal to any child with a love of mystery.

OTHER BOOKS BY FRANCES HODGSON BURNETT
A Little Princess; *Little Lord Fauntleroy*

READ-ONS
Tom's Midnight Garden, by Philippa Pearce

SECRET WORLD OF POLLY FLINT, THE

by Helen Cresswell; illustrated by Shirley Felts (Puffin, 1983)
Interest level: 9–11/Reading age: 9+
FANTASY ● GHOSTS

POLLY Flint has always been able to see things that other people couldn't see – such as angels, and people from earlier times. When she arrives in the Nottinghamshire village of Wellow, where her father has been sent to convalesce after a mining accident, she isn't particularly surprised to encounter some strange people in the woods near her home, who call themselves 'Time Gypsies'; or to see, very early on May Day, children from long ago dancing around a maypole . . . Cresswell's evocative story will delight any child who has ever daydreamed about going back in time.

OTHER BOOKS BY HELEN CRESSWELL
Up the Pier; *The Bagthorpe Saga*; *Stonestruck*

READ-ONS
The Mirror Image Ghost, by Catherine Storr

SHAKESPEARE STORIES

Volumes I & II; retold by Leon Garfield; illustrated by Michael
Foreman (Gollancz, 1994)
Interest level: 10–13/Reading age: 10+/Key Stage: 3

YOUNGER readers often find Shakespearean language difficult, even
though the plots, once grasped, are easy to enjoy. Leon Garfield's
sensitive and colourful retelling of the stories of Shakespeare's most famous
plays gives full rein to the imaginative power of the original, while simplifying
some of the more difficult language and ideas. Michael Foreman's lively
illustrations also help to bring the text alive.

OTHER BOOKS BY LEON GARFIELD
Smith; *Devil-in-the-Fog*; *The December Rose*; *Black Jack*; *The Wedding
Ghost*

READ-ONS
plays of William Shakespeare

SHOUT, WHISPER AND SING
101 POEMS TO READ ALOUD

Compiled by Beverley Mathias; illustrated by Victor Ambrus
(Bodley Head, 1989)
Interest level: 8–12/Reading age: 9+
POETRY

THIS collection of classical and contemporary verse has something for
everyone: poems 'to be whispered while waiting at airports and railway
stations'; poems 'to shout aloud when walking'; poems, above all, to be
enjoyed. Wordsworth, Keats, Tennyson, Longfellow, Browning and a host of
others are collected here, providing an excellent introduction to the pleasures of language for children of all ages.

SILVER SWORD, THE

by Ian Serraillier (Puffin, 1956)
Interest level: 11–13/Reading age: 11 +
ADVENTURE • WAR

S ERRAILLIER'S exciting and moving novel about a family of Polish refugees escaping the Nazis has become a classic of children's literature about the Second World War. Three children, Ruth, Edek and Bronia, journey to Switzerland in the hope of being reunited with their parents, after the token of a silver penknife – the 'silver sword' of the title – has been given to them, which they believe to be from their father.

READ-ONS

* *When Hitler Stole Pink Rabbit*, by Judith Kerr; *The Dolphin Crossing*, by Jill Paton Walsh

STIG OF THE DUMP

by Clive King; illustrated by Edward Ardizzone (Puffin, 1963)
Interest level: 9–11/Reading age: 9 +
ADVENTURE

O NE day when he is playing on the edge of the chalk-pit where the rubbish is dumped, Barney feels the ground give way – and before he knows what is happening, he is lying at the bottom of a cave. It is then that he meets Stig – a boy of about his own age who comes from the Stone Age. No one else believes in Stig, but to Barney he is totally real. Together they have the most wonderful adventures – until the time comes for Stig to rejoin his own people . . . Clive King's delightful story has seldom been out of print since it was first published. A story which will appeal to any child with an imagination – and a taste for adventure.

READ-ONS

* *The Indian in the Cupboard* series, by Lynne Reid Banks

STITCH IN TIME, A

. . . .

by Penelope Lively (Mammoth, 1976)
Whitbread Award
Interest level: 10–12/Reading age: 10+
GHOSTS • LONELINESS • VICTORIANS

H OLIDAYING in Lyme Regis with her parents, eleven-year-old Maria Foster finds herself increasingly fascinated by the life of a previous inhabitant of the house where they are staying – a girl about her own age called Harriet, who lived there over a hundred years ago, and whose interest in fossils Maria shares . . . Penelope Lively's gentle ghost story is as much about the loneliness of being an only child as it is about an actual haunting. Thoughtful and evocative, it will appeal to any imaginative child who has ever been thrown on her own resources for a summer.

OTHER BOOKS BY PENELOPE LIVELY

The Ghost of Thomas Kempe; *The House in Norham Gardens*

READ-ONS

Tom's Midnight Garden, by Philippa Pearce

STONE MENAGERIE, THE

. . . .

by Anne Fine (Mammoth, 1980)
Carnegie Medal
Interest level: 11–13/Reading age: 11+
MENTAL ILLNESS

E VERY Sunday, Ally and his parents go to visit Aunt Chloe in the mental hospital where she lives, which is set in beautiful grounds. Ally hates these visits, which alternately bore and frighten him – until the day he looks out of the window and sees a girl dressed in outlandish clothes on the other side of the lake. As he watches, he sees that the girl is sending him a message – her name, written in plants. Ally can't rest until he finds out who she is and, through her, learns the secret of the Stone Menagerie . . . Anne Fine's sensitive story explores the nature of delusion, and raises some thought-provoking questions about society's treatment of the mentally ill.

OTHER BOOKS BY ANNE FINE

Goggle Eyes; *Madame Doubtfire*; *Flour Babies*; *Bill's New Frock*

READ-ONS

An Angel for May, by Melvin Burgess

STONESTRUCK
. . . .

by Helen Cresswell (Puffin, 1995)
Interest level: 10–13/Reading age: 10+
GHOSTS ● LONELINESS ● WAR

EVACUATED from London during the Blitz, Jessica finds herself living in a huge Welsh castle, with only the gardener and housekeeper for company. Here, while she is wandering around the grounds, she stumbles across a strange and terrifying secret. For hidden in the castle gardens are gangs of children, like herself, who have been bewitched – or 'stonestruck' – by a sinister Green Lady. Can Jessica break the spell and release the lost children or will she, too, be turned to stone? Spellbinding and poetic, Helen Cresswell's story juxtaposes striking images of life and death in a powerful wartime fable.

OTHER BOOKS BY HELEN CRESSWELL
Lizzie Dripping; *The Secret World of Polly Flint*; *Up the Pier*; *The Bagthorpe Saga*

READ-ONS
The Children of Green Knowe (and sequels), by Lucy M. Boston

STORY OF THE TREASURE SEEKERS, THE
. . . .

by E. Nesbit (Puffin Classics, 1899)
Interest level: 8–11/Reading age: 9+
ADVENTURE

THE first in Nesbit's classic series of books about a London family, *The Treasure Seekers* has become an established favourite with young readers, as much for the humour with which it portrays the relationships between the six Bastable siblings as for the liveliness with which it describes their adventures. Much of the humour stems from the fact that Oswald Bastable, the narrator of this and subsequent books, is also one of the protagonists, whose fondness for heroic literature and (pardonable) tendency to present his own part in events in the most flattering light are jokes only the reader can appreciate. The book's opening chapters set the action firmly in time and place: 1890s London. The Bastable children – Dora, Oswald, Dicky, Alice and Noel, who are twins, and Horace Octavius (a.k.a. 'H.O.') live with their widowed father in a large house 'in the Lewisham Road'.

It transpires that, following their mother's death, the children's father has been let down by his business partner and is suffering financial difficulties. It is in response to this that Oswald and his siblings embark on a series of schemes – some more practical than others – to help the family fortunes. These range from digging up the garden in search of hidden treasure, to turning to crime detection; these and other money-spinning schemes fail to achieve the desired end, but an encounter with the 'Indian Uncle' – an elderly relative whom the children suppose to be down on his luck but who is actually very wealthy – gives a fairy-tale happy ending to the story. With this exception, the plot is determinedly realistic, with the ever-present threat of financial ruin hanging over the family and the children's comic efforts to alleviate the problem sharpened by this knowledge. The attractive realism with which Nesbit portrays her characters, especially the engaging Oswald, is another reason for the book's enduring success; her refusal to condescend to her readers is another.

OTHER BOOKS IN THIS SERIES BY E. NESBIT
New Treasure Seekers; *The Wouldbegoods*

SWALLOWS AND AMAZONS
. . . .
by Arthur Ransome (Jonathan Cape, 1930)
Interest level: 9–12/Reading age: 9+
ADVENTURE • FAMILIES • PIRATES

First in a series of eleven books about the adventures of a group of children – Susan, John, Titty (Letitia) and Roger Walker – who are spending their summer holidays in a cottage on Lake Windermere in the Lake District. Here they enjoy the idyllic pleasures of camping, fishing and sailing a small boat, the *Swallow*, in which they explore the lake, and in particular the little island they call Wild Cat Island. While they are camping on the island, they encounter some other children, Peggy and Nancy Blackett – the 'Amazons' of the title – with whom they later join forces against the (supposed) hostilities of 'Captain Flint', who is actually a writer, but whom they imagine to be a retired pirate. The book is delightful both for the way it enters into the children's imaginative world, and for its attentiveness to detail, ranging from nautical terminology to the minutiae of setting up camp on an uninhabited island. This book is essential reading for any child with imagination and a sense of adventure. Summer holidays will never seem the same again.

OTHER BOOKS BY ARTHUR RANSOME
The Big Six; *The Coot Club*; *Great Northern*; *Missee Lee*; *The Picts and the Martyrs*; *Pigeon Post*; *Secret Water*; *Swallowdale*; *We Didn't Mean to Go to Sea*; *Winter Holiday*; *Peter Duck*

READ-ONS
* *The Treasure Seekers* (and sequels), by E. Nesbit

SWEET VALLEY SERIES
. . . .
by Francine Pascal (Bantam, from 1984)
Interest level: 11–14/Reading age: 11 +

H UGELY successful series about an American high school, aimed at girls. See also * *Babysitters' Club* series.

TALE OF TIME CITY, A
. . . .
by Diana Wynne Jones (Mammoth, 1987)
Interest level: 9–12/Reading age: 9 +
ADVENTURE ● SCIENCE FICTION

V IVIAN has been kidnapped – snatched away by her friends, Jonathan and Sam, to a city of the future. Trying to get home, she becomes caught up in the plight of the crumbling Time City, which is falling apart in front of her very eyes. Can she track down the man who built it – the legendary Faber John – and restore the city to its former glory? Or will the dreaded Time Lady get there first? Diana Wynne Jones's fantasy novel incorporates time travel, mystery and alternative universes in a strange and fascinating mixture. A gripping read for any young science fiction addict.

OTHER BOOKS BY DIANA WYNNE JONES
The Lives of Christopher Chant; *Fire & Hemlock*; *The Homeward Bounders*; *Archer's Goon*

READ-ONS
* *The Time and Space of Uncle Albert*, by Russell Stannard

TARKA THE OTTER

by Henry Williamson (Puffin, 1927)
Interest level: 9–12/Reading age: 10+
ANIMALS

A LTHOUGH not originally written for children, Williamson's story about a man's relationship with the young otter he saves from death and rears by hand has been popular with young readers since it was first published and has become a classic of its kind, dealing as it does with the natural world and our relation to it.

READ-ONS
Watership Down, by Richard Adams

TEAM MASCOT

by Michael Hardcastle (Mammoth, 1987)
Interest level: 9–11/Reading age: 9+
FOOTBALL

W HEN Damian Tennant is chosen by his local Football League club to be their mascot, it is the best day of his life. But his selection causes jealousy among his team-mates and threatens his captaincy of Sunday League side Darton United. How can he prove he is the leader they need – and get his friends back on his side? One of a highly popular series aimed at young football fans, this offers an exciting read – and plenty of details about the game.

OTHER BOOKS BY MICHAEL HARDCASTLE
Away from Home; *Free Kick*; *In the Net*; *United!*; *Soccer Special*

READ-ONS
Napper's Luck and others in the series, by Martin Waddell

TIME AND SPACE OF UNCLE ALBERT, THE

by Russell Stannard (Faber & Faber, 1989)
*Shortlisted for the Whitbread Award
and the Science Book Award*
Interest level: 9–12/Reading age: 9+
ADVENTURE ● SCIENCE

As Professor of Physics at the Open University, Russell Stannard is better placed than most to explain the intricacies of particle physics to young readers. This entertaining adventure, in which Gedanken and her uncle Albert explore the peculiarities of time and space in an imaginary space ship, sets out to make Einstein's Theory of Relativity comprehensible to non-scientists – and succeeds admirably. Other books in the series deal with black holes, quantum theory and other daunting subjects, which are made to seem not only fascinating but fun.

OTHER BOOKS BY RUSSELL STANNARD
Black Holes and Uncle Albert; *Uncle Albert and the Quantum Quest*; *Letters to Uncle Albert*

TIME OF FIRE, A

by Robert Westall (Macmillan, 1994)
Interest level: 11–14/Reading age: 11+
DEATH ● WAR

WHEN Sonny Prudhoe's mother is killed in a German bombing raid on his Tyneside village, his life – and that of his whole family – is devastated. Consumed by guilt because he believes that his carelessness may have contributed to his mother's death, Sonny spends his time searching the sky for the German plane he is convinced was responsible. His father carries this personal vendetta a stage further by signing up as an air-gunner, in the hope of getting his revenge on the enemy in a one-to-one confrontation. Westall's account of wartime life is as detailed and realistic as ever; and his depiction of individual tragedy utterly convincing.

OTHER BOOKS BY ROBERT WESTALL
The Machine Gunners; *Blitzcat*; *The Kingdom by the Sea*

READ-ONS
Goodnight, Mr Tom, by Michelle Magorian

TIMESNATCH
. . . .

by Robert Swindells (Yearling, 1994)
Interest level: 10–14/Reading age: 10+
ENVIRONMENT • SCIENCE FICTION

TEN-YEAR-OLD Kizzy Rye and her brother Fraser are at first amazed and delighted when their physicist mother invents a time-machine which can bring back extinct creatures from previous times. With the aid of this fantastic device, they can restock the oceans and the earth with marvellous creatures and save the planet from becoming an arid wasteland. But then a sinister organization gets wind of Harper Rye's time-machine, and decides to employ it for their own evil ends . . . Swindells's thought-provoking story raises issues about the environment, as well as those of a more disturbing nature about the way science is used in our society.

OTHER BOOKS BY ROBERT SWINDELLS
Room 13; *Daz 4 Zoe*; **Unbeliever*

READ-ONS
The Time Machine, by H.G. Wells

TOM'S MIDNIGHT GARDEN
. . . .

by Philippa Pearce (Oxford University Press, 1958)
Carnegie Medal
Interest level: 9–12/Reading age: 9+
GHOSTS • GROWING UP • LONELINESS • VICTORIANS

PEARCE's novel tells the story of Tom, who is forced to spend the summer holidays with his well-meaning but dull uncle and aunt when his brother comes down with measles. Aunt Gwen and Uncle Alan have no children, so there is no one for Tom to play with; worse still, the house where they live – a Victorian mansion converted into flats – doesn't even have a garden. But then one night Tom finds himself disturbed by the striking of the grandfather clock in the hall, and when he goes downstairs it is to find that everything looks different. For when he goes outside he finds himself in a beautiful garden, with spreading lawns and trees to climb. Best of all, there are other children there – three boys and a girl named Hatty. The strangest thing is that only Hatty is able to see Tom, and no one takes any notice of Hatty because she is a girl . . . Redolent of a vanished era of childhood, this lyrical story has dated very little since it was first published, and still retains its power to enthrall.

OTHER BOOKS BY PHILIPPA PEARCE
The Way to Sattin Shore; *A Dog So Small*

READ-ONS
The Secret Garden, by Frances Hodgson Burnett

TREASURE ISLAND
. . . .
by Robert Louis Stevenson (Magnet Classics, 1883)
Interest level: 9–11/Reading age: 9+
ADVENTURE ● PIRATES

R OBERT Louis Stevenson's classic tale of skulduggery on the high seas, first
published over a hundred years ago, remains one of the most exciting
ever written for children. The narrator, Jim Hawkins, a West Country
innkeeper's son, encounters the pirate, Billy Bones, in his father's pub,
the Admiral Benbow. Bones, it transpires, is in possession of a secret, which
is hidden in his old sea-chest. After he dies of an apoplectic fit, Jim retrieves
the key of the chest and discovers a map, describing the location of buried
treasure, hidden amongst its contents. It is this which forces him to flee for his
life, when Bones's former shipmates, acting on the orders of the fearsome
Captain Flint, arrive at the inn. Jim joins forces with the kindly Doctor Livesey
and Squire Trelawney to get up an expedition to find the treasure. They are
joined in this endeavour by Long John Silver, a one-legged seaman who is
engaged as ship's cook. Jim's suspicions about him are confirmed as soon as
they are at sea, when he overhears Silver planning a mutiny against the ship's
captain, in order to secure the treasure for himself and his cronies. This plan
is not carried out until the ship's company have landed on the island where
the treasure is located, after which a terrifying battle of wits ensues. The story
ends, after many casualties on both sides, with the mutineers routed and the
treasure recovered. But such is Stevenson's gift for suspense that this is never
a foregone conclusion.

OTHER BOOKS BY ROBERT LOUIS STEVENSON
Kidnapped; *Doctor Jekyll and Mr Hyde*; *A Child's Garden of Verses*

READ-ONS
Hornblower stories, by C.S. Forester

TRUCKERS
. . . .
by Terry Pratchett (Corgi, 1989)
Interest level: 9–12/Reading age: 10+
ADVENTURE ● FANTASY

TERRY Pratchett's wonderfully quirky fantasy adventure story takes place in a large department store, which is home to thousands of inch-high humans called 'nomes'. To Masklin and his fellow nomes, the store is the only world they have ever known, and the thought of a universe outside seems like nothing more than a far-fetched myth – until the day they discover that their world is about to be demolished. Then it is up to the resourceful Masklin to think of an escape plan . . . Pratchett's mixture of humour, adventure and inventiveness has been a winning combination for many young readers, for whom his books are the *only* thing to read. Fortunately, he has published a lot of books.

OTHER BOOKS BY TERRY PRATCHETT
*The Colour of Magic; The Carpet People; The Light Fantastic; *Diggers; Equal Rites; Wings*

READ-ONS
The Hitch-hiker's Guide to the Galaxy (and sequels), by Douglas Adams

TURBULENT TERM OF TYKE TYLER, THE
. . . .
by Gene Kemp (Puffin, 1977)
Carnegie Medal
Interest level: 9–12/Reading age: 9+
FAMILIES ● GENDER STEREOTYPING

WHEN Tyke Tyler is around, anything can happen – and frequently does. Tyke's best friend Danny, who is far from being the brightest boy in the class, steals a ten-pound note from a teacher's purse – and Tyke has the task of replacing it without anybody noticing. Then there is the little matter of Danny's pet mouse, which goes AWOL in the middle of school assembly and has to be recaptured. But by far her most spectacular stunt is the time Tyke decides to climb the school bell-tower and ring the bell – a dare which lands her in hospital.

Gene Kemp's prize-winning novel was one of the first to feature a female character who is every bit as tough and resourceful as her male contemporaries.

Tyke's gender is deliberately unspecified until the last two pages of the book; even the illustrations, which show a short-haired child in jeans and T-shirt, don't give the game away. The novel makes a good starting point for class discussion of sexual stereotyping – as well as being one which children of both sexes will enjoy.

OTHER BOOKS BY GENE KEMP

Tamworth Pig stories; *The Clock Tower Ghost*; *Dog Days and Cat Naps*; *Gowie Corby Plays Chicken*; *No Place Like*; *Ducks and Dragons* (ed.); *Charlie Lewis Plays for Time*; *Jason Bodger and the Priory Ghost*; *Juniper*; *I Can't Stand Losing*; *The Well*; *Roundabout*; *Zowey Corby's Story*

READ-ONS

* *Proper Little Nooryeff*, by Jean Ure

TWO WEEKS WITH THE QUEEN
································
by Morris Gleitzman (Macmillan, 1990)
Interest level: 10–14/Reading age: 10+
AIDS • DEATH

COLIN's eight-year-old brother, Luke, has cancer. The doctors have given up hope; even his parents seem to think he is going to die. Colin is determined to prove them all wrong. When his parents send him from his home in Australia to England to stay with his uncle and aunt, he decides to take matters into his own hands. Failing to get a personal audience with the Queen on his first visit to Buckingham Palace, he tries telephoning her; when this, too, fails, he resorts to writing a letter, in which he asks Her Majesty whether he can 'borrow' her most eminent doctor for a few days, in order to cure his brother's cancer. Predictably enough, he receives no immediate reply – and time, Colin knows, is of the essence. So he decides to find his own doctor, and goes to the most famous cancer hospital he can find. There, once again, he fails in his mission, but finds a new friend instead. This is Ted, a young gay man, whose lover is dying; it is he, more than anyone else, who helps Colin come to terms with death. Despite its sombre subject, this is a very funny book, which treats its central character's predicament with just the right mixture of sensitivity and humour.

OTHER BOOKS BY MAURICE GLEITZMAN

Misery Guts; *Blabbermouth*

UP THE PIER
. . . .

by Helen Cresswell; illustrated by Gareth Floyd
(Faber & Faber, 1971)
Interest level: 9–11/Reading age: 9+
GHOSTS

S TAYING at her aunt Esther's small hotel in an out-of-season Welsh seaside
town, while her parents go house-hunting, ten-year-old Carrie feels
herself at a loose end. With the weather too cold for the beach and no
other children to play with, she is reduced to taking solitary walks along the
sea-front to the deserted pier. Then one day, on the pier, she sees the boy and
his dog – and from then on all kinds of surprising things start to happen.
Carrie finds she can see people whom nobody else can see – not only that,
but they can see her! Helen Cresswell's atmospheric depiction of a seaside
town in winter seems exactly right for her story's blend of mystery and gentle
humour.

OTHER BOOKS BY HELEN CRESSWELL
Moondial; *The Secret World of Polly Flint*; *Bagthorpes Unlimited*; *Stone-struck*

READ-ONS
The Haunting, by Margaret Mahy

WATER BABIES, THE
. . . .

by Charles Kingsley (Penguin, 1863)
Interest level: 10–16/Reading age: 10+
ADVENTURE ● DEATH

K INGSLEY's extraordinary fable about a little chimney-sweep who is
transformed into a 'water baby' after falling into a river, and eventually
achieves spiritual redemption, used at one time to be standard reading for
quite young children, although its mixture of *Alice-in-Wonderland*-type
fantasy and social commentary can be hard for even an adult to understand. The novel opens with a small boy, Tom, being taken by his cruel
master, Grimes, to help sweep the chimneys at Harthover, a grand mansion in
the North of England. Here, he encounters Ellie, the squire's little daughter,
whom he disturbs while she is asleep. She screams at the sight of him and
Tom runs away, coming to rest at last beside a river, where, exhausted by his

flight, he falls asleep in the water and is drowned. Reborn as a water baby – an amphibious creature which lives for ever – he undertakes a series of journeys and transformations, which end with him being reunited with the angelic Ellie, who has also become a water baby. While the Christian symbolism of Kingsley's novel may strike a modern reader as unpalatable, there is no doubt that the book had a profound effect on nineteenth-century attitudes towards child labour; indeed, within a year of its publication, a law was passed banning the use of children as chimney-sweeps.

WATERSHIP DOWN

by Richard Adams (Puffin, 1972)
Interest level: 10–13/Reading age: 10 +
ANIMALS • ENVIRONMENT

WHEN a housing development sweeps away the burrow where Hazel and his fellow rabbits have lived for generations, he decides to lead an expedition across the countryside, in search of a place where they will all be safe. But on the way, there are many dangers to contend with . . . Adams's powerful fable about a community of rabbits escaping the destructive forces which threaten them, in order to found a new society, has obvious parallels with Orwell's *Animal Farm*, particularly in the way its various animal protagonists reflect different types of human behaviour while remaining recognizable as animals.

OTHER BOOKS BY RICHARD ADAMS
The Tyger Voyage (with Nicola Bayley); *The Plague Dogs*

READ-ONS
The Earth Giant, by Melvin Burgess

WAY HOME

by Libby Hathorn; illustrated by Gregory Rogers (Red Fox, 1996)
Kate Greenaway Medal
Interest level: 9–12/Reading age: 9 +
HOMELESSNESS

HATHORN's powerful story about homelessness is given added impact by Gregory Rogers's haunting and disturbing illustrations. Street-kid Shane finds a stray cat in an alley and must overcome a series of obstacles presented by the night city, ranging from marauding street gangs to a fierce dog, before he and the Cat with No Name can reach the safety of 'home' – which turns out to be a cardboard box. Although the picture-book format suggests that this could be read by a younger readership, the language and underlying message of the book is definitely more appropriate for older children. Moving and unsettling, this is a book whose implications linger in the mind long after the last page has been turned.

READ-ONS
The Baby and Fly Pie, by Melvin Burgess

WAY TO SATTIN SHORE, THE

by Philippa Pearce; illustrated by Charlotte Voake (Puffin, 1983)
Interest level: 9–11/Reading age: 9+
FAMILIES

THERE is a mystery about Kate Tranter's family which no one will explain to her – but but she knows it is in some way connected to Sattin Shore, and the terrible events which took place there ten years before. She stumbles upon the first clue when she is exploring the area on her bike, and comes across a tombstone in the local churchyard on which her father's name is inscribed. More than that, the date of his death is the same as that of Kate's own birth . . . Philippa Pearce's gripping drama of family rivalries and secrets is full of twists and turns, which will keep young readers riveted until the final page.

OTHER BOOKS BY PHILIPPA PEARCE
Tom's Midnight Garden; *A Dog So Small*; *The Battle of Bubble and Squeak*

WEIRDSTONE OF BRISINGAMEN, THE

by Alan Garner (Collins, 1960)
Interest level: 9–12/Reading age: 9+
ADVENTURE ● FANTASY ● MAGIC

COLIN and Susan are spending the summer in the Yorkshire village of Highmost Redmanhey, staying on a farm with their mother's old nurse, Bess, while their parents are abroad. Here, while exploring the ridge of hills called 'the Edge' which overlooks the farm, they stumble on a fantastic secret.

The hills are honeycombed with caves – an underground world, inhabited by supernatural beings. Returning home one night, they are almost seized by a fearsome tribe of cave-dwelling goblins – the 'svarts' – who seem to want something from them. Saved from the svarts by Cadellin, a powerful wizard, they learn what it is that has put them in such danger. For on Susan's favourite bracelet is a magic charm – and it is this that the svarts and their master, the evil Grimnir, intend to have for themselves . . . Alan Garner's classic tale of sorcery and adventure has dated very little since it was first published. The Yorkshire settings are vividly rendered, and the atmosphere of breathless suspense sustained until the final page. A sequel, *The Moon of Gomrath*, contains further adventures.

OTHER BOOKS BY ALAN GARNER
*The Owl Service; *Elidor*

READ-ONS
*The Dark is Rising trilogy, Susan Cooper

WHEN HITLER STOLE PINK RABBIT
. . . .
by Judith Kerr (Collins, 1971)
Interest level: 9–11/Reading age: 10 + /Key Stage: 2
FAMILIES ● WAR

THIS story, the first in a trilogy collectively entitled *Out of the Hitler Time*, concerns nine-year-old Anna, a Jewish girl growing up in Germany during the early 1930s. When Hitler and the Nazi party come to power in 1933, Anna's father – a prominent radical journalist – decides that life in Berlin is much too dangerous for the family. Evading capture by the Nazis by a matter of days, they move first to Switzerland and then to Paris, where Anna and her brother Max attend a French school. Later, when things become too risky for them there, they journey to England and the next stage of their new life . . . Judith Kerr, well known as the author of the popular **Mog* series, writes movingly – and from first-hand experience – about how it felt to be a refugee during the war years. Her central character, Anna, is an ordinary little girl with ordinary concerns (such as the loss of her favourite toy rabbit) who nevertheless understands how much is at stake in the struggle against fascism.

OTHER BOOKS BY JUDITH KERR
A Small Person Far Away; *The Other Way Around*

READ-ONS

The Silver Sword, by Ian Serraillier; *The Dolphin Crossing*, by Jill Paton Walsh

WHITBY WITCHES, THE

by Robin Jarvis (Simon & Schuster, 1991)
Interest level: 11–13/Reading age: 11+
FANTASY ● WITCHES

J ENNET and Ben arrive at the seaside town of Whitby to stay with Alice Boston, an eccentric 92-year-old, who has adopted them. Ben has the gift of second sight, and can see things hidden from the eyes of ordinary folk. He soon learns that Alice and her friends are not entirely as they seem – in fact they, and some of the other inhabitants of Whitby, are very bizarre indeed . . . Jarvis's fantasy adventure, the first volume in a series, offers plenty of thrills and chills for young mystery addicts with reading stamina.

OTHER BOOKS BY ROBIN JARVIS

The *Deptford Mice* trilogy, the *Deptford Histories*

READ-ONS

The Witches, by Roald Dahl; *Nothing to be Afraid Of*, by Jan Mark

WIND IN THE WILLOWS, THE

by Kenneth Grahame; illustrated by E.H. Shepard (Magnet, 1908)
Interest level: 7–11/Reading age: 9+
ADVENTURE ● ANIMALS

M OST of us can remember the first time we read *The Wind in the Willows*; it is one of those books which remain indelibly fixed in the mind, as fresh and delightful now as when it was first published ninety years ago. The story has appeared in numerous different versions, from an award-winning stage play to a film, but the original is still the best. The opening chapter, in which Mole takes a break from his spring-cleaning and finds himself by the riverbank, is one of the most evocative accounts of the delights of open-air life ever written. As Mole's friend Ratty would put it: 'there is *nothing* – absolutely nothing – half so much worth doing as simply messing about in boats.' Mole and Rat's subsequent adventures and their encounters with the other main characters in the book – crusty but loveable Badger and boastful, excitable Toad – make fascinating reading for adults as well as children, reflecting as they do the social upheavals of Edwardian England, and the conflict between the old and the new – epitomized by up-to-date Toad's addiction to the motor-car. Children of course read the stories for their humour and adventure, and for the thrill of identifying with wilful, disobedient Toad – surely one of the most anarchic figures in children's literature.

WITCHES, THE

by Roald Dahl (Puffin, 1983)
Whitbread Award
Interest level: 9–12/Reading age: 9+
WITCHES

R OALD Dahl's boisterous sense of humour is very much to the fore in this story, in which a boy and his grandmother foil the dastardly schemes of a gang of witches bent on turning all the children in England into mice. That, in fact, is the entire plot; as with his other works, characterization is minimal (his narrator doesn't even have a name) and background description virtually non-existent, as the author gets on with the job of making the reader squirm. Certainly his coven of bald, bewigged witches, with their two-inch claws concealed by gloves and their pathological hatred of children, are amongst his most repellent creations. But – for an adult reader at least – there is something rather feeble about the whole performance, which puts one in mind of a jolly uncle, intent on scaring the kiddies into fits.

WOLVES OF WILLOUGHBY CHASE, THE

by Joan Aiken (Red Fox, 1962)
Interest level: 9–11/Reading age: 9+
ADVENTURE • FANTASY

S ET in an imaginary nineteenth century (the reign of James III in the 1830s), the novel describes an England overrun with wolves – which have returned to Britain from the Continent via the newly opened Channel Tunnel. As the novel opens, landowner Sir Willoughby and his ailing wife decide to go abroad, leaving their daughter and her cousin in the care of the villainous governess, Miss Slighcarp, who is determined to get her hands on the Willoughby inheritance by any means possible – including doing away with the children ... With its larger-than-life Dickensian characters and Gothic imagery, the book established Joan Aiken as one of the foremost writers of historical fantasy for children.

OTHER BOOKS BY JOAN AIKEN
Blackhearts in Battersea; *Midnight is a Place*; *The Night Birds on Nantucket*; *Arabel*

READ-ONS
A Little Princess, by Frances Hodgson Burnett

WONDERFUL WIZARD OF OZ, THE

by L. Frank Baum; illustrated by W.W. Denslow (Puffin, 1900)
Interest level: 9–11/Reading age: 9+
ADVENTURE ● FANTASY

FAMILIAR to many from the 1939 film starring Judy Garland, *The Wizard of Oz* tells the story of Dorothy, an orphan, who lives with her kindly aunt and uncle on their farm in Kansas. One memorable day, Dorothy is blown by a cyclone to the magical land of Oz, where she is told that the only way to get home again is to enlist the aid of a great and powerful Wizard, who lives in the Emerald City. On her way to the city, she encounters a Scarecrow, a Tin Man and a Cowardly Lion – all of whom have reasons of their own for needing the Wizard's help. Before any of the four can achieve their heart's desire, however, they must first defeat the Wicked Witch of the West . . . Baum's all-American fable was written with the express intention of providing an alternative to what the author perceived as the 'blood-curdling' morality of traditional fairy tales. What his book offers instead has less to do with European myths of sacrifice and redemption and more to do with American ideals of self-improvement and the pursuit of happiness.

READ-ONS
The Phantom Tollbooth, by Norton Juster

WORD-SPELLS
....

by Judith Nicholls; illustrated by Alan Baker (Faber & Faber, 1988)
Interest level: 9–11/Reading age: 9+
POETRY

A wonderfully imaginative anthology of classical and modern poetry that any child will respond to, including poems by William Shakespeare, Christina Rossetti and *Walter de la Mare, as well as those by contemporary writers such as *Ted Hughes and *Grace Nichols. Exquisitely illustrated by Alan Baker, this is a collection you and your child will want to read again and again.

OTHER BOOKS BY JUDITH NICHOLLS
Dragonsfire and other poems

READ-ONS
Moon-whales, by Ted Hughes

Zoo
.....

by Anthony Browne (Red Fox, 1992)
Kate Greenaway Medal
Interest level: 9–11/Reading age: 9+
ANIMALS

IN the continuing debate on the validity or otherwise of keeping animals in zoos, Anthony Browne is unequivocally of the opposition point of view. This powerful book about a family's visit to London Zoo, in which the human beings appear in every respect to be more 'bestial' than the beasts, pulls no punches in its indictment of the conditions under which animals are kept. As always in Browne's work, this is shown principally through his meticulously detailed and unsettling pictures – which in this case depict various animals against their anything-but-natural setting. Giraffes are shown camouflaged against brickwork, a rhinoceros dwarfed by the monolithic buildings of the Elephant House and, most poignant of all, an orang-utan huddled in a corner of its cage, averting its gaze from jeering human spectators. This is a book which should prompt classroom discussion, and which will appeal to any child with an interest in changing the way we treat our fellow inhabitants of the planet.

READ-ONS
The Bath Rat, by Sian Lewis

Secondary School – Becoming an Independent Reader

YEAR SEVEN: 11–12 YEARS

Starting secondary school is one of the most momentous changes your child will ever experience in the whole of her school career. Getting to grips with a different routine and a new environment, with its unfamiliar rules, can make those first few weeks seem very intimidating – and that's even without the work! Of course some children thrive on it, adapting almost overnight to a more demanding curriculum and taking great pride in everything about their new routine, from wearing a uniform to having to do proper homework. Others are less enthusiastic. 'I'm so *tired*,' was my son's heartfelt complaint during his first term. 'There's no time for anything – except work, work, work!'

All this has implications for the amount of reading – curriculum-based or otherwise – your child will have time for. Many children coping with their first year at secondary school just don't have the energy to read. After getting through a mountain of homework every night, the last thing most of them feel like doing is taxing their brains with what seems like more work. For those children who have not already established the habit of reading for pleasure, it's even harder to get the message across that – far from being an arduous or unpleasant addition to their already overburdened timetables – reading can actually help you to relax.

Some parents, for understandable reasons, have a tendency to overemphasize the worthier aspects of reading, directing their children only towards those books which are related to particular topics at school and banning 'unsuitable' books and comics from the house. While this, like attempts to limit children's television-watching, may be effective in the short term, the end result may be counter-productive. Giving a child the idea that there is something swotty about reading is the surest way to put her off the whole activity for life.

While it is obviously a good idea to keep up with what your child is studying and to offer additional support with appropriate reading material, it is also essential to let her choose the kind of books she enjoys as part of her leisure activities – even if this means she reads stuff of no literary merit at all. Comics and comic-strip format stories, series books and spin-offs from favourite films and TV programmes all have their place in keeping your child reading, at a time when most of her energy is taken up with school.

YEAR 8: 12–13 YEARS

Early adolescence can be a difficult time for both children and parents. Children are growing up fast, and are being offered a range of possibilities which may seem bewildering. The certainties of childhood may have been left behind, but it is often hard to know what to replace them with. Questions about the kind of world they are growing up in, and the kind of decisions they will have to make about their lives, arise every day for most young people. *Why* do I have to go to school? What's the *point* of exams? Why do people have to work? If work is so important, why don't some people have jobs?

These and other, more fundamental questions are an important part of growing up – of discovering where one fits in the scheme of things. The early teenage years are a time when children become aware of all kinds of serious issues, such as divorce, racism, religious intolerance, child abuse – issues with which some of them have to deal in their daily lives.

Reading about other people's experiences, and other ways of dealing with the world, won't stop your child worrying about such things, but it may help her to come to terms with what the world is like. Developing understanding through reading is one of the best ways there is of encouraging tolerance and calming fears. Some of the best books for children I have read recently deal with topics which would have seemed unthinkable even a few years ago. Children are asking questions – about AIDS, about war, about injustice – and writers are producing books which, without claiming to offer all the answers, at least try to address the issues in a sensitive and non-patronizing way.

YEAR 9: 13–14 YEARS

Of course, not all good fiction for teenagers is preoccupied with real-life issues – indeed, a lot of it deals with subjects which are quite literally out of this world. This is an age when many young readers are discovering science fiction and its related category, fantasy – finding in both a breadth of ideas and an imaginative scope often missing from more down-to-earth narratives. Young readers who enjoyed the more fantastical kind of children's classics, such as the *Narnia stories and the novels of Alan Garner, may find themselves drawn to the more grown-up fantasies purveyed by Terry Pratchett and Ursula Le Guin. When homework and domestic chores are getting you down, what could be better than a book about an alternative universe – where school is unheard of and no one ever has to do the washing-up?

YEAR 10: 14–15 YEARS

Books about the world we live in, books about other worlds . . . Whatever your child's preference, the chances are that by her mid-teens she will be reading an increasingly wide range of material, some of it of considerable sophistication. As part of the first year of her

GCSE course, she will be studying a number of set books, which will include Shakespeare plays and classic novels by Jane Austen, Charles Dickens and Charlotte Brontë, as well as more modern authors such as Thomas Hardy and George Orwell. With these and related texts, she will be learning how to deal with the complexities of character, plot and style, and getting used to expressing her ideas in essay form.

Reading works of classic literature is the surest way of developing an appreciation of good writing, as well as one of the most enjoyable. Far from being boring or difficult, novels such as Dickens's *Great Expectations* or Austen's *Pride and Prejudice* are full of humour, excitement and suspense – the ingredients of any good read! The spate of recent film and television adaptations of Austen, George Eliot and Dickens is further indication – if any were needed – of the enduring popularity of their books. Nor should reading the classics be dismissed as escapist or irrelevant to our own times. As well as offering an analysis of human motives and desires, great works of fiction give us insight into the conditions under which people lived in former times, enabling us to understand the way our own society has developed. But such justifications are beside the point – which is that there are few things in life as pleasurable as reading, and the better the book, the more enjoyable it is.

YEAR 11: 15–16 YEARS

By the age of fifteen or sixteen, reading tastes are pretty much formed, and your child will require little help from you in choosing the kind of books she wants to read. These are unlikely to be books specifically written for children – although cross-over writers such as Terry Pratchett and Douglas Adams are popular with this age group. What can be useful for readers still experimenting with adult fiction is some suggested further reading. Instead of the latest Stephen King, why not try Mary Shelley's *Frankenstein* or Edgar Allan Poe's *Tales of Mystery and Imagination*? As an alternative to Danielle Steel, how about Emily Brontë's *Wuthering Heights* or Evelyn Waugh's *Brideshead Revisited*? By this age, there are no limits to what your child is capable of reading – and some of the books she chooses may surprise or even dismay you. Don't worry – half the fun of becoming an independent reader is discovering what you *don't* like, and making informed choices. Once established, the reading habit is going to be with her for a very long time.

ADVENTURES OF HUCKLEBERRY FINN, THE

by Mark Twain (Wordsworth Classics, 1884)
Interest level: 12–16/Reading age: 12+
ADVENTURE

WRITTEN as a sequel to the equally brilliant *Tom Sawyer* but readable as a self-contained novel, *Huckleberry Finn* is narrated by its eponymous hero (a departure from the third-person narrative of the earlier book) and tells the story of his adventures after he takes off on a raft along the Mississippi, to escape from his drunken and potentially murderous father, accompanied by Jim, a runaway slave. Hoping to reach the tributary of the Ohio River and to proceed from there to the Free States (where slavery has been abolished), the two are accidentally diverted from their course and carried deeper into the slave-owning South. Here, they fall in with a pair of confidence tricksters, styling themselves the 'King' and the 'Duke', who take over the raft and compel Huck and Jim to join forces with them in their unscrupulous schemes. After a number of hair-raising adventures during which Jim only narrowly evades capture, he is taken prisoner by a local farmer, a relation of Tom Sawyer, it emerges – who providentially arrives at the farm on a visit. The two boys concoct a fanciful plan to free Jim from captivity, which later turns out to be unnecessary, as it transpires that he has already been granted his freedom by his former owner, who has since died. As wonderfully written, funny and exciting as its companion volume, Twain's novel offers a scathing indictment of slavery, which is all the more powerful because it is seen through the eyes of a child of the Deep South. At the beginning of the novel, Huck is unquestioning in his acceptance of slave-owning; later, he comes to understand how much Jim has suffered, and to reject the idea that one human being can ever be the property of another.

OTHER BOOKS BY MARK TWAIN

Adventures of Tom Sawyer; *The Prince and the Pauper*

ADVENTURES OF TOM SAWYER, THE

by Mark Twain (Wordsworth Classics, 1876)
Interest level: 12–16/Reading age: 12+
ADVENTURE

MARK Twain's classic tale about Tom and his friends Joe Harpur and *Huckleberry Finn is set in the Deep South, a few years before the abolition of slavery. Tom, an orphan, lives with his brother Sid and his Aunt Polly in the Mississippi village of St. Petersburg, where he constantly plays truant from school and gets into mischief – some of it of a highly dangerous variety. One night he and Huck Finn witness a murder in the local graveyard, after which they feel it politic to disappear for a while. Accordingly they slip away to an island in the river, where they live for several days. Presumed drowned by their nearest-and-dearest, on returning home they find themselves just in time to attend their own funerals. The book ends with the discovery, by Tom and Huck, of a treasure-chest hidden by the murderer, Injun-Joe, as a result of which they become very rich – a fate later deplored by Huckleberry, in the sequel which bears his name.

Twain's novel and its sequel are among the funniest and most imaginative books ever written for children, and contain some of the most exciting episodes in any work of fiction. The scene in which Tom and Huck overhear the murder taking place, and the no less harrowing episode in which Tom and his friend Becky Thatcher become lost in a network of limestone caves and nearly die as a result, seem as vivid and memorable now as they were for young readers at the end of the last century. Foolhardy and fond of exaggeration and story-telling as he is, Tom is a very likeable hero, whose fundamental decency and generosity have endeared him to generations of readers.

BABY AND FLY PIE, THE

by Melvin Burgess (Andersen Press, 1993)
Interest level: 13–16/Reading age: 13+
HOMELESSNESS

SET in a future dystopia in which society has broken down to the extent that rich and poor seem almost to belong to different species, Burgess's sombre tale is narrated by the eponymous Fly Pie, a boy who has been abandoned or lost by his parents and who ekes out a living with other

'Rubbish Kids', by scrounging what he can from rubbish tips and handing over what he finds to one of the 'Mothers' who control the tips, in exchange for a night's food and lodging. Everything changes when Fly Pie and his mate Sham stumble across a wounded gangster, who has kidnapped a baby and is holding it to ransom. The gangster dies, and the two boys are left – literally – holding the baby, realizing too late that this puts them in mortal danger . . . What follows is an absorbing and at times harrowing depiction of a society in chaos, as the two boys and Fly Pie's older sister, Jane, find themselves on the run from a variety of pursuers, ranging from the police to the gang-leaders in charge of the criminal underworld in which Fly Pie and the others have grown up, and from which they try vainly to escape. Burgess offers no comforting resolution to his dark fable, whose disturbing ending breaks the 'happy ever after' convention of most children's fiction. This is a book which will make young readers think – and may raise serious questions about social justice.

OTHER BOOKS BY MELVIN BURGESS
An Angel for May; *The Cry of the Wolf*; *Burning Issy*; *Loving April*

READ-ONS:
1984, by George Orwell; *The Dispossessed*, by Ursula Le Guin

BLACK JACK

by Leon Garfield (Puffin, 1968)
Interest level: 12–15/Reading age: 12+
ADVENTURE

REMINISCENT in style of both Dickens and Fielding (for whose novels the author professed great admiration), Garfield's novel is set in eighteenth-century London, and concerns the relationship between the eponymous villain and Tolly, the young apprentice who is forced to assist him in his career of crime. Only Tolly's love for Belle, a young girl suffering from a nervous illness, whom he saves from being committed to an asylum, gives him the courage to break away from Black Jack . . . Beautifully written, and as full of exciting incident as his earlier novels, this is a book that will seize the imagination of young readers, both for its sympathetic portrayal of its young hero's dilemma and for its vivid account of the past.

READ-ONS
Tom Jones, by Henry Fielding; *A Tale of Two Cities*, by Charles Dickens

BULLY
. . . .

by Yvonne Coppard (Red Fox, 1990)
Shortlisted for Children's Book Award
Interest level: 12–15/Reading age: 12 +
BULLYING • DISABILITY

W HEN her parents move her to a new school, following a car accident
which has left her with a damaged leg, thirteen-year-old Kerry Hollis
becomes the target of vicious bullying by a group of older boys, led by the
thuggish Billy Taggart. Humiliated by their taunts but afraid to tell anyone at
school in case it makes things worse, Kerry finds herself trapped in a
nightmarish situation. Then, quite by chance, she discovers something about
Billy Taggart's past which gives her a hold over him; suddenly the roles are
reversed and Kerry is the one with the power ... Yvonne Coppard's
thoughtful and provocative exploration of the damage bullying inflicts on
both perpetrator and victim makes this a gripping read, and provides some
valuable insights into what has become a disturbingly common phenomenon
in schools.

OTHER BOOKS BY YVONNE COPPARD
Copper's Kid; *Hide and Seek*; *Simple Simo*; *The Rag-Bag Family*

CHRISTMAS CAROL, A
. . . .

by Charles Dickens; illustrated by John Leech
(World's Classics, 1843)
Interest level: 12–16/Reading age: 12 +
GHOSTS • VICTORIANS

D ICKENS's classic story was the first of his highly popular Christmas
Books series. It has been adapted for film and television, and illustrated
by numerous artists – but none so effectively as the original, John Leech. The
story – a simple morality tale with Dickensian embellishments – takes place
on Christmas Eve, and concerns the spiritual regeneration of an old miser,
Ebenezer Scrooge. The story opens as Scrooge is closing up shop in his
counting-house in the City, after grudgingly allowing his down-trodden clerk,
Bob Cratchitt, to take Christmas Day off. That night in Scrooge's run-down
lodgings, he is visited by the ghost of his late partner, Jacob Marley, who
warns him against the sins of avarice and cupidity of which both have been

guilty and for which Jacob is paying the price in the afterlife; later the same night, Scrooge receives further visitations. The first of these is from the Spirit of Christmas Past, an elfin figure, who conducts Scrooge to the scenes of his boyhood and youth, showing the contrast between his innocent former self and the hard and cruel man he has become. Next, the jovial Spirit of Christmas Present takes Scrooge on a tour of some of his acquaintances' households as they are preparing for the festivities: foremost among these is that of the Cratchitt family, presided over by the sickly but much-beloved Tiny Tim. The final visitation is from the spectral Ghost of Christmas Yet to Come, who shows the hapless Scrooge a vision of his own, unmourned death. The story ends with Scrooge awaking on Christmas morning a changed man, determined to mend his ways and to make the lives of those around him better. In its own way, and bearing in mind that this was a highly condensed form for a writer whose natural length was the three-decker novel, this is as perfect a story as Dickens ever wrote, displaying all the characteristics for which his writing is renowned: a warm and humorous appreciation of human diversity, wonderfully vivid characters and settings, and a passionate concern for the poor and dispossessed.

READ-ONS
David Copperfield and *Great Expectations*, by Charles Dickens

COLOUR OF MAGIC, THE
. . . .
by Terry Pratchett (Corgi, 1983)
Interest level: 12–16/Reading age: 12 +
FANTASY ● SCIENCE FICTION

TERRY Pratchett's *Discworld* series has become hugely popular with teenage readers for its blend of surreal fantasy, magic and humour. The saga follows the adventures of sundry witches and wizards, barbarians and heroes who all live on a huge disc, supported by four exceptionally large elephants standing on the shell of Great A' Tuin, a turtle of unimaginable size – the whole contraption of course hurtling through space. *The Colour of Magic* – the first book in the series – introduces us to Rincewind, a failed wizard from the capital city of Ankh-Morpork. Commissioned to act as a guide for a tourist named Twoflower from the other side of the Disc, his adventures begin with the destruction of a city – and don't stop there . . . Exciting and hilarious, Terry Pratchett's epic adventures will appeal to anyone who wants to lose themselves in another, fantastic world.

OTHER BOOKS BY TERRY PRATCHETT

The Light Fantastic (sequel to *The Colour of Magic*); *Equal Rites*; **Truckers*; *The Carpet People*; *Only You Can Save Mankind*; *Johnny and the Dead*; *Johnny and the Bomb*

READ-ONS

**Hitch-hiker's Guide to the Galaxy*, by Douglas Adams

DARK IS RISING, THE

. . . .

by Susan Cooper (Puffin, 1965–77)
Newbery Medal
Interest level: 11–15/Reading age: 11+
ADVENTURE ● FANTASY ● MAGIC

THIS sequence of five novels includes *Over Sea, Under Stone*; *The Dark is Rising*; *Greenwitch*; *The Grey King* and *Silver on the Tree*. Loosely based on the Arthurian legends but set in the modern world, Susan Cooper's compelling series begins (in *Over Sea, Under Stone*) when three children holidaying in Cornwall discover a Grail. In the second book in the series, *The Dark is Rising*, eleven-year-old Will Stanton finds out that he has a special destiny – to help defeat the forces of Darkness which threaten the world. *Greenwitch* takes up the saga with the theft of the Grail by the forces of the Dark, and (like Alan Garner's *The Owl Service) concerns the making of a woman out of leaves, who turns out to have occult powers. *The Grey King* and *Silver on the Tree* are both set in Wales, and concern Will's continuing struggle against evil. In these, as in the earlier books, elements of fantasy and legend are mingled with descriptions of everyday life. Will may represent the forces of good, but he is also an ordinary boy. Lyrical and haunting, these books offer a good introduction to myth and fable for young readers interested in the supernatural.

READ-ONS

**The Weirdstone of Brisingamen*, by Alan Garner; **The Lion, the Witch and the Wardrobe* and sequels, by C.S. Lewis; **The Lord of the Rings*, by J.R.R. Tolkien

DEAD HOUR, THE
· · · · · · · · · · · · · · · ·

by Pete Johnson (Mammoth, 1995)
Interest level: 13–16/Reading age: 13 +
FEAR ● GHOSTS ● HORROR

WHEN seventeen-year-old Richard and his best friend Danny decide to go on a ghost-hunt, to impress Danny's girlfriend Angie and her friend Louise, they regard it as a bit of a joke. Surely there can't be anything in the rumour that the deserted church on Abbotts Hill is haunted? But then Richard sees something he can't explain – something he fears may be an evil spirit – and what's more, he finds that Louise has seen it too. What follows is a suitably creepy – but also humorous – exploration of the tricks the imagination can play, which ends on a comfortingly positive note. Johnson's *Friends Forever* series provides a popular alternative to its American counterparts (e.g. *Sweet Valley High*), offering well-written versions of popular genres such as horror and romance. Johnson, who lists J.D. Salinger's *Catcher in the Rye* and P.G. Wodehouse's *Jeeves* stories among his favourite books, has expressed his awareness of the importance of providing good fiction for teenage readers which is neither condescending nor overtly moralizing.

OTHER BOOKS BY PETE JOHNSON
We the Dead; *Ten Hours to Live*

READ-ONS
The Stones of Muncaster Cathedral, by Robert Westall

DEAR NOBODY
· · · · · · · · · · · · · ·

by Berlie Doherty (Collins, 1991)
Carnegie Medal
Interest level: 14–16/Reading age: 14 +
FAMILIES ● PREGNANCY ● SINGLE PARENTHOOD

CHRIS and his girlfriend Helen are both eighteen, and looking forward to going to university. But then, after one careless sexual encounter, Helen discovers she is pregnant, and suddenly her plans for the future look very different. If she decides to go through with having the baby – her little 'Nobody' – she can say goodbye to Music College – and perhaps to her relationship with Chris . . . Powerful and moving, Berlie Doherty's novel uncompromisingly gets to grips with the realities of teenage pregnancy. This is a book every young adolescent ought to read.

OTHER BOOKS BY BERLIE DOHERTY

The Snake Stone; *Spellhorn*; *Granny was a Buffer Girl*

READ-ONS

*The Millstone, by Margaret Drabble

DINOTOPIA
· · · · · · · · · · ·

by James Gurney (Dorling Kindersley, 1992)
Interest level: 11–15/Reading age: 11+
DINOSAURS

I N 1860, during a daring voyage of exploration, American biologist Arthur Denison and his son Will stumble across a unique civilization, in which humans and dinosaurs live in peaceful co-existence. This book is the chronicle of their adventures ... Gurney's wonderfully detailed account of a remarkable utopian society reads like a cross between William Morris and Conan Doyle's **The Lost World*. His intricate and colourful paintings of Dinotopia and its citizens will delight any reader with an interest in dinosaurs – or, indeed, in alternative societies.

READ-ONS

*The Lost World, by Sir Arthur Conan Doyle; *News from Nowhere*, by William Morris; *Erewhon*, by Samuel Butler

DIVORCE EXPRESS, THE
· ·

by Paula Danziger (Mammoth, 1982)
Interest level: 12–15/Reading age: 12+
DIVORCE ● FRIENDS

F OURTEEN-YEAR-OLD Phoebe Brooks has had two homes since her parents' divorce – one with her mother, in New York City, the other with her father, in rural Woodstock. Every weekend she commutes between the two, on the Divorce Express, the bus service which carries other children like herself from one family to another. One of these fellow passengers is Rosie, who lives in Woodstock with her mother, and attends the same school as Phoebe. A friendship develops, through which Phoebe learns that there can be advantages as well as disadvantages to being the child of divorced parents, and that she needn't feel guilty about being hurt or angry. Paula

Danziger confronts some of the painful truths about what happens when marriages end, with her customary warmth and humour. Inevitably, the story has dated a little since it was first published (notably in the descriptions of the teenagers' clothes), but it still retains much of its appeal.

OTHER BOOKS BY PAULA DANZIGER

Can You Sue Your Parents for Malpractice?; *Everyone Else's Parents said Yes!*; *Make Like a Tree and Leave*

EAGLE OF THE NINTH, THE
. . . .

by Rosemary Sutcliff (Puffin, 1954)
Interest level: 11–14/Reading age: 11+
ADVENTURE ● ROMANS

SET in Britain during the Roman occupation, this exciting and historically accurate novel (the first of a trilogy about the Romans in Britain which also includes *The Silver Branch* and *The Lantern Bearers*) concerns a young centurion, Marcus, who is invalided out of the army after being wounded in battle and decides to go in search of the Ninth Legion, which some years before was ordered into the uncharted territory beyond Hadrian's Wall to quell an uprising, and never seen again. Also lost with the legion (which was commanded by Marcus's father) was the standard or Eagle of the Ninth. Determined to find the Eagle, and also to clear his father and the rest of the legion of suspected cowardice, Marcus ventures beyond the Wall, accompanied by the former slave, Esca, and finds himself in a dangerously unfamiliar world . . . As gripping and believable in its recreation of life in Roman Britain as it was when first published in the 1950s, this novel established Rosemary Sutcliffe as one of the foremost writers of historical novels for children and adults.

OTHER BOOKS BY ROSEMARY SUTCLIFF

Black Ships before Troy; *The Silver Branch*; *The Lantern Bearers*; *Warrior Scarlet*; *Blood Feud*; *Dawn Wind*; *The Mark of the Horse Lord*; *Frontier Wolf*; *Outcast*; *The Shining Company*

READ-ONS

Song for a Tattered Flag, by Geoffrey Trease; *Horned Helmet*, by Henry Treece

FEVER PITCH
. . . .

by Nick Hornby (Indigo, 1992)
Interest level: 12–16/Reading age: 12+
FOOTBALL

Nick Hornby's autobiography about his life as an Arsenal football club supporter will appeal to football fanatics of all ages, conveying as it does the excitement, enjoyment and occasional disappointment of being a football fan. Beginning with a description of the first match he attended, when he was eleven, Hornby's nostalgic and very funny account is a history both of his favourite club and of the era in which he grew up. An ideal read for any football-mad youngster.

OTHER BOOKS BY NICK HORNBY
High Fidelity

FIREWEED
. . . .

by Jill Paton Walsh (Puffin, 1969)
Interest level: 13–15/Reading age: 13+/Key Stage: 3
WAR

Bill and Julie are both fifteen, and are both on the run from the authorities in wartime London. For Bill, there is a stark choice between returning to Wales as an evacuee, or going back to live with his unsympathetic aunt. For Julie, rescued from a torpedoed ship on its way to Canada, the choice is more problematic still: should she return to her wealthy family, who believe she is out of harm's way – or continue enjoying a life of freedom? Jill Paton Walsh's gripping adventure conveys the excitement as well as the horror of wartime, as seen through the eyes of its teenage protagonists.

OTHER BOOKS BY JILL PATON WALSH
*A Parcel of Patterns; *The Dolphin Crossing*; **The Butty Boy*; *Gaffer Samson's Luck*

READ-ONS
*Back Home and **Goodnight, Mr Tom*, by Michelle Magorian

FLOUR BABIES
· · · · · · · · · · · · ·

by Anne Fine (Puffin, 1992)
Carnegie Medal
Interest level: 11–14/Reading age: 11+
BABIES ● DIVORCE ● FAMILIES

W HEN the annual school science project turns out to be Flour Babies, Class 4C is not amused. What on earth is the point of lugging around a six-pound bag of flour and caring for it as if it were a baby? Surely they could have had more fun with exploding custard tins or a maggot farm? But then Simon Martin, the least promising member of the school's most unpromising class, finds that he may be learning something from the exercise after all . . . Anne Fine's wonderfully funny and moving story shows how, given the right encouragement, everyone can be brilliant at something.

OTHER BOOKS BY ANNE FINE
Stranger Danger?; *Bill's New Frock*; **Madame Doubtfire*; **Goggle Eyes*; **The Stone Menagerie*

FRIENDS, THE
· · · · · · · · · · · · ·

by Rosa Guy (Puffin Modern Classics, 1973)
Interest level: 13–16/Reading age: 12+
FRIENDS ● RACIAL STEREOTYPING

G UY'S hard-hitting novel about a young West Indian girl growing up in Harlem was ahead of its time in addressing the issue of race from a child's perspective. Phyllisia Cathy and her parents and older sister have arrived from the Caribbean and are making their way in New York. It is the era of Civil Rights, and the city is in ferment – a mood which has spread to the school where Phyllisia is a pupil. Here she encounters prejudice not only from her white teachers but also from her black classmates. When she is beaten up by the school bully on her way home, she is befriended by Edith, a black girl from a poor family. But when Phyllisia tries to introduce Edith to her own family, she experiences prejudice of a different kind from her domineering father, Calvin, who tells her that Edith is not good enough for her. Then Rowena, Phyllisia's mother, becomes seriously ill, and the two friends are drawn even closer together by tragedy . . .

More than twenty years after it was first published, Guy's novel still seems relevant to the problems many children experience both at home and at school. Its insistence on the value of friendship in the face of bigotry is all the more heartening because it does not gloss over how insidious this can be.

READ-ONS
Roll of Thunder, Hear My Cry, by *Mildred D. Taylor*; *The Colour Purple*, by Alice Walker

GATHERING DARKNESS, THE
. . . .
by Paula Fox (Orion, 1995)
Interest level: 13–16/Reading age: 12+
AIDS ● DEATH

L IAM Cormac is thirteen years old and lives in New York City with his mother, Katherine. He is in his first year at high school, he has lots of friends and he likes rock music and a girl in his class called Delia. Liam also has a secret: his father, Philip, is dying of AIDS. Liam tells his friends his father has cancer – a euphemism even Philip's family and friends seem willing to accept. Katherine tells Liam that his father contracted his illness when he received infected blood during a routine transfusion – but Liam suspects the truth may be very different. On a weekend visit to his father's cabin on the New England coast, he confronts Philip with his suspicions that his father has been involved in a homosexual relationship. Philip confirms that Liam is right. At first angry and shocked, Liam is eventually able to come to terms with this knowledge, and with his father's inevitable death.

Paula Fox's sensitive exploration of living with AIDS and the repercussions the illness has on a family, is more than just another 'issues' novel. All three main characters are sympathetically portrayed, although the character of Liam – in all his anger and confusion – is particularly well drawn. This is a book which raises many important issues to do with tolerance and understanding, but which does so with great subtlety.

OTHER BOOKS BY PAULA FOX
Western Wind

GOGGLE EYES
. . . .

by Anne Fine (Penguin, 1989)
Interest level: 12–15/Reading age: 12 +
DIVORCE ● FRIENDS

WHEN Kitty Kilin's best friend Helen turns up at school distraught by the news that she is to have a new stepfather, Kitty is able to sympathize. Hasn't she had to deal with exactly the same situation? As she tries to comfort Helen, she tells her how awful *she* felt the day she first met her mother's new boyfriend, Gerald – or 'Goggle-eyes', as Kitty calls him. What on earth could her mum see in someone so boring? Anne Fine's funny and thought-provoking story dramatizes the tensions which often occur when parents of adolescent children try to form new relationships with the opposite sex.

OTHER BOOKS BY ANNE FINE
Madame Doubtfire; *Bill's New Frock*; *Stranger Danger?*

GRANNY WAS A BUFFER GIRL
. . . .

by Berlie Doherty (Mammoth, 1986)
Carnegie Medal
Interest level: 12–16/Reading age: 12 +
FAMILIES

SEVENTEEN-YEAR-OLD Jess is about to leave her close-knit working-class family for the first time to go away to college. As the time of her departure approaches, she finds herself listening with even greater attention to the family stories she has always loved, stories which reflect several generations of Sheffield life. Such as the story about her maternal grandmother Bridie, who worked as a 'buffer girl' in a Sheffield cutlery factory after the First World War. Berlie Doherty's family saga is full of affectionate and moving anecdotes about a fascinating period of English history.

OTHER BOOKS BY BERLIE DOHERTY
Children of Winter; *Dear Nobody*; *Spellhorn*

READ-ONS
Sons and Lovers, by D.H. Lawrence

HITCH-HIKER'S GUIDE TO THE GALAXY, THE

by Douglas Adams (Pan, 1979)
Interest level: 12–16/Reading age: 12+
ADVENTURE ● FANTASY ● SCIENCE FICTION

ALTHOUGH not written as a children's book, Douglas Adams's hilarious spoof of science fiction 'space operas' has become such a cult with teenage readers that – like the novels of *Terry Pratchett – its omission from any reading list for the under-sixteens would be unthinkable. As any fan will tell you, the series (currently standing at five books) concerns the travels of one Arthur Dent around an increasingly chaotic and surprising universe. In the first book, Arthur is forced to leave his home on Earth when the entire planet is demolished to make way for an intergalactic motorway; subsequent adventures involve him in encounters with strange, poetry-reading aliens, a two-headed, three-armed superstar and the rulers of the universe – a colony of white mice. The zany quality of the book is hard to convey in a few words; the best advice to prospective readers is probably that of the eponymous Guide itself (a combination of travel book and encyclopaedia to which Arthur refers in times of trial): 'DONT PANIC!'

OTHER BOOKS BY DOUGLAS ADAMS
The Restaurant at the End of the Universe; *Life, the Universe and Everything*; *So Long, and Thanks for All the Fish*; *Mostly Harmless*

READ-ONS
**The Colour of Magic* and *Truckers*, by Terry Pratchett

HOBBIT, THE

by J.R.R. Tolkien (Unwin Paperbacks, 1937)
Interest level: 12–16/Reading age: 13+
ADVENTURE ● FANTASY

PUBLISHED fifty years ago, J.R.R. Tolkien's fantasy adventure story has become a cult book, inspiring a host of imitators and admirers of his blend of magic, myth and adventure story. Its reluctant hero, the Hobbit – one Bilbo Baggins of Bag End – is thrown into the adventure head-first when he is recruited by Gandalf, a powerful wizard, and his band of Dwarves, to help search for a missing hoard of gold. Bilbo's journey takes him through

Mirkwood, which is inhabited by giant spiders, over treacherous mountains, where he encounters the slimy Gollum and acquires a magic ring, and through many strange lands until he reaches the lair of a large and dangerous dragon named Smaug . . . At the time the book was written, Tolkien was Professor of Anglo-Saxon at Oxford University, and drew heavily on his knowledge of Norse myth and legend for his own work. Despite its author's scholarly background, the book is far from heavy, and indeed reads more like an exciting mystery story than an exercise in archaic narrative.

OTHER BOOKS BY J.R.R. TOLKIEN

The Lord of the Rings (three-part sequel to *The Hobbit*); *The Silmarillion*; *The Adventures of Tom Bombadil*; *Farmer Giles of Ham*

HOUSE IN NORHAM GARDENS, THE
. . . .
by Penelope Lively (Mammoth,1974)
Interest level: 12–15/Reading age: 12 +
GROWING UP

FOURTEEN-YEAR-OLD Clare lives with her two elderly great-aunts in a vast Victorian mansion in North Oxford, whose rooms are stuffed with old clothes, furniture and curiosities brought back by Clare's anthropologist great-grandfather at the turn of the century. While the household struggles to make ends meet, taking in lodgers to supplement the family income, Clare confronts anxieties of a different kind, in the disturbing dreams which oppress her every night. Could the dreams be linked to the ceremonial shield she has discovered in the attic, which rightly belongs to the New Guinea tribe from which her great-grandfather took it all those years ago? If so, what can Clare do to make things right? Penelope Lively's haunting novel offers some memorable images, and some thoughtful insights into the loneliness of adolescence.

OTHER BOOKS BY PENELOPE LIVELY

The Ghost of Thomas Kempe; *A Stitch in Time*; *The Revenge of Samuel Stokes*

JURASSIC PARK
. . . .

by Michael Crichton (Arrow, 1991)
Interest level: 12–16/Reading age: 13+
ADVENTURE • DINOSAURS

W HEN John Hammond, eccentric millionaire head of InGen, a biotech-
nological company, uses genetic engineering to revive a race of
dinosaurs extinct for 65 million years, he invites a hand-picked team of
palaeontologists to view the result. But the experiment goes horribly wrong
when Dennis Nedry, an embittered computer genius sent to infiltrate
Hammond's dinosaur park, switches off the electric fences which keep
the dinosaurs at bay. As a result, the dinosaurs escape and start wreaking
havoc on their surroundings and on their neighbours . . . Michael Crichton's
electrifying thriller was filmed by Steven Spielberg in 1993.

OTHER BOOKS BY MICHAEL CRICHTON
The Lost World (sequel to *Jurassic Park*)

READ-ONS
*The Lost World, by Sir Arthur Conan Doyle

LITTLE WOMEN
. . . .

by Louisa M. Alcott (Puffin, 1868)
Interest level: 12–16/Reading age: 12+
FAMILIES

A LCOTT'S classic novel about four sisters growing up in a Massachusetts
village during the American Civil War achieved widespread popularity
on its publication for its realistic portrayal of family life – in particular, the
relationships between the sisters, Meg, Jo, Amy and Beth. One of the reasons
for the book's enduring success (it has been filmed and adapted for
television several times) is the crispness with which Alcott defines her
characters – pretty, domesticated Meg, independent bluestocking Jo, vain,
frivolous Amy and sweet, uncomplaining Beth – who might be regarded as
types of mid-nineteenth-century womanhood. Of the four, it is Jo – the
tomboyish intellectual of the family – who emerges as the real heroine of the
book. Alcott was ahead of her time in presenting a feminist viewpoint, and in
refusing to show marriage as 'the only end and aim of a woman's life' she set a
precedent for much that was to follow in women's writing.

OTHER BOOKS BY LOUISA M. ALCOTT
Good Wives

READ-ONS
What Katy Did, by Susan Coolidge

LIZARD
. . . .

by Dennis Covington (Bloomsbury, 1991)
Interest level: 12–15/Reading age: 12 +
DISABILITY

THIRTEEN-YEAR-OLD Lucius Sims – or 'Lizard' as he prefers to be known – is different from other boys his age. Born with a facial malformation which means his eyes are set on either side of his face rather than close together, he is used to being shunned by other people, who think that because of his looks he must be mentally slow. But when a troupe of travelling actors puts on a performance at the institution for retarded boys where Lizard is an inmate, he knows he has found his vocation. Leaving the hateful institutional life behind, he follows Callahan and Sallie and their dog Mac to the bright lights of Birmingham, Alabama, where the troupe is putting on a production of Shakespeare's *The Tempest*, in which Lizard has a starring role . . . Dennis Covington's novel sensitively evokes his main character's point of view, showing how it feels to be different from other people, and how important it is to be accepted for what you are and not how you look.

LORD OF THE RINGS
. . . .

by J.R.R. Tolkien (Penguin, 1954)
Interest level: 12–16/Reading age: 12 +
ADVENTURE ● FANTASY

WRITTEN as a sequel to *The Hobbit* but vastly outstripping it in length and scope, Tolkien's epic work combines elements of medieval romance, adventure story and Icelandic saga, and has captured the imagination of children and adults throughout the world. The narrative follows the attempts by its hobbit-hero, Bilbo, accompanied by a group of friends, to retrieve a magic ring from the evil Gollum, who has stolen it, and to take the ring back to its rightful owner, evading all subsequent attempts on the part of the forces of darkness to steal it back. The book is distinguished by some exciting set-pieces, including the description of Bilbo and his friends escaping across the Shire from the malevolent Black Riders, and of the ensuing battle. Many readers have been captivated by its mixture of high-sounding language and comic incident, but for others the work's enduring appeal is harder to explain.

OTHER BOOKS BY J.R.R. TOLKIEN
* *The Hobbit*; *The Silmarillion*; *Farmer Giles of Ham*; *The Adventures of Tom Bombadil*

LOST WORLD, THE

by Sir Arthur Conan Doyle (Puffin, 1912)
Interest level: 12–16/Reading age: 12 +
ADVENTURE ● DINOSAURS

THE plot of Michael Crichton's * *Jurassic Park* owes a good deal to this 1912 novel, in which a team of explorers on an expedition down the Orinoco discover a region cut off from the rest of the world, where dinosaurs roam free and humanity is still in a primitive state. As well as its terrifyingly real account of the encounters between twentieth-century scientists and prehistoric monsters, the book is notable for the vividness and accuracy of its descriptions of the Venezuelan landscape, although Conan Doyle in fact never visited the country, basing his account on lectures he had heard at the Royal Geographic Society.

READ-ONS
* *Jurassic Park*, by Michael Crichton

MAKE LEMONADE

by Virginia Euwer Wolff (Faber & Faber, 1993)
Interest level: 13–16/Reading age: 13 +
FAMILIES ● PREGNANCY ● SINGLE PARENTHOOD

LAVAUGHN is fourteen and one of the brightest in her class at high school. Determined to save the money to go to college, she takes a babysitting job, working for Jolly, a seventeen-year-old single parent who lives with two young children, Jeremy and Jilly, in conditions of depressing squalor – but who is, in her own way, determined to make her life work. When Jolly loses her job after being sexually harassed by her boss, the future looks bleak for the little family. Terrified that her children will be taken away from her, Jolly refuses to go on Welfare, persuading LaVaughn to look after her children for free while she tries to find work. When this proves futile, LaVaughn encourages Jolly to join a community education programme for young mothers, as a result of which Jolly is able to take the first steps towards an independent life.

Virginia Euwer Wolff's moving novel is told from the point of view of fourteen-year-old LaVaughn, and captures the speech rhythms and thoughts of her young heroine exactly. The book conveys a passionate belief in the importance of education as an enabling force, and shows how even a little effort at the right time in someone's life can bring about great changes.

MAPHEAD
. . . .
by Lesley Howarth (Walker Books, 1994)
Guardian Children's Fiction Award
Interest level: 12–16/Reading age: 12 +
FANTASY • SCIENCE FICTION

TWELVE-YEAR-OLD Maphead is a visitor from another world, who arrives with his father, Ran, in search of Maphead's human mother. For Maphead – whose name refers to his ability to 'blush' a map of wherever he is across his domed forehead – the first problem is going to be fitting in with the indigenous population. This means learning to eat human food and wearing the clothes that humans wear, to say nothing of learning their language. With these elements mastered, his next task is to track down his mother – but will she recognize him? Lesley Howarth's offbeat story offers some surprising insights into how it feels when you don't belong. A must for all young science fiction buffs.

OTHER BOOKS BY LESLEY HOWARTH
Weather Eye; *The Flower King*

NORTHERN LIGHTS
. . . .

by Philip Pullman (Scholastic, 1995)
Carnegie Medal
Interest level: 12–16/Reading age: 12 +
FANTASY ● SCIENCE FICTION

THE first part of a projected trilogy (collectively entitled *His Dark Materials*), Pullman's breathtaking saga is set in an alternative civilization which resembles our own – but with certain striking differences. One of these is that all human beings are accompanied by their 'daemon' or familiar spirit, which takes the form of an animal or bird. Lyra, the novel's twelve-year-old protagonist, has a daemon called Pantalaimon, who sometimes looks like a moth and sometimes like an ermine. At the beginning of the novel, Lyra and her daemon are living in Oxford, under the protection of the master of Jordan College. Here, she is petted and indulged by all the Scholars, and allowed to run wild with her friend Roger the kitchen boy. But then one day Roger disappears – one of an increasing number of unexplained disappearances. Lyra decides to go to his rescue, and in doing so, learns the truth about who she really is – knowledge which may put her in mortal danger . . . Pullman's multi-layered and intriguing work is a compelling read, and a fine introduction to the pleasures of imaginative writing.

READ-ONS
The Dispossessed, by Ursula Le Guin; *The Colour of Magic*, by Terry Pratchett

PARCEL OF PATTERNS, A
. . . .

by Jill Paton Walsh (Kestrel, 1983)
Interest level: 13–16/Reading age: 12 + /Key Stage: 3
DEATH ● TUDORS & STUARTS

THE plague comes to the Derbyshire village of Eyam when a parcel of dress patterns arrives from London in September 1665. The journeyman tailor, George Vicars, is the first to fall ill, setting in motion a terrible train of events which only comes to an end when all but a few of the village's three hundred and fifty souls are dead. Based on actual events, Paton Walsh's moving and evocative novel is narrated by seventeen-year-old Mall Percival, a girl from a Quaker family, who is betrothed to Thomas Torre, a local shepherd. Mall watches in horror as friends and later family succumb to the sickness, never losing her devout religious faith until the very end, when the person she loves the most is taken from her . . . Traumatic historical events are brought vividly to life in this powerful work, made all the more compelling by its simple but direct narrative style.

READ-ONS

Diaries, by Samuel Pepys

POINT HORROR

Series editor: Anne Finnis (Scholastic, from 1991)
Interest level: 12–16/Reading age: 12 +
HORROR

L ove them or loathe them – and most parents loathe them – this series of horror stories aimed at young teens has proved highly popular with its target readership since it was first launched in the UK in 1991. Authors such as the appropriately named D.E. Athkins, Caroline B. Cooney and Diane Hoh have produced over forty of these gruesome chillers, whose titles – *The Carver*, *The Stalker*, *Vampire Love* – say it all. The success of the *Point Horror* books, which until recently have been decidedly American in setting and style, has prompted an English spin-off, *Point Horror Unleashed*, with references to GCSEs and cups of tea instead of High School and pizzas to alleviate the suspense.

READ-ONS

Tales of Mystery and Imagination, by Edgar Allan Poe; *Dracula*, by Bram Stoker; *Ghost Stories of an Antiquary*, by M.R. James

SMITH

by Leon Garfield (Constable, 1967)
Interest level: 12–16/Reading age: 12 + /Key Stage: 3
ADVENTURE

T welve-year-old Smith is an orphan, making his living by his wits and by picking pockets in the streets of his native London. So far he has managed to evade the hangman's noose – until the day he witnesses the murder of an elderly man whose pocket he has just picked, and finds himself in possession of a document he suspects may hold the clue to the killing.

Unfortunately for Smith, several other people also want to get hold of the document – including a mysterious Man in Black. Realizing that he cannot trust his two grown-up sisters Fanny and Bridget with the secret, Smith decides to go to ground in another part of the city. Here he encounters an old blind man, Mr Mansfield, whose misguided attempts to help the homeless orphan only lead him deeper into trouble. Garfield's account of his young hero's predicament is told with great verve and excitement, and his portrayal of the novel's eighteenth-century setting is wonderfully evocative. This is a book which will grip any young reader's imagination, creating a vivid picture of life in one of the most turbulent and colourful eras in English history.

READ-ONS

Tom Jones, by Henry Fielding; *David Copperfield*, by Charles Dickens

SWORD IN THE STONE, THE
. . . .
by T.H. White (Fontana, 1938)
Interest level: 12–16/Reading age: 12+
ADVENTURE ● MAGIC

THE first part of T.H. White's epic Arthurian tetralogy *The Once and Future King* is the most accessible to younger readers. The story concerns the boyhood of King Arthur (irreverently known as the 'Wart'), and his schooling in the arts of kingship and magic by the magician Merlyn. Brought up as companion and squire to Sir Ector's son, Kay, Wart shows an early aptitude for the teachings of Merlyn, which include being changed into various different animals in order to experience life from the point of view of another species – an idea which seems very much in tune with recent environmental thinking. When all the other knights fail to draw the magical sword from the stone, Wart succeeds, and in doing so reveals himself as the future king. White's retelling of Malory's *Le Morte D'Arthur* humanizes the story, portraying Arthur as a sympathetic and peace-loving character, and Merlyn as an engaging eccentric. It offers a wonderfully detailed and entertaining introduction to the Arthurian legends.

OTHER BOOKS BY T. H. WHITE

The Witch in the Wood; *The Ill-Made Knight*; *The Candle in the Wind*

READ-ONS

Tales of King Arthur, by Roger Lancelyn Green

TRIPODS, THE
. . . .

by John Christopher (Puffin, 1967)
Interest level: 12–15/Reading age: 12+
ADVENTURE ● SCIENCE FICTION

*T*HE *Tripods*, John Christopher's classic trilogy (comprising *The White Mountains, The City of Gold and Lead* and *The Pool of Fire*), describes his young hero Will's struggle against the Masters, alien beings which have come to dominate the human race and which resemble huge metal tripods. With his friends Henry and Beanpole, Will determines to rid the earth of the Tripods by joining forces with the rebels in a distant camp in the White Mountains. Recently adapted for television, this dramatic story was a landmark in children's science fiction.

READ-ONS
The Day of the Triffids, by John Wyndham

TROKEVILLE WAY, THE
. . . .

by Russell Hoban (Jonathan Cape, 1996)
Interest level: 12–15/Reading age: 12+
FANTASY ● GROWING UP

*T*WELVE-YEAR-OLD Nick Hartley is on his way home from school, after being knocked out in a fight with school bully Harry Buncher. He's still feeling strangely light-headed when he encounters Moe Nagic, a down-and-out magician, who sells him an unusual jigsaw made from a cut-up painting depicting a road leading to the mysterious Trokeville. Moe shows him a technique for getting into the painting, but warns him that he may not like what he finds when he gets there. Undaunted by this, Nick succeeds in finding a way into the painting to explore the Trokeville Way and becomes involved in a series of strange adventures, in which he is forced to confront his deepest fears – and also his anxieties about first love.

Renowned for his poetic fantasies for adults as well as children, Hoban is a master of the surreal world between waking and dreaming. This book explores the unknown territory of the unconscious mind in a way that even younger readers will understand, and sensitively handles the conflicts of adolescence.

OTHER BOOKS BY RUSSELL HOBAN

*The Mouse and His Child; *Riddley Walker*; **Bedtime for Frances*; *The Twenty Elephant Restaurant*; *Court of the Winged Serpent*

READ-ONS

*The Phantom Tollbooth, by Norton Juster; *The Catcher in the Rye*, by J.D. Salinger

UNBELIEVER

. . . .

by Robert Swindells (Hamish Hamilton, 1995)
Interest level: 13–16/Reading age: 12 +
DEATH • FAMILIES • RELIGION

A NNABEL Henshaw's mother is dying of cancer – a fact which, in itself, is putting her family under enormous pressure. But then her father, Malcolm, turns to religion as a way of coping with his grief – and Annabel's life is turned upside-down. First Malcolm tries to forbid her to go out with her friends; then he has her removed from her Comparative Religion class at school, because its non-denominational approach conflicts with the dogmatic teachings of the fundamentalist sect, The Little Children, of which he has become a member. Worst of all, he seems determined to win over Annabel's younger sister, Sarah, to his beliefs. Annabel's reaction is to run away from home. She ends up in London, and is taken in by a volunteer with the Samaritans, who persuades her to get in touch with her family. Things take a turn for the worse when she learns that her sister has gone away on a weekend retreat with The Little Children, and that she may be in danger of being sexually abused by the leader of the sect. Annabel enlists the aid of her Good Samaritan and the story ends happily, with Annabel's mother in remission and her father renouncing his extremist beliefs.

This typically hard-hitting novel deals with a number of contemporary issues in a plausible and compelling way. As well as his more realistic fiction, Swindells is renowned for dystopian fantasies, such as his prize-winning *Daz 4 Zoe* and **Timesnatch*, about the effects of genetic engineering.

OTHER BOOKS BY ROBERT SWINDELLS
Room 13; *The Thousand Eyes of Night*; *Daz 4 Zoe*; *Dracula's Castle*; *Hydra*; *Inside the Worm*; **Timesnatch*; *Stone Cold*

READ-ONS
The Crucible, by Arthur Miller

WAR OF JENKINS' EAR, THE

by Michael Morpurgo (Mammoth, 1993)
Shortlisted for Smarties Prize
Interest level: 12–14/Reading age: 12+
FRIENDS ● GROWING UP ● RELIGION

S ET at a boy's preparatory school in 1952, Michael Morpurgo's compelling story explores the relationship between two friends, twelve-year-old Toby Jenkins and a new boy, Simon Christopher. Before long, it becomes apparent that there is something different and even a little strange about Simon. He isn't afraid of anyone – not even the headmaster – and he can make things happen, just by saying they will. But is he really as special as he claims to be – or has Toby fallen under the spell of a charlatan? Morpurgo's novel powerfully conveys the claustrophobic atmosphere of boarding-school life, as well as the intensity of adolescent friendships.

OTHER BOOKS BY MICHAEL MORPURGO
*My Friend Walter; *Mr Nobody's Eyes*; *Why the Whales Came*

READ-ONS
*Catcher in the Rye, by J. D. Salinger

WEATHER EYE

by Lesley Howarth (Walker Books, 1995)
Interest level: 13–16/Reading age: 12+
ENVIRONMENT ● FAMILIES ● SCIENCE FICTION

H OWARTH's millennial fable is set on a remote Welsh windfarm, where wind is harnessed to make electricity; it is here that Teresa Craven – or Telly as she likes to be called – lives with her parents and younger brother, Race. Telly is a member of the Weather Eye club – an international organization for young people concerned about recent developments in the world's weather, which communicates on the Internet. One night during one of the violent storms which have become increasingly frequent, Telly is injured by a piece of flying debris; when she wakes up again, in hospital, it is with the knowledge that only she – and her friends – can save the world . . .

Lesley Howarth's story will appeal to any young teenager with an interest in environmental matters – or an understanding of the Internet. Her book deals with serious topics, but with enough humour to make it very readable.

OTHER BOOKS BY LESLEY HOWARTH
The Flower King; **Maphead*

WIZARD OF EARTHSEA, A

by Ursula Le Guin (Puffin, 1967)
Interest level: 12–16/Reading age: 12+
FANTASY ● GHOSTS ● SCIENCE FICTION

First in an acclaimed trilogy, set in an imaginary world, concerning the trials of young Ged, a sorcerer's apprentice studying magic at a college for magicians, who inadvertently brings to life a spirit of the dead, which is intent on his destruction. Only after Ged has learned wisdom, and can control his own powers, is he able to restrain the spirit. Later books in the *Earthsea* trilogy (which includes *The Tombs of Atuan* and *The Farthest Shore*) deal with Ged's further adventures in the realms of magic. Despite its ostensible concern with the occult, this is a book about growing up, and learning to cope with one's own untried powers. Young readers with an interest in fantasy and magic may find this bridges the gap between **The Lord of the Rings* and adult science fantasy.

READ-ONS
The Dispossessed, by Ursula Le Guin

WOLF

by Gillian Cross (Puffin, 1990)
Carnegie Medal
Interest level: 12–14/Reading age: 12+

Cassy lives with her nan, because her mum, feckless and childlike Goldie, doesn't want the responsibility of looking after her. But one day Cassy is told she must go and stay with Goldie, now living in a squat with her latest boyfriend, and that she must stay there until it is safe for her to return. Above all, she mustn't ask questions – such as who is the visitor who arrived very late one night at her nan's flat? And what is the connection between this mysterious visitor and the play about wolves Goldie and her boyfriend Lyall are putting on, and in which Cassy will play a leading role? Gillian Cross's novel skilfully evokes an atmosphere of menace and unease, as the events of its young heroine's drama move inexorably towards their terrifying conclusion.

OTHER BOOKS BY GILLIAN CROSS

The Demon Headmaster; The Revenge of the Demon Headmaster; The Prime Minister's Brain; *The Great Elephant Chase; Twin and Super-Twin; *The Crazy Shoe Shuffle

Suggested Further Reading for Age 12–16+

Ackroyd, Peter – *Chatterton*
Alain-Fournier – *Le Grand Meaulnes*
Aldiss, Brian – *Last Orders*
Allende, Isabel – *The House of the Spirits*
Amis, Kingsley – *Lucky Jim*
Amis, Martin – *The Rachel Papers, Money*
Angelou, Maya – *I Know Why the Caged Bird Sings*
Atkinson, Kate – *Behind the Scenes at the Museum*
Atwood, Margaret – *The Handmaid's Tale*
Austen, Jane – *Pride and Prejudice, Sense and Sensibility, Emma,*
   Persuasion, Mansfield Park, Northanger Abbey
Bainbridge, Beryl – *An Awfully Big Adventure*
Baldwin, James – *Go Tell It on the Mountain*
Ballard, J.G. – *Empire of the Sun*
Balzac, Honoré de – *Lost Illusions, Eugenie Grandet, Old Goriot*
Barnes, Julian – *Metroland*
Beckett, Samuel – plays
Beerbohm, Max – *Zuleika Dobson*
Bennett, Arnold – *Anna of the Five Towns*
Benson, E.F. – *Trouble for Lucia, Lucia's Progress*
Blake, William – poems
Bowen, Elizabeth – *The Death of the Heart*
Boyd, William – *An Ice-Cream War*
Bradbury, Malcolm – *The History Man*
Bradbury, Ray – *The Day It Rained Forever*
Braine, John – *Room at the Top*
Brontë, Charlotte – *Jane Eyre*
Brontë, Emily – *Wuthering Heights*
Brookner, Anita – Hotel du Lac
Browning, Robert – poems
Buchner, Georg – plays
Burgess, Anthony – *A Clockwork Orange*
Butler, Samuel – *Erewhon*

Byatt, A.S. – *Possession*
Byron, Lord George Gordon – poems
Calvino, Italo – *The Ancestors, If on a Winter's Night a Traveller*
Camus, Albert – *The Outsider, The Plague*
Carey, Peter – *Oscar and Lucinda*
Carter, Angela – *Nights at the Circus*
Cervantes, Miguel de – *Don Quixote*
Chandler, Raymond – *The Big Sleep, Farewell My Lovely, The Long Goodbye*
Chesterton, G.K. – *Father Brown* stories, *The Man Who was Thursday*
Christie, Agatha – *Hercule Poirot, Miss Marple* stories
Colegate, Isabel – *The Shooting Party*
Colette – *Claudine* stories
Collins, Wilkie – *The Moonstone, The Woman in White*
Compton-Burnett, Ivy – *A House and Its Head*
Conan Doyle, Sir Arthur – *Sherlock Holmes* stories
Conrad, Joseph – *The Secret Agent, Lord Jim, Under Western Eyes*
Coolidge, Susan – *What Katy Did*
Defoe, Daniel – *Robinson Crusoe*
Dickens, Charles – *Nicholas Nickleby, Bleak House, Oliver Twist, Little Dorrit*
Dostoevsky, Fyodor – *Crime and Punishment*
Drabble, Margaret – *The Millstone, A Summer Bird-cage*
Du Maurier, Daphne – *Rebecca*
Eco, Umberto – *The Name of the Rose*
Eliot, George – *Middlemarch, The Mill on the Floss, Silas Marner*
Eliot, T.S. – *The Waste Land*
Ellis, Brett Easton – *Less than Zero*
Faulkner, William – *The Sound and the Fury, Sanctuary*
Faulks, Sebastian – *Birdsong*
Fielding, Henry – *Tom Jones*
Fitzgerald, F. Scott – *The Great Gatsby, Tender is the Night*
Flaubert, Gustave – *Madame Bovary*
Fleming, Ian – *James Bond* books
Forester, C.S. – *Horatio Hornblower* stories
Forster, E.M. – *Howards End, A Passage to India, A Room with a View*
Frank, Anne – Diary
Galsworthy, John – *The Forsyte Saga*
Gerhardie, William – *Futility*
Gibbons, Stella – *Cold Comfort Farm*
Gissing, George – *New Grub Street*
Golding, William – *Lord of the Flies*
Graves, Robert – *Greek Myths*; *I, Claudius, Goodbye to All That, King Jesus*
Green, Henry – *Loving*

Greene, Graham – *Brighton Rock, The Power and the Glory*
Hamilton, Patrick – *The Slaves of Solitude*
Hardy, Thomas – *Far from the Madding Crowd, Tess of the D'Urbervilles, The Mayor of Casterbridge, Jude the Obscure*
Heaney, Seamus – poems
Heller, Joseph – *Catch-22*
Hemingway, Ernest – *For Whom the Bell Tolls, A Farewell to Arms*
Hornby, Nick – *High Fidelity*
Huxley, Aldous – *Point Counter Point*
James, Henry – *Turn of the Screw, The Portrait of a Lady, The Ambassadors*
James, M.R. – *Ghost Stories of an Antiquary*
Joyce, James – *Dubliners, A Portrait of the Artist as a Young Man*
Kafka, Franz – *The Trial*
Keane, Molly – *Devoted Ladies*
Keats, John – poems
Kesey, Ken – *One Flew Over the Cuckoo's Nest*
Kipling, Rudyard – stories
Larkin, Philip – poems
Lawrence, D.H. – *Sons and Lovers, Women in Love*
Le Guin, Ursula – *The Dispossessed*
Lee, Harper – *To Kill a Mocking-bird*
Lehmann, Rosamund – *A Note in Music*
Lessing, Doris – *The Golden Notebook*
Lewis, Wyndham – *The Revenge for Love*
Lodge, David – *Nice Work*
Lowry, Malcolm – *Ultramarine, Under the Volcano*
Mann, Thomas – *The Magic Mountain, Buddenbrooks*
Manning, Olivia – *The Balkan Trilogy*
Mansfield, Katherine – stories
Marlowe, Christopher – plays
Marquez, Gabriel Garcia – *One Hundred Years of Solitude*
Maugham, Somerset – *Cakes and Ale*; stories
McCullers, Carson – *The Heart is a Lonely Hunter*
Melville, Herman – *Moby Dick*
Meredith, George – *The Egoist*
Miller, Arthur – *The Crucible*
More, Thomas – *Utopia*
Morris, William – *News from Nowhere*
Murdoch, Iris – *The Bell, A Severed Head*
Nabokov, Vladimir – *Lolita*
O'Brien, Flann – *The Third Policeman*
Orwell, George – *Animal Farm, Homage to Catalonia, 1984*

Owen, Wilfred – poems
Pepys, Samuel – Diaries
Plath, Sylvia – *The Bell Jar*
Poe, Edgar Allan – *Tales of Mystery and Imagination*
Powell, Anthony – *A Dance to the Music of Time*
Proust, Marcel – *In Search of Lost Time*
Rhys, Jean – *Wide Sargasso Sea*
Roth, Philip – *Goodbye, Columbus*
Rushdie, Salman – *Midnight's Children, Haroun and the Sea of Stories*
Saki – stories
Salinger, J.D. – *Catcher in the Rye*
Sartre, Jean-Paul – *The Age of Reason* trilogy
Shakespeare, William – *Hamlet, Macbeth, King Lear, Romeo and Juliet, A Midsummer Night's Dream,* Sonnets
Shelley, Mary – *Frankenstein*
Smith, Stevie – *Novel on Yellow Paper*
Spark, Muriel – *The Prime of Miss Jean Brodie*
Sterne, Laurence – *The Adventures of Tristram Shandy*
Stoker, Bram – *Dracula*
Swift, Jonathan – *Gulliver's Travels*
Taylor, Elizabeth – *The Soul of Kindness*
Thackeray, William Makepeace – *Vanity Fair*
Thomas, Dylan – *Under Milk Wood*
Tolstoy, Leo – *War and Peace, Anna Karenina*
Townsend, Sue – *The Secret Diary of Adrian Mole*
Tremain, Rose – *Restoration*
Trevor, William – stories
Trollope, Anthony – *Barchester Towers, Can You Forgive Her?*
Verne, Jules – *Around the World in Eighty Days*
Walker, Alice – *The Colour Purple*
Warner, Sylvia Townsend – stories
Waugh, Evelyn – *Brideshead Revisited*
Weldon, Fay – *The Life and Loves of a She-devil*
Wells, H.G. – *The Invisible Man, The War of the Worlds*
Welsh, Irvine – *Trainspotting*
Wharton, Edith – *The Age of Innocence*
Wodehouse, P.G. – *Jeeves* stories
Woolf, Virginia – *To the Lighthouse, Mrs Dalloway*
Wordsworth, William – poems
Wyndham, John – *The Day of the Triffids*
Yeats, W.B. – poems

Information Books
– the Whys and Wherefores

There was a time when reference books were something your child brought home from school, or got out of the local library for specific projects. Not any more. Now, thanks to the revolution in reference book publishing which has taken place over the past decade, most families can boast a more than adequate non-fiction library of their own, with books on every topic from microbiology to the origins of the universe. The sheer numbers of books on every conceivable subject which are published every year can make this a daunting area for parents wanting to select the right information books for their child's particular needs. After all, most of us have to work within a budget!

For many parents, building a good reference library is something which can be done over a number of years, as their child grows up. The wide range of early learning books available to help develop first skills can eventually give way to more complex and detailed material which will lay the foundation for a child's school career, so that by the time your child is ready to tackle the demands of the National Curriculum, she will already be familiar with many of the things expected of her – such as the ability to carry out simple scientific experiments, or gather information.

As with the process of teaching your child to read, learning how to use information books is something which can be done quite gradually. And of course it can be a lot of fun, for both parents and children. Answering your preschooler's questions about the world is only a step away from encouraging her to look up the answers herself. Fortunately, most publishers now have a section devoted to very young children's needs, as well as those of school-age children. The high quality of illustration which is often to be found in even those books aimed at the under-fives is an added incentive for your child to get to grips with factual books as well as story books from an early age.

So what are the things to look for in a reference book? Is it better to wait until a child has reached the appropriate stage in her learning ability before buying a reference book – or is it a good idea to have a stock of books on hand for those awkward questions about life, the universe and everything?

While it is undoubtedly true that a good, basic library of a few essential books is a useful resource, there is no need to go to a lot of expense in the first instance. A good children's dictionary (there are some excellent illustrated ones on the market), an illustrated atlas and a well-illustrated, general encyclopaedia are books you and your child will refer to time and again – so it makes sense to get the best available (this does not necessarily mean the most expensive!). Other than this, you will find that the child's own needs will determine the way your library grows. From a fairly early age, some children just can't seem to get enough of factual information – about stars and planets, about natural history, about the workings of the combustion engine or the microchip. Whatever the current area of interest, you can be sure there is a book available which will suit your child's reading ability.

The earliest kinds of reference books are those which deal with simple concepts: numbers, colours, nature study and simple science. Look for colourful, high-quality pictures or photographs and clear, simple text rather than anything too complicated. For children starting school, the same principles apply. A first encyclopaedia or number book will help them get used to basic learning concepts, while a few 'fun' books on favourite topics such as dinosaurs or castles will encourage them to develop their interests at home. It is also a good idea to have a few inexpensive 'Make and Do' books around, for those days when inspiration (yours or the child's) is at a low ebb. For preschool children, this is especially important, as a way of getting them used to the idea of working independently.

As your child progresses up the school, certain subjects will become increasingly prominent in her school career, and it is then that it makes sense to acquire some more challenging fact books. Again, look for high-quality photographs or illustrations, clear presentation of facts and a systematic approach to a given topic. These can all be found in the wonderful range of illustrated guides to science, art, history, geography and other essential areas of your child's learning, published by Dorling Kindersley, Usborne, Kingfisher and others. A school project on the Romans can now be researched by exploring a Roman town, using Kingfisher's imaginative guide, or studying the architecture and technology of Roman times in the DK *Eyewitness Guide to Ancient Rome*, or finding out what it was like to be a soldier in the Roman army in Macdonald's 'Peoples of the Past' series. There is even a Roman newspaper in Usborne's 'Newspaper History' series, giving the 'latest' headlines about Roman conquests!

For older children, the sheer range of books available is breathtaking, with books on every subject they will be expected to cover at school up to and beyond GCSE level. Nor are these works confined to academic subjects such as Chemistry and Physics, although science is very well represented in most publishing lists. Books on art and music, on fashion, sport, pop music, politics and the environment cater for the wide variety of interests your child will be developing in addition to her studies. Also available are an increasing number of reference works on CD-ROM, offering an invaluable (and exciting) resource for work and general interest.

With so vast a selection of reference books to choose from, it is difficult to do more than offer a very brief selection here, although I hope that I have included some of the best. Many of the works mentioned, such as the admirable 'Eyewitness' guides already referred to, are part of a large and steadily growing series, and are listed on the back cover of each work. Since the introduction of the 'Key Stage' system (gradings according to the National Curriculum: Key Stage 1: age 5–7; Key Stage 2: age 7–11; Key Stage 3: age 11–14), many publishers have responded to popular demand by producing handbooks on all the main topics, from mathematics to the plays of Shakespeare. If your child has to find out about a particular topic for his or her schoolwork – or just because he or she needs to *know* – you can bet there is a book about it.

NOTE ON PUBLICATIONS

Reference books are often produced by teams of editors and illustrators, rather than a single author. In these instances, the name listed is that of the senior editor. However, since this kind of book is revised and updated so frequently, it seemed unnecessary to provide dates of publication, as has been done elsewhere.

ALL WAYS OF LOOKING AT: WEATHER

by Jane Walker (Aladdin)
Interest level: 7–9/Reading age: 7+/Key Stage: 2
SCIENCE

ONE of a series about natural history topics, this clearly illustrated book examines different aspects of the weather from a historical, anthropological and scientific point of view, including simple experiments for measuring rainfall and wind-speed, and interesting facts about freak weather conditions. A useful book for helping with those Key Stage 2 science projects.

OTHER BOOKS IN THE SERIES
The Seashore; *Rocks and Minerals*; *Flowers*; *Seeds, Bulbs and Spores*

AMAZING SCHEMES WITHIN YOUR GENES

by Dr Fran Balkwill; illustrated by Mic Rolph (Collins)
Science Book Prize
Interest level: 8–11/Reading age 8 + /Key Stage: 2–3

F IRST in an award-winning series about microbiology, which shows exactly what goes on inside your cells, and why your eyes are a certain colour and your hair another. Mic Rolph's attractive pictures help convey the information with clarity and humour. Other books in the series demystify the mind-boggling intricacies of DNA and cell biology. An essential read for any budding research scientist.

BE AN EXPERT ENVIRONMENTALIST

by John Stidworthy (Aladdin/Gloucester Press)
Interest level: 10–13/Reading age: 10 + /Key Stage: 2–3
ENVIRONMENT • SCIENCE

M ANY young people are concerned about the harmful effects on the environment of our consumer society – in particular the unnecessary wastage of fuels and packaging which takes place in most households. This useful book offers a range of practical, small-scale changes which can be made in the running of an ordinary home, with suggestions for ways of saving resources and conserving energy which will appeal to the environmentally conscious child.

OTHER BOOKS IN THE SERIES
Be an Expert Astronomer; *Be an Expert Naturalist*; *Be an Expert Weather Forecaster*

BIG BOOK OF HOW THINGS WORK, THE

by Peter Lafferty (Hamlyn)
Interest level: 8–12/Reading age: 8 + /Key Stage: 2–3

A N invaluable no-nonsense guide to the inner workings of some everyday things, ranging from nuclear power plants to skyscrapers, from motor cars to X-rays. Each section is clearly laid out, with detailed diagrams and cut-away drawings. A book that will save a lot of time when it comes to finding things out for school projects.

BOOK OF NATURAL DISASTERS, THE

by Jane Walker (Aladdin/Shooting Star Press)
Interest level: 8–12/Reading age: 8+/Key Stage: 2–3

ONE of a series of books on science and natural history, this illustrated guide offers some stunning insights into the power of volcanoes, hurricanes, earthquakes, tidal waves and other natural forces which have overwhelmed parts of the earth throughout history. This account is mingled with some thoughtful analysis of the destructive effects of global warming and other man-made disasters, and the implications of this and other environmental changes for life on the planet.

OTHER BOOKS IN THE SERIES
Encyclopedia of Great Civilizations; *Encyclopedia of Science*; *The Book of Natural History*

CHILDREN JUST LIKE ME

by Barnabas and Anabel Kindersley (Dorling Kindersley in association with United Nations Children's Fund)
Interest level: 7–11/Reading age: 7+

A celebration of children around the world, which brings out the similarities as well as the differences between children from many cultures. UNICEF receives a royalty for every copy sold.

CHILDREN'S ENCYCLOPEDIA, A

(Kingfisher)
Interest level: 8 upwards/Reading age: 8+/Key Stage: 2–3

PACKED with detailed information on a wealth of key topics, the Kingfisher encyclopedia is a must-have for any reference library. Interactive experiments and 'Strange but True' panels offer lots of help with school projects and plenty of incentive to browse.

CHILDREN'S FIRST ATLAS, THE

by Neil Morris; illustrated by S. Boni and L. R. Galante
(Horus Editions)
Interest level: 7–10/Reading age: 7+/Key Stage: 2

TWENTY-ONE different maps showing the countries of the world, including their main geographical, industrial, agricultural, geological and cultural features.

CLOSER LOOK AT VOLCANOES

(Watts Books)
Interest level: 10–12/Reading age: 10+/Key Stage: 2–3
ENVIRONMENT ● SCIENCE

ONE of a series which takes a closer look at aspects of the environment, ranging from rainforests to tidal waves, this colourfully illustrated book gives a detailed and fascinating account of what causes volcanic activity, and the devastation it can bring.

OTHER BOOKS IN THE SERIES
The Ozone Hole; *The Greenhouse Effect*; *Earthquakes*; *Hurricanes and Typhoons*

COLLINS ILLUSTRATED CHILDREN'S DICTIONARY

(Collins)
Interest level: 5–8/Reading age: 5/Key Stage: 1–2

OVER 5,000 words are defined in clear, familiar language, with additional explanations to put them in context, and 250 illustrations to clarify their meaning further. Collins publish a range of dictionaries tailored for each age group, beginning with their *First Word Book* (aimed at preschool children) and progressing through primary and junior school levels, up to secondary school (11+). From about five – or as soon as children start to get more confident about reading – it is a good idea to encourage them to use a dictionary. This not only helps with spelling, but enables them to build up new vocabulary.

COLLINS LITTLE GEMS

. . . .

(Collins)
Interest level: 5–7/Reading age: 5+

FINDING out about your favourite subject needn't cost the earth, with this pocket-size and pocket-money-priced series of fact-finder books. Essential facts about a range of topics, including cars, dogs, dinosaurs and horses, are contained within an attractively illustrated format.

CROSS-SECTIONS: CASTLE

. . . .

by Stephen Biesty (Dorling Kindersley)
Interest level: 7–13/Reading age: 7+/Key Stage: 2–3

ONE of a brilliant series of books featuring wonderfully detailed cut-away drawings, showing the interior of various structures. Here, a four-teenth-century castle is revealed in all its fascinating complexity. A book that will keep your child occupied for hours – as well as providing a wealth of knowledge about the everyday life of the period.

OTHER BOOKS IN THE SERIES
Cross-sections: Man-of-War; *Cross-sections: Buildings and Machines*

DICTIONARY OF SCIENCE

. . . .

by Neil Ardley (Dorling Kindersley)
Interest level: 10 upwards/Reading age: 10+/Key Stage: 2–3

OVER 2,000 key words to do with science and its workings are explained in this absorbing work, which covers all the main aspects of physics, chemistry, technology and mathematics, and includes biographies of major scientific innovators. Lucidly written, with lots of helpful illustrations, this is an invaluable asset to any reference library.

DISCOVERIES: UNDER THE SEA

(Macdonald)
Interest level: 8–10/Reading age: 8+/Key Stage: 2–3

Part of the *Discoveries* series about the earth and its inhabitants, this attractively laid out book offers an insight into the way that the oceans of the world work as eco-systems, with detailed descriptions and full-colour photo-spreads of their varied and fascinating creatures.

OTHER BOOKS IN THE SERIES
Native Americans; *Dangerous Animals*; *Flight*; *Volcanoes*; *Dinosaurs*

ENCYCLOPEDIA OF GREAT CIVILIZATIONS

(Aladdin/Shooting Star Press)
Interest level: 8–12/Reading age: 8+/Key Stage: 2–3

This vivid introduction to the great civilizations of the world offers a clear and concise account of the origins of each separate civilization, tracing its history and influence on our own culture from prehistoric times to the present day. Egypt, China, Japan, Greece, Rome and the Aztecs are just some of the civilizations covered in full-colour detail, with plenty of maps, photographs and paintings to break up the text. This is a book which will grip the imagination of any child with an interest in other cultures.

EYEWITNESS ART: IMPRESSIONISM

by Jude Welton; in association with the Art Institute of Chicago
(Dorling Kindersley)
Interest level: 9–15/Reading age: 9+/Key Stage: 2–3

One of an inspiring series offering detailed analysis of a range of famous paintings, in conjunction with full-colour illustrations and historical background on artists ranging from Van Gogh to Monet. Of all art movements in history, Impressionism is probably the one which children respond to most immediately – perhaps because its combination of real-life subjects with a vividly expressive approach to colour and style is one with which they can identify.

OTHER BOOKS IN THE SERIES
Van Gogh; *Manet*; *Monet*; *Post-Impressionism*

EYEWITNESS ART: LOOKING AT PAINTINGS

by Jude Welton; in association with the National Gallery
(Dorling Kindersley)
Interest level: 9–15/Reading age: 9 + /Key Stage: 2–3

L EARNING to look at paintings is something which comes with practice – as any parent who has ever dragged a bored toddler around an art gallery will agree! However, most children do have an instinctive appreciation of colour and shape, which develops, as they get older, into a more mature understanding of the complexities of line, form and tonal values – a development which is often reflected in their own work. Jude Welton's illuminating book – one of an excellent series on art appreciation – focuses on a range of famous paintings from various historical periods, giving a detailed analysis of exactly what is going on in each.

EYEWITNESS ART: THE RENAISSANCE

by Alison Cole; in association with the National Gallery
(Dorling Kindersley)
Interest level: 12–16/Reading age: 12 + /Key Stage: 3

A s lavishly illustrated as ever, DK's guide to the Renaissance provides an in-depth account of the period's importance in Western cultural history, with detailed reference to a range of famous artists, from Michelangelo to Dürer. Fascinating information on techniques, styles and materials is interspersed with analysis of individual works, together with biographical data on the artists and the historical background of this exciting era.

OTHER BOOKS IN THE SERIES
Impressionism; *Gauguin*; *Goya*; *Manet*; *Monet*; *Looking at Paintings

EYEWITNESS GUIDES: ANCIENT ROME
. . . .

by Simon James (Dorling Kindersley)
Interest level: 9–13/Key Stage: 2–3

THE crisp, clean layout and stunning photographs of the Eyewitness series – now including over sixty titles on a huge range of subjects – has made them an essential part of any child's reference library. In this volume, for example, information on Ancient Rome and its people (a Key Stage 2 topic) is conveyed in short, lucid chapters, interspersed with lots of clearly labelled illustrations. Every aspect, from the rise of the Roman city-state to the kind of things wealthy Romans had for dinner, is covered in fascinating detail. Other titles in the series, which covers scientific, historical, geological and cultural topics, are equally well done.

OTHER BOOKS IN THE SERIES
Ancient Greece; *Ancient Egypt*; *Knights*; *Pirates*; *Inventions*; *Cinema*; *Amphibians*; *Fossils*; *Rocks & Minerals*; *Pond & River*; *Africa*; *China*

EYEWITNESS SCIENCE: EVOLUTION
. . . .

by Linda Gamlin (Dorling Kindersley)
Interest level: 9–15/Reading age: 9+/Key Stage: 2–3

How did life begin? Is evolution just a theory? Why did the dinosaurs die out? What is DNA? All these and many more questions are dealt with in satisfying detail in this book, one of an exceptional series dealing with a whole range of topics your child is likely to encounter at Key Stage 3 and beyond. With their crisp layouts and high-quality photographs, these books have changed the face of children's reference publishing.

OTHER BOOKS IN THE SERIES
Electricity; *Light*; *Force & Motion*; *Matter*; *Energy*; *Chemistry*; *Human Body*; *Electronics*

EYEWITNESS VISUAL DICTIONARIES: BUILDINGS

(Dorling Kindersley)
Interest level: 9–14/Reading age: 9 + /Key Stage: 2–3

STUNNING photographs and detailed labelling make this a wonderfully thorough introduction to architecture and how it works. Explore famous buildings such as St Paul's Cathedral and the Colosseum from the inside out, using the exploded views and cut-away photographs on every page. Children love the sheer wealth of information in these books, which are invaluable for school projects at every level.

OTHER BOOKS IN THE SERIES
Everyday Things; *Human Body*; *Ships & Sailing*; *Animals*; *Plants*; *Cars*; *Military Uniforms*; *Flight*

FAX FINDER SERIES

(Collins)
Interest level: 7–11/Reading age: 7 + /Key Stage: 2

THE insatiable desire for facts some children feel can be satisfied with this attractively packaged series, which comes with its own personal organizer file. Each topic – including *Great Inventions*, *Major Disasters*, *Animals* and *Unsolved Mysteries* – comes in its own separate section, illustrated throughout with colour photographs. Masses of fascinating 'Did You Knows' with which to keep the rest of the family guessing.

FIRST SCHOLASTIC ENCYCLOPEDIA

(Scholastic)
Interest level: 8–11/Reading age: 8 + /Key Stage: 2

FOUR attractively illustrated volumes – on *Animals and Nature, How Things Work, All About People* and *A First Atlas* – are contained in a strong protective cover for easy reference.

FOCUS ON ANCIENT EGYPTIANS

by Anita Ganeir (Aladdin)
Interest level: 9–12/Key Stage: 2–3

ONE of a series of around thirty titles dealing with a range of topics from ancient civilizations to natural history. Clearly illustrated with full-colour photographs, maps and drawings, these thought-provoking guides offer some useful insights into their given subject. Here, for example, you can find out how a pyramid was constructed, learn about paper-making and hieroglyphics and discover what Ancient Egyptian life was like in the home. A must for budding archaeologists.

OTHER BOOKS IN THE SERIES
Romans; *Vikings*; *Ancient Greeks*; *Aztecs and Incas*

FOCUS ON INSECTS

(Aladdin)
Interest level: 9–12/Reading age: 9+/Key Stage: 2–3

ONE of a series of books with a natural history theme, offering a detailed look at the weird and wonderful world of insects. As well as the kind of scientific lore one might expect, the book gives additional information on the role insects have played in art, music and literature, with references ranging from Rimsky-Korsakov's 'Flight of the Bumble Bee' to Charles Dickens's 'Cricket on the Hearth'.

OTHER BOOKS IN THE SERIES
Birds; *Trees*; *Reptiles*; *Weather and Climate*

FRENCH FOR BEGINNERS

by Angela Wilkes; illustrated by John Shakhell (Usborne Language Guides)
Interest level: 11 upwards/Reading age: 11+/Key Stage: 3

ONE of an excellent series of beginners' guides to languages, incorporating the basics of grammar, vocabulary and useful phrases to cover a range of everyday situations. The comic-strip format is easy to read and fun. The books are also accompanied by a tape.

OTHER BOOKS IN THE SERIES
German for Beginners; *Italian for Beginners*; *Spanish for Beginners*; *Latin for Beginners*

FUN WITH SIMPLE SCIENCE
. . . .
(Kingfisher)
Interest level: 5–9/Reading age: 5 + /Key Stage: 1–2

S CIENCE is made easy and fun for younger children, in this series of attractively designed reference books, each of which takes a different phenomenon and explains its workings, with simple experiments to illustrate the text.

OTHER BOOKS IN THE SERIES
Batteries and Magnets; *Floating and Sinking*; *Shadow and Reflection*; *Sound and Music*

GREAT ANIMAL SEARCH, THE
. . . .
by Caroline Young; illustrated by Ian Jackson (Usborne)
Interest level: 8–10/Reading age: 8 + /Key Stage: 2

Y OUNG animal lovers are encouraged to spot their favourite creatures – ranging from prehistoric dinosaurs to present-day farm animals – in this ingenious picture-puzzle book, with animals hidden on every page.

GREAT COMPOSERS
. . . .
by Piero Ventura (Hamlyn)
Interest level: 9–12/Reading age: 9 + /Key Stage: 2–3
MUSIC

A clear, concise introduction, with plenty of colourful illustrations, to the lives of great composers such as Mozart, Beethoven, Hadyn, Schubert and many more, up to and including twentieth-century composers such as Benjamin Britten and even the Beatles. Interesting glossaries provide information on different musical genres, instruments and styles.

GROWING UP

. . . .

(Usborne)

Times Educational Supplement Information Book Award
Interest level: 11–14/Reading age: 11 + /Key Stage: 3
GROWING UP • SCIENCE

O NE of a series of lively information books describing the changes which take place when a person reaches puberty – and how to deal with them! Unpatronizing advice on sex, personal hygiene and emotional development is accompanied by clear line drawings explaining the finer points. A worthy successor to the equally good *Facts of Life*.

OTHER BOOKS IN THE SERIES
Babies; *Facts of Life*

HISTORICAL FACTS: WORLD WAR II

. . . .

by Richard O'Neill (Crescent Books)
Interest level: 11–14/Reading age: 11 + /Key Stage: 3
HISTORY

O VER 200 colour spreads and a wealth of archive photographs are the main feature of this illustrated guide, which sets out to explain the causes and consequences of the Second World War.

HISTORY OF BRITAIN: THE TUDORS

. . . .

by Andrew Langley (Heinemann Children's Reference)
Interest level: 11–14/Reading age: 11 + /Key Stage: 3
HISTORY

I NVALUABLE series of clearly laid out information books charting the history of Britain from the Romans to the present day. Excellent for school projects in these essential Key Stage areas.

OTHER BOOKS IN THE SERIES
Queen Victoria; *Modern Britain*

HORRIBLE HISTORIES

by Terry Deary (Scholastic)
Interest level: 8+/Reading age: 8+/Key Stage: 2
HISTORY

TERRY Deary's wickedly anarchic series informatively covers all the bits the history books gloss over! Encompassing a range of periods from Ancient Greece to Modern Britain, each book gives a potted history of each era, complete with tongue-in-cheek explanations and enjoyably gruesome pictures.

OTHER BOOKS IN THE SERIES
The Awesome Egyptians; *The Blitzed Brits*; *The Groovy Greeks*; *The Rotten Romans*; *The Slimy Stuarts*; *The Terrible Tudors*; *The Vicious Vikings*; *The Vile Victorians*

HUMAN BODY, THE

by L. Dilner (Reader's Digest Children's Books)
Interest level: 8–11/Reading age: 8+/Key Stage: 2–3
SCIENCE

THE ingenious see-through format of this picture book allows the structures and systems of the human body to be uncovered, layer by layer, as each page is turned. In addition to the stunning illustrations, the text is packed with information on the body and how it works.

HUTCHINSON TREASURY OF CHILDREN'S LITERATURE, THE

Edited by Alison Sage; foreword by Quentin Blake (Hutchinson)
Interest level: All ages/Reading age: 8+

A richly illustrated introduction to the wonders of children's literature, beginning with nursery rhymes and stories for the very young and ending with extracts from classics for older children such as Dickens's *A Christmas Carol*, Arthur Ransome's *Swallows and Amazons* and many more.

I LIKE MUSIC

by Barrie Carson Turner (Kingfisher)
Interest level: 8–11/Reading age: 8 + /Key Stage: 2–3
MUSIC

A N attractively illustrated introduction to the world of music, covering all its aspects from orchestral instruments to pop music. As well as the informative introductions to each section, there are pages of teach-yourself advice for a range of different instruments, including suggested music.

OTHER BOOKS IN THE SERIES
I Like Painting

IF I DIDN'T HAVE ELBOWS

by Sandi Toksvig; illustrated by David Melling (De Agostini)
Interest level: 8–11/Reading age: 8 +
SCIENCE

I F you didn't have elbows, you'd have to give up arm wrestling – and that's just for starters! Life wouldn't be the same without elbows, or skin, or blood – or all the other things we take for granted about our bodies. The jokey, strip-cartoon format of this lively 'what if' book conveys a lot of fascinating facts and hard information about your body and how it works. Science has never seemed so much fun.

ILLUSTRATED FACTOPEDIA, THE

(Dorling Kindersley)
Interest level: 11–15/Reading age: 11 + /Key Stage: 3

F ROM science and technology to animals and plants, from musical instruments to computers – Dorling Kindersley's imaginatively laid out guide offers concise but detailed information on a huge range of topics, illustrated with the clarity and thoroughness with which DK books have become identified. One of the best encyclopaedias currently available.

ILLUSTRATED USBORNE DICTIONARY, THE

by Rachel Wardley and Jane Bingham (Usborne)
Interest level: 5–8/Reading age: 5 + /Key Stage: 1–2

OVER 2,500 words are defined in clear, simple English, with attractive drawings and photographs to reinforce the message. Spelling tips, word games and puzzles make the learning process an enjoyable one.

INGREDIENTS OF MUSIC, THE

by Elizabeth Sharma (Wayland)
Interest level: 7–11/Reading age: 7 + /Key Stage: 2
MUSIC

AN informative, illustrated guide to music around the world, incorporating photographs of musicians from a variety of different cultures, together with simple analysis of music theory, tunes for readers to try out for themselves, listening suggestions and a reading list.

LADYBIRD DISCOVERY: DINOSAURS

by Dougal Dixon; illustrated by S.Boni and L.R. Galante (Ladybird)
Interest level: 7–10/Reading age: 7 + /Key Stage: 2
DINOSAURS • SCIENCE

ONE of a series of inexpensive full-colour guides to nature, science and history, this handy-size book (slightly larger in format than the traditional Ladybird pocket guide) gives young readers the low-down on *Allosaurus, Brachiosaurus* and the rest of the dinosaur clan.

OTHER BOOKS IN THE SERIES
Castles; *Clothes and Costume*; *Volcanoes and Earthquakes*; *The Sea*; *Polar Animals*

LADYBIRD HISTORY OF BRITAIN: THE TUDORS

by Tim Wood; illustrated by Peter Dennis (Ladybird)
Interest level: 8–11/Key Stage: 2–3

ONE of a very useful and reasonably priced series on English history from the Romans to the present day, containing key facts on the reigns of the Tudor monarchs, as well as photographs and detailed drawings of artefacts, clothing and architecture of the period.

OTHER BOOKS IN THE SERIES
Romans; *Saxons and Normans*; *The Middle Ages*; *The Stuarts*; *The Georgians*; *The Victorians*; *Britain 1901–1945*

LADYBIRD YOUNG DISCOVERY: ANIMAL HOMES

by Priscilla Hannaford; illustrated by John Dillon and L.R. Galante
(Ladybird)
Interest level: 5–7/Reading age: 5+/Key Stage: 1

ONE of a series of clearly illustrated, inexpensive pocket guides, providing an introduction to the world of nature and science for younger readers. The series features a glossary of scientific terms at the end of each book. Their handy small size and simple but attractive illustrations have made Ladybird books popular with generations of children; recent updating of the tried-and-tested format has resulted in improved layout and better colour.

OTHER BOOKS IN THE SERIES
Our Planet

LADYBIRD, THE

by Pascale de Bourgoing; illustrated by Sylvaine Perols (Gallimard Jeunesse/Moonlight Publishing)
Interest level: 3–6/Reading age: 6+/Key Stage: 1
SCIENCE

ORIGINALLY published in France, the *First Discovery* series offers a simple but accurate introduction to science and natural history. The illustrations are the main attraction: clear and bold without sacrificing too much detail, they are printed on laminated paper with transparent overlays which lift up to reveal the next layer of information. Children from two years upwards love turning the brightly coloured pages for themselves (the books are ring-bound, to make this easier), and there is plenty of information to interest older children: how ladybirds reproduce, what they like to eat and how to distinguish them from other sorts of insect. Young readers may need help with some of the vocabulary.

OTHER BOOKS IN THE SERIES
The Egg; *The Tree*; *The Flower*; *Cats*; *Vegetables*; *Weather* and *Colours*

LOOK AT YOUR BODY: SKELETON

by Steve Parker (Watts Books)
Interest level: 9–12/Key Stage: 2–3

O NE of a series dealing with the human body, this attractively illustrated guide uses a mixture of photographs, diagrams and drawings to explain the workings of the skeleton, with detailed descriptions of each bone and what it is for.

OTHER BOOKS IN THE SERIES
Lungs; *Senses*; *Digestion*

MAN-MADE DISASTERS: ATMOSPHERE IN DANGER

by Jane Walker (Aladdin)
Interest level: 10–12/Key Stage: 2–3

T HE catastrophic effect of unchecked industrialization on the environment is the subject of this thought-provoking analysis, which is aimed at young readers but which many adults will find no less disturbing. With full-page spreads dealing with aspects of environmental damage from global warming to acid rain, the book gives a worrying picture of what human beings have done to the planet, as well as suggestions as to how the problems we have created might be alleviated. A good text to focus class discussion of this all too urgent topic.

OTHER BOOKS IN THE SERIES
The Ozone Hole; *Vanishing Habitats and Species*; *Earthquakes*; *Tidal Waves and Flooding*; *Hurricanes and Typhoons*

Masters of Art: Leonardo Da Vinci

by Francesca Romei (Macdonald Young Books)
Interest level: 10–14/Reading age: 10+/Key Stage: 3

ARTIST, inventor and scientist, Leonardo da Vinci was one of the greatest figures of the Renaissance and, indeed, of all time. This superbly illustrated guide to his life and work – one of a series about great artists from the Renaissance to the twentieth century – describes the conditions under which Leonardo's works were painted, as well as the materials, equipment and methods of working which were current at the time. All this is related to a selection of the artist's most famous works, which are reproduced in full colour, with detailed analysis. The book and its companion volumes offer a thorough and fascinating introduction to art history, written in clear and precise language.

OTHER BOOKS IN THE SERIES
The Impressionists; *Van Gogh*; *Picasso*; *Renoir*; *Monet*; *Degas*

Microbes, Bugs and Wonder Drugs

by Fran Balkwill; illustrated by Mic Rolph
with Victor Darley-Usmar (Portland Press)
Interest level: 11–14/Reading age: 11+/Key Stage: 3

FIRST in a new series of science books for children, this illustrated guide to the wonder drugs that have shaped human health and history includes information on both the beneficial and the harmful effects of drugs.

Most Amazing Pop-up Science Book, The

by Jay Young (Franklin Watts)
Interest level: 8–13/Reading age: 8+/Key Stage: 2–3
SCIENCE

PREPARED in association with the Science Museum, this fantastic pop-up book contains seven working models to illustrate key concepts about sound, magnetism, magnification, photography, time, colour and light. A clear and detailed text gives expert information for budding scientists.

MYTHS AND LEGENDS FROM AROUND THE WORLD

by Sandy Shepherd; illustrated by Tudor Humphries (Evans)
Interest level: 9–11/Reading age: 9+/Key Stage: 2–3

INDIA, Africa, China, South America and Australia are just some of the places whose myths and legends are retold here, with Tudor Humphries's evocative illustrations.

PASTEUR'S FIGHT AGAINST MICROBES

by Beverley Birch; illustrated by Christine Bingham (Gollancz)
Interest level: 9–11/Reading age: 9+/Key Stage: 2–3
SCIENCE

ONE of a useful and thought-provoking series about great scientists and their discoveries, beautifully illustrated with Christine Bingham's pastel drawings. The combination of clear, precise text and imaginative illustration really brings the subject alive.

OTHER BOOKS IN THE SERIES
Marie Curie's Search for Radium; *Marconi's Battle for Radio*; *Benjamin Franklin's Adventures with Electricity*

PIRATES AND TREASURE

by Saviour Pirotta (Wayland)
Interest level: 10–14/Reading age: 10+/Key Stage: 2–3
PIRATES • HISTORY

WHAT were pirates really like? Were they the romantic figures of popular imagination, or were they no more than bloodthirsty criminals? Were there ever women pirates? This exciting and informative book – part of an illustrated series looking at particular aspects of the past – uses anecdotes, quotations, stories and legends as well as historical facts to make the text come alive.

OTHER BOOKS IN THE SERIES
Monsters of the Deep; *Voyages of Exploration*; *The Whalers*

QUESTIONS AND ANSWERS ABOUT SUN, STARS AND PLANETS

by James Muirden (Kingfisher)
Interest level: 8–11/Reading age: 8+/Key Stage: 2–3
SCIENCE

WHAT is a Black Hole? What is the Big Bang? The simple question-and-answer format offers a wealth of detailed information about the universe and its mysteries – an invaluable aid for school projects.

OTHER BOOKS IN THE SERIES
Questions and Answers about the Human Body

RAINFOREST ANIMALS

by Paul Hess (De Agostini)
Interest level: 2–4/Reading age: 2+

ONE of a beautifully illustrated series aimed at very young children, combining humorous rhymes with subtly coloured, naturalistic paintings of animals in their rainforest setting. Tree frogs and toucans, jaguars and monkeys make an exciting alternative to the kinds of animals often shown in books for this age group.

OTHER BOOKS IN THE SERIES
Safari Animals; *Polar Animals*; *Farmyard Animals*

RECYCLING

by Jo Gordon (Watts Books/Gloucester Press)
Interest level: 11–14/Key Stage: 3
ENVIRONMENT • SCIENCE

AN invaluable guide to recycling and how it works, illustrated with photographs and diagrams, and offering lots of useful advice on how we can all become more energy-efficient and conservation-conscious.

OTHER BOOKS IN THE SERIES
Acid Rain; *Deforestation*; *Nuclear Waste Disposal*; *Toxic Waste*; *The Greenhouse Effect*

SCIENCE FOR FUN: MAKING THINGS FLOAT AND SINK

by Gary Gibson (Aladdin)
Interest level: 7–9/Reading age: 7+/Key Stage: 2

O NE of an attractively illustrated series on simple science, with experiments which can be carried out in the home, using inexpensive, everyday materials (ask first before you borrow!). This book offers lots of suggestions for fun things to do with paper-clips, scissors, cardboard and plastic bottles, to make a range of floating and non-floating objects.

OTHER BOOKS IN THE SERIES
Light and Colour; *Hearing Sounds*; *Understanding Electricity*; *Making Things Change*

SEE INSIDE SERIES

(Kingfisher)
Interest level: 10+/Reading age: 10+/Key Stage: 2–3
HISTORY

E XPLORE an Ancient Greek or a Roman town, using the detailed illustrations in these illuminating guides, which offer an imaginative way of getting to grips with history.

OTHERS BOOKS IN THE SERIES
An Egyptian Town

THINK OF AN EEL

by Karen Wallace; illustrated by Mike Bostock (Walker Books)
Kurt Maschler Award/
Times Educational Supplement Book Award
Interest level: 5–8/Reading age: 5+/Key Stage: 1–2
SCIENCE

B EAUTIFULLY illustrated by Mike Bostock, this award-winning book follows the life cycle of an eel from its beginnings in the Sargasso sea to its return, three years later, to the river where its parents lived.

TUDORS AND STUARTS: LIFE AT SEA

by Margaret Rule (Wayland)
Interest level: 7–11/Reading age: 7 + /Key Stage: 2–3
TUDORS & STUARTS ● HISTORY

O NE of a series about key aspects of history, this attractive illustrated guide offers a wealth of information. Lively pictures of contemporary artefacts, buildings and paintings provide a varied and interesting source of evidence about this area of the past, with timelines, glossaries of specialized vocabulary and lots more.

OTHER BOOKS IN THE SERIES
Clothes; *Country Life*; *Exploration*; *Food*; *Homes*

ULTIMATE DINOSAUR BOOK, THE

by David Lambert; in association with the Natural History Museum
(Dorling Kindersley)
Interest level: 9–13/Reading age: 9 + /Key Stage: 2–3

L AVISH illustrations and precise, detailed information about a topic which fascinates most children at some stage in their lives gives DK's guide to dinosaurs an edge over many other books on the market. Here is material for even the most demanding school project, all wrapped up in the attractively laid out style pioneered by the company.

UNDERSTANDING MUSIC

by Judy Tatchell (Usborne)
Interest level: 11–14/Reading age: 11 + /Key Stage: 3
MUSIC

A lively and informative guide to the history and theory of music, giving detailed analysis of principal musical styles and movements, and illustrations of musicians and musical instruments from a variety of different cultures and times.

OTHER BOOKS IN THE SERIES
Understanding Modern Art

UNDERSTANDING YOUR BRAIN

by Rebecca Treays; illustrated by Christyan Fox (Usborne)
Interest level: 8–11/Reading age: 8+/Key Stage: 2–3
SCIENCE

USBORNE's lively, well-illustrated format provides an excellent introduction to the processes that take place inside the brain, every time people carry out a range of activities. As lucid, readable and reasonably priced as all the Usborne titles, this guide is one of a new series called 'Science for Beginners'.

OTHER BOOKS IN THE SERIES
Electricity and Magnetism; *Atoms and Molecules*; *Machines*

USBORNE ILLUSTRATED ATLAS OF THE 20TH CENTURY

by Lisa Miles and Mandy Ross (Usborne)
Interest level: 9–13/Reading age: 9+/Key Stage: 2–3
HISTORY

TWENTIETH-CENTURY history from the First World War to the Millennium is the subject of this fascinating book, covering a whole range of topics such as the Great Depression, the Rise of Fascism, Votes for Women, the Rise and Fall of Communism and much more. Clear illustrations and lots of interesting maps make this an ideal reference work for school projects.

VISUAL DICTIONARY

by Jane Bunting; illustrated by David Hopkins (Dorling Kindersley)
Interest level: 5–8/Key Stage: 1–2

ATTRACTIVELY illustrated in DK's crisp and colourful style, with definitions of more than 2,500 words and over 700 pictures to help explain their meaning, with sections on School, Home, Travel, Animals, Hobbies and lots more.

ALSO AVAILABLE
My First French Word Book

VISUAL DICTIONARY OF DINOSAURS, THE
. . . .
Eyewitness Guides (Dorling Kindersley)
Interest level: 8–11/Key Stage: 2–3

A LL you ever wanted to know about stegosaurs, iguanodons, carnosaurs, sauropods – that is, dinosaurs of all kinds. Most children go through a stage of being completely obsessed by the loveable beasts, so this book is the perfect answer. For anyone who *still* hasn't had enough, Dorling Kindersley's *Ultimate Book of Dinosaurs* offers a yet more detailed approach to the topic.

WAYLAND ATLAS OF THE WORLD, THE
. . . .
by Mary Jane Gerber (Wayland)
Interest level: 8–14/Key Stage: 2–3

F ULLY revised and up-to-date, the *Wayland Atlas* consists of sixteen full-colour world maps (double-page spreads) giving detailed information about the earth, its geography and its political configurations; twelve pages of maps featuring the UK, Ireland and Europe; fifteen regional maps giving a detailed picture of the world's different regions and an eight-page section on statistics.

WHAT LIFE WAS LIKE: FISHBOURNE – A DAY IN A ROMAN PALACE
. . . .
by T.D. Tiggs (Wayland)
Interest level: 7–11/Reading age: 7+/Key Stage: 2–3
ROMANS • HISTORY

O NE of an attractively illustrated series, giving a detailed picture of what life was like at certain key stages in history. In this, a clear, lively text offers the reader a fly-on-the-wall look at daily life as it was lived in a Roman villa, with cut-away illustrations of Fishbourne in its heyday, and photographs of artefacts found at the site.

OTHER BOOKS IN THE SERIES

A Day in a Medieval Mansion; *A Day in a Tudor Mansion*; *A Day in a Victorian Town House*

WHAT SHALL I DO TODAY?

(Usborne)
Interest level: 4–8

THREE colourful volumes – *What Shall I Draw?*, *What Shall I Paint?* and *What Shall I Make?* – offer lots of creative suggestions for the young make-and-do enthusiast.

WHAT'S INSIDE BUILDINGS?

by Steve Parker (Macdonald)
Interest level: 10–12/Reading age: 10 + /Key Stage: 2–3

ONE of a series which offers a detailed and enlightening insight into the workings of some things we take for granted in our world – in this case, the buildings which go to make up our towns and cities. Large, cut-away illustrations and precise information give plenty of material for young minds to work on.

OTHER BOOKS IN THE SERIES
What's Inside Aeroplanes?; *What's Inside Plants?*; *What's Inside the Human Body?*

YEAR I WAS BORN, THE

by Sally Tagholm; illustrated by Michael Wood (Puffin)
Interest level: 8–12/Reading age: 8 + /Key Stage: 2

AN irresistible birthday present for anyone born since 1980 – which is when the series starts. Interesting facts about a given year are mingled with amusing anecdotes, to build up a lively and entertaining picture of the times.

YOUNG OXFORD BOOK OF CINEMA, THE

David Parkinson (Oxford University Press)
Interest level: 12–14/Reading age: 12+

THIS full-colour guide, published to coincide with cinema's centenary, covers the history of film from the earliest shadow-shows to the latest Academy Awards, providing a wealth of detailed information for the young movie buff.

YOUNG PERSON'S GUIDE TO MUSIC, A

by Neil Ardley; music composed by Poul Ruders (Dorling Kindersley)
Interest level: 10–15/Reading age: 10+/Key Stage: 3
MUSIC

AN informative and entertaining guide to music and instruments, which comes complete with its own CD of specially composed tunes to demonstrate sounds and styles. Stylishly laid out colour photographs and illustrations enhance the appeal.

CD-ROMs

Many homes now have personal computers with CD-ROM, which can be a valuable resource for your child to develop co-ordination and recognition skills and to extend his or her knowledge of a wide range of subjects, from space exploration to the human body. Used in addition to traditional learning methods, the specially designed software now available for these computers can help give your child a head-start in tomorrow's world. In response to the increasing demand for children's software, publishers have started to produce a range of attractive educational packages which can be used in exactly the same way as one would use a conventional reference book. The difference is that where *The Oxford English Dictionary* or the *Encyclopaedia Britannica* might once have filled twenty volumes, it can now be contained on a single disc.

Using CD-ROM is no more difficult than using a conventional CD player; the only difference is that there are pictures as well as sound. After inserting the disc into the computer, you simply click on the appropriate symbol to open the 'book', which will then offer you a list of 'menus' or choices very similar to those of an ordinary index. Having made your selection, you can then enter the section you wish to read. Many programs, especially those designed for children, are interactive, allowing the participant to sample different aspects of a particular topic, and even to create new material – drawings, sounds and stories – which can then be stored in the computer's memory.

Although it would be a pity if computers were ever to replace books altogether, it is certainly true – especially in the field of reference – that CD-ROM can offer some exciting alternatives to more established learning resources. Children's familiarity with television images leads them to expect that pictures will move, and that pictures are accompanied by sounds. They are therefore instantly at home with the kind of technology now available on computer which makes pictures 'come alive' and words 'speak'. And publishers of conventional reference books have not been slow to respond to the CD-ROM revolution. A glance at any recent work of reference tells the same story: brighter and bolder layouts, more detailed information and better design are now the norm, not the exception. Maybe computers have their uses, after all.

NOTE ON COMPATIBILITY OF SOFTWARE

The availability of *Windows 95* has meant that most programs now offered can be used on either an Apple Macintosh computer or a PC. If in doubt, check the packaging for the appropriate guidelines.

A CHRISTMAS STORY

by Brian Wildsmith; narrated by Martin Jarvis
(Oxford University Press Multimedia)
PC and Macintosh compatible
Interest level: 3–8

WILDSMITH'S enchanting illustrations to the Christmas story are animated for the very young, with a range of interactive puzzles to enhance the effect. A miniature book telling the story is also supplied.

DORLING KINDERSLEY CHILDREN'S DICTIONARY

CD-ROM for Windows (Dorling Kindersley)
Interest level: 7–10

CARRYING on from where DK's *First Incredible Amazing Dictionary* left off, this illustrated multimedia dictionary offers definitions of over 37,000 words, 17,500 sounds and pronunciations and lots more. Reading the dictionary has never been so much fun.

EYEWITNESS ENCYCLOPEDIA OF NATURE
. . . .

CD-ROM for Windows (Dorling Kindersley)
Interest level: 9–15

WITH over 700 photographs and illustrations of every conceivable creature from tree frogs to tigers, and every kind of life form from ferns to rainforests, DK's animated guide to the wonders of nature will open up a whole new world for young animal lovers.

EYEWITNESS ENCYCLOPEDIA OF SPACE AND THE UNIVERSE
. . . .

CD-ROM for Windows (Dorling Kindersley)
Interest level: 9–15

EXPLORE the mysteries of space with this absorbing reference guide, including over 80 animations, 400 photographs and illustrations as well as a wealth of sound effects, interactive features, games and quizzes to test your knowledge of the universe.

EYEWITNESS HISTORY OF THE WORLD
. . . .

CD-ROM for Windows (Dorling Kindersley)
Interest level: 9–15

OVER 30 video sequences and 100 animations feature in this illustrated multimedia guide to the world's history from the days of sailing ships to the era of space exploration. High-quality graphics and photographs and detailed information about every aspect of the past make this a fascinating and valuable educational resource.

THE FISH WHO COULD WISH

. . . .

by John Bush and Korky Paul – Narrated by Robbie Coltrane
(Oxford University Press Multimedia)
PC and Macintosh compatible
Interest level: 4–6

ENTER the weird and wonderful underwater world of the fish whose wishes come true – at the click of a 'mouse'. Play in the fish's dream castle and see him drive his sports car and his yellow submarine. Hours of interactive fun, complete with narrative and sound effects.

MAGIC THEATRE CARTOON MAKER

. . . .

CD-ROM Multimedia (Random House)
Interest level: 6–8

CREATE your own cartoons with this exciting 'paintbox' package, using a range of colourful backgrounds such as a forest, a castle or outer space and a selection of characters you can animate yourself – with sound effects to add the finishing touch!

MY FIRST AMAZING WORLD EXPLORER

. . . .

CD-ROM for Windows (Dorling Kindersley)
Interest level: 3–7

DK's electronic atlas can transport you to another world, with the aid of animated maps giving detailed information about the geography, climate and culture of a particular country. More than twenty different journeys whizz you to the ends of the earth and back, and there are activities and games to add to the enjoyment of finding out. Best of all, the package comes with a personalized passport, sticker book and postcards to send, to enhance the authentic feel.

MY FIRST ENCYCLOPEDIA

CD-ROM Microsoft Windows compatible (Random House)
Interest level: 3–6

CREATED for early and pre-readers, this programme targets ten key learning areas such as Space, the Body, Earth and Nature, Animals, Sport and Famous People, all arranged as branches of a Tree of Knowledge. Interactive games, sound effects and animations add to the fun.

MY FIRST INCREDIBLE AMAZING DICTIONARY

CD-ROM for Windows (Dorling Kindersley)
Interest level: 3–7

OVER a thousand first words and their meanings are explained in this interactive programme, designed to help early readers on the path to reading confidence, using sound effects, word games, animation and the mixture of high-quality photographs and colourful graphics for which Dorling Kindersley has become renowned.

P.B. BEAR'S BIRTHDAY PARTY

CD-ROM for Windows (Dorling Kindersley)
Interest level: 3–5

DESIGNED to promote first reading skills, this interactive story allows children to take part in planning P.B. Bear's birthday treat – with easy-to-read vocabulary, sound effects and animation to add to the fun of learning.

STOWAWAY!

CD-ROM for Windows (Dorling Kindersley)
Interest level: 9–13

STEPHEN Biesty's *Incredible Cross-sections* are brought to life in this interactive multimedia package, which enables you to get inside a sailing ship of the Napoleonic period and to see a sailor's life at first hand – in all its glorious, gory detail!

ULTIMATE HUMAN BODY, THE

CD-ROM for Windows (Dorling Kindersley)
Interest level: 10–15

Part of DK's 'Ultimate Image' series, this multimedia program enables children to get to grips with all aspects of human anatomy, from the skeleton and cardio-vascular system to the workings of the brain. Over 1,000 illustrations and 100 animations make this a useful resource for children up to GCSE level.

OTHER CD-ROM PACKAGES IN THE SERIES
Cats; *Wild Animals*; *Birds*; *Children*

Some Outstanding Contributors

I N a book of this size, it would have been impractical to have provided biographies of every author and illustrator whose work is mentioned, however excellent it might be. Some names, however, occur so often and are so renowned that their omission seemed unthinkable. Authors and illustrators of long-established classics and more recent works that are already regarded as classics are included here, as well as other writers and historians – Peter and Iona Opie, for example – whose pioneering studies have helped to put children's literature on the map, and without whom this book would not have been written.

AHLBERG, Allan
(b 1938) Author
Allan Ahlberg's work is distinguished by its humour and inventiveness. Apart from the well-known series of children's picture books produced with his wife Janet (including *The Baby's Catalogue, *The Jolly Postman, etc.), he is responsible for the popular *Happy Families series of reading books, in conjunction with illustrators such as Joe Wright, André Amstutz and *Colin McNaughton.

AHLBERG, Janet
(1944–94) Illustrator
Chiefly renowned for her work with her husband, *Allan Ahlberg; together they produced a remarkably fresh and innovative range of picture books for young children, including *Each Peach Pear Plum, *Peepo!, *The Baby's Catalogue and *The Jolly Postman. Janet Ahlberg's delicate watercolour illustrations combined nostalgic detail with a sense of fun, often mingling characters from nursery rhyme and traditional children's stories with those from real life.

AIKEN, Joan
(b 1924) Author

Best known for her gothic fantasies for older children, of which *The Wolves of Willoughby Chase* is perhaps the most famous, she has also published books for younger children, including a series about Arabel and her talking raven.

ALCOTT, Louisa May
(1832–88) Author

The daughter of a New England philosopher and experimental education-alist, she is most famous for *Little Women* and its sequel *Good Wives*, about a family of girls growing up in Boston.

ANDERSEN, Hans Christian
(1805–75) Author

Danish author of over 150 fairy stories, both of his own invention and drawn from folk tales, Andersen was one of the most influential figures in the history of children's literature. His lyrical, romantic and occasionally horrific stories have been translated into many languages, and have been illustrated by numerous distinguished illustrators, including *Arthur Rackham and *Errol Le Cain.

ARDIZZONE, Edward
(1900–79) Author and illustrator

Best known for his illustration of classics such as *Peacock Pie* and *J.M. Barrie's Peter and Wendy*, he also produced a series of books about a little boy, Tim, and his friend Lucy, developed from stories he told his own children.

BARRIE, Sir J(ames) M(atthew)
(1860–1937) Author

A successful playwright during the Edwardian era, he is chiefly known for *Peter Pan* (1904), a highly popular play about a boy who refuses to grow up, which is still regularly performed and which was later recast as a novel, *Peter and Wendy* (1911) – one of the most influential works of children's literature ever written.

BAWDEN, Nina
(b 1925) Author

Also renowned as an adult novelist, she began publishing children's fiction in the late 1950s. *Carrie's War (1973), based on her own experiences as a wartime evacuee, and *The Peppermint Pig (1975) are among her best-known works.

BAYNES, Pauline
(b 1922) Illustrator

Her illustrations for *J.R.R. Tolkien's Farmer Giles of Ham (1949) and *C.S. Lewis's *The Lion, the Witch and the Wardrobe (1950) established her as one of the most talented children's illustrators of her generation. In 1960, she produced illustrations for Amabel Williams-Ellis's Fairy Tales from the British Isles.

BELLOC, Hilaire
(1870–1953) Author

Best known for his comic verses for children, The Bad Child's Book of Beasts (1896), More Beasts for Worse Children (1897) and Cautionary Tales (1907), which are distinguished by their macabre flavour. Recent illustrators include *Quentin Blake.

BLAKE, Quentin
(b 1932) Author and illustrator

A former head of the Illustration Department at the Royal College of Art, Quentin Blake is one of the most distinguished author/illustrators working in children's literature, who has illustrated books for some of its best writers, including *Joan Aiken, *Russell Hoban, *Michael Rosen and *Roald Dahl. His best-loved books include *Mister Magnolia (1980), *Cockatoos (1992) and *All Join In (1990).

BLYTON, Enid
(1897–1968) Author

Still one of the most commercially successful children's authors ever, she is now best known for her collections of adventure stories for children, *The Famous Five (1942) and The Secret Seven (1949), and for the Little Noddy series about an elf and his friend Big Ears – once castigated for its alleged racism, but more recently republished in a 'cleaned-up' form.

BOND, Michael
(b 1926) Author

Best known for the *Paddington stories, about a small bear living with a London family.

BOSTON, Lucy M(aria)
(1892–1990) Author

Best-known for *The Children of Green Knowe (1954), a lyrical book about a small boy staying in a haunted house, and its various sequels.

BRIGGS, Raymond
(b 1934) Author and illustrator

Best known for his lyrical story-without-words, *The Snowman (1979), and for his two *Father Christmas books (1973 and 1975), which also use a comic-strip format. Other notable books include When the Wind Blows (1982), a post-holocaust picture book considered too horrifying for young children.

BRUNA, Dick
(b 1927) Author and illustrator

Born in Holland, he is best known for his highly successful and influential illustrated books for very young children, including the *Miffy books.

BURNETT, Frances Hodgson
(1849–1924) Author

Renowned for *The Secret Garden (1909), which deals, as several of her books do, with a child's loneliness and unhappiness. *A Little Princess (1902) and Little Lord Fauntleroy (1885) are also well known.

BURNINGHAM, John
(b 1936) Author and illustrator

Burningham's distinctive illustrative style – which is deliberately naive and childlike – has won him many admirers. *Mr Gumpy's Outing (1970) was his first exercise in this form; it was followed by others, which have established him as one of the best-loved and most distinguished author/illustrators currently working.

CARROLL, Lewis (Charles Lutwidge Dodgson)
(1832–98) Author

Although his most enduring claim to fame is as the author of *Alice's Adventures in Wonderland (1865) and its sequel, Through the Looking-glass (1871), Carroll was also a mathematics don at Oxford; his fascination with mathematical and logical problems can be discerned in his writing for children, which abounds with puns, jokes and philosophical conundrums.

COOPER, Susan
(b 1935) Author

Best known for her fantasy sequence, *The Dark is Rising* (1965–77), a retelling of the Arthurian legends.

CRESSWELL, Helen
(b 1934) Author

Best known for her comic series *The Bagthorpe Saga* (from 1977) and for her fantasies for children, such as *The Secret World of Polly Flint*.

CROMPTON, Richmal
(1890–1969) Author

Famous for the *William* books, about a naughty schoolboy, of which the first was published in 1922 and the last posthumously in 1970.

DAHL, Roald
(1916–90) Author

After establishing himself as a writer of adult fiction, he began his career as a children's author with *James and the Giant Peach* (1961), a fantasy based on a story told to his own children. This was followed by *Charlie and the Chocolate Factory* (1964), *Fantastic Mr Fox* (1970), *Danny the Champion of the World* (1975), *George's Marvellous Medicine* (1981), *The BFG* (1982) and many others – all characterized by the gruesomely comic inventiveness and anarchic humour with which the author has become identified.

DE LA MARE, Walter
(1873–1956) Author

Renowned for his haunting and imaginative stories and verse, not all of it specifically written for children, including *The Listeners and other poems* (1912) and *Peacock Pie* (1913).

GARFIELD, Leon
(1921–96) Author

Best known for his powerful and evocative historical novels for children, many of which are set in the eighteenth century. They include *Jack Holborn* (1964), *Devil-in-the-Fog* (1966), *Smith* (1967), *Black Jack* (1968) and numerous others. He also published a two-volume retelling for children of the plays of Shakespeare.

GARNER, Alan
(b 1934) Author

Best known for his series of fantasy novels for children, which incorporate elements from Arthurian legend and the *Mabinogion* into contemporary stories. His books include *The Weirdstone of Brisingamen* (1963) and its sequel *The Moon of Gomrath, Elidor* (1965), *The Owl Service* (1967), *Red Shift* (1973) and *The Stone Book* (1976).

GRAHAME, Kenneth
(1859–1932) Author

Famous as the author of *The Wind in the Willows* (1908), an idyllic celebration of the bucolic life enjoyed by a group of woodland creatures, including Mole, Ratty and Badger, and the disruption of their settled existence by the foolishly adventurous Toad.

GREEN, Roger Lancelyn
(1918–87) Author and historian

Renowned for his biographical studies of various influential figures in children's literature, such as *Andrew Lang, *C.S. Lewis, *J.M. Barrie and *Lewis Carroll, he has also published anthologies such as *A Book of Dragons* (1970) and retellings of traditional tales and legends including *King Arthur and his Knights of the Round Table* (1953), *The Adventures of Robin Hood* (1956) and *Heroes of Greece and Troy* (1960).

GREENAWAY, Kate
(1846–1901) Author and illustrator

Renowned as the author and illustrator of several books of verse for children, including *Under the Window* (1879), *Mother Goose or The Old Nursery Rhymes* (1881) and *Marigold Garden* (1885). As with all her work, these are characterized by their charmingly old-fashioned illustrations of children in stylized eighteenth-century costume, and the gentle unworldliness of their sentiments.

GRIMM, Jacob (1785–1863) and Wilhelm (1786–1859)
Collectors of folk tales and *fairy stories

Famous for their collection of over 200 fairy tales, first published in 1812 as *Nursery and Household Tales* but now more widely known as *Grimm's Fairy Tales*.

HOBAN, Russell
(b 1925) Author

Renowned as the author of a whole range of children's books, from the 'Frances' series for very young children, of which the first, *Bedtime for Frances*, appeared in 1960, to more complex and thought-provoking novels for older children, such as *The Mouse and His Child* (1967).

HUGHES, Shirley
(b 1929) Author and illustrator

After leaving art school in the 1950s, she began illustrating her own picture books, of which the most renowned are the 'Lucy and Tom' series, about the everyday adventures of a brother and sister, and the 'Alfie' series, about the escapades of a small boy – of which the first (*Alfie Gets in First*) was published in 1981.

HUGHES, Ted
(b1930) Author and poet

One of the most distinguished post-war poets, he has written verse and prose for adults and children. A fantasy novel, *The Iron Man* (1968) is perhaps his most famous work for children; *Moon-whales and other poems* (1976) is a collection of verse about animals.

HUGHES, Thomas
(1822–96) Author

Best-known as the author of *Tom Brown's Schooldays* (1857), a fictional account of his own experience as a pupil at Rugby, under the headmastership of Thomas Arnold.

JONES, Diana Wynne
(b 1934) Author

Best known for her fantasy novels for children, including *The Lives of Christopher Chant*, which typically incorporate elements of myth and the supernatural into everyday settings.

KINGSLEY, Charles
(1819–75) Author

Famous as the author of *The Water Babies* (1863), a fable about a little chimney-sweep transformed into a water-sprite, which did much to bring about the reform of the laws governing child labour in the nineteenth century.

KIPLING, Rudyard
(1865–1936) Author

A distinguished author of fiction and poetry for adults, he published several outstanding works for children, including *The Jungle Book* (1894); *Stalky & Co* (1899), a collection of school stories; *Kim* (1901), which is set in India; *Just So Stories* (1902); *Puck of Pook's Hill* (1906), a fantasy set in rural Sussex; and its sequel, *Rewards and Fairies* (1910).

LANG, Andrew
(1844–1912) Folklorist and author

Chiefly renowned for his *Fairy Book* series, of which the first, *The Blue Fairy Book*, was published in 1889 and was followed by eleven others. These collections were enormously influential in establishing the importance of fairy and folk tales as a subject for study, as well as something to be enjoyed by children.

LE CAIN, Errol
(1941–89) Illustrator

Errol Le Cain's illustrations of classic stories by the Brothers *Grimm, *Hans Christian Andersen, *Perrault and others are distinguished by their intricate, jewel-like style and richness of colour. Each page offers a feast for the eyes, with the emphasis on pattern and stylized forms rather than on naturalism. The illustrations for *Aladdin* (1981), for example, are reminiscent of Moorish art, with each picture framed in an elaborate border.

LEAR, Edward
(1812–88) Author and illustrator

Renowned during his lifetime as a landscape painter, Lear is now chiefly remembered for his extraordinary nonsense verse, which began with *A Book of Nonsense* in 1846. This was followed by several other collections of limericks and nonsense rhymes, many of them illustrated by the author. Of these, several – including the delightfully rhapsodic 'The Owl and the Pussy-cat' – have become an established part of most children's reading; others, such as The Dong with a Luminous Nose, convey a more melancholy side to Lear's eccentric personality.

LEWIS, C(live) S(taples)
(1898–1963) Author

An academic by profession (he was a Fellow of Magdalen College, Oxford and Professor of Medieval Literature at Cambridge), C.S. Lewis is also renowned as the author of the *Narnia* books for children, of which the first was *The Lion, the Witch and the Wardrobe* (1950). These set a standard for children's fantasy writing which has seldom been equalled, and which still ensures his books a wide readership.

LIVELY, Penelope
(b 1933) Author

A distinguished writer of fiction for both children and adults, she is best known for her thoughtful explorations of the relationship between past and present, which often have an element of the supernatural – such as the award-wining *The Ghost of Thomas Kempe* (1973) and *A Stitch in Time* (1976).

LOFTING, Hugh
(1886–1947) Author and illustrator

Best known for the *Doctor Dolittle* books, about an eccentric zoologist, the first of which was published in 1922.

MASEFIELD, John
(1878–1967) Author and poet

A distinguished poet and playwright, he published several outstanding fantasy novels for children, including *The Midnight Folk* (1927) and *The Box of Delights* (1935).

MILNE, A(lan) A(lexander)
(1882–1956) Author

Famous as the author of the *Winnie-the-Pooh* (1926) and *The House at Pooh Corner* (1928), about a small boy's adventures with his friends Pooh Bear, Piglet, Eeyore and Tigger, as well as for his collections of verse, *When We Were Very Young* (1924) and *Now We Are Six* (1927), which were written, like the Pooh stories, for his son, Christopher Robin.

NESBIT, E(dith)
(1858–1924) Author

Renowned in her lifetime for her progressive views (she was a founder member of the Fabian Society), E. Nesbit is now best known for her stories about the magical adventures of a family of five children in *Five Children and It* (1902) and its sequels, *The Phoenix and the Carpet* (1904) and *The Story of the Amulet* (1905), as well as for the more realistic tales about the Bastable family in *The Treasure Seekers* (1899), *The Wouldbegoods* (1901) and others.

NORTON, Mary
(1903–92) Author

Best known as the author of the comic fantasy *Bedknobs and Broomsticks* (1947) and for *The Borrowers* (1952) and its sequels, about a family of tiny people living under the floorboards of a great house, which established her as one of the leading children's writers of the post-war era.

OPIE, Peter (1918–82) and Iona (b 1923)
Anthropologists and editors

Renowned for their definitive studies of nursery rhymes (*The Oxford Dictionary of Nursery Rhymes*, 1951) and fairy tales (*The Classic Fairy Tales*, 1974) and for their ground-breaking research into children's games and slang (*The Lore and Language of Schoolchildren*, 1959; *Children's Games*, 1969).

PEARCE, Philippa
(b 1920) Author

The author of several outstanding children's books, including the Carnegie Prize-winning *Tom's Midnight Garden* (1958), *A Dog So Small* (1962) and *The Way to Sattin Shore* (1982).

POTTER, Beatrix
(1866–1943) Author and illustrator

Famous as the author of *The Tale of Peter Rabbit* (1901) and its successors, including *The Tailor of Gloucester* (1903), *The Tale of Squirrel Nutkin* (1903), *The Tale of Mrs Tiggywinkle* (1904) and many others, all of which were illustrated by Potter herself.

RACKHAM, Arthur
(1867–1939) Illustrator

Renowned for his wonderfully fantastic and even grotesque drawings and paintings, he is best known as the illustrator of *Grimm's Fairy Tales* (1900) *Peter Pan in Kensington Gardens* (1906), *Hans Andersen's Fairy Tales* and others, all of which display his characteristic style, a mixture of Pre-Raphaelite medievalism and the more decadent *fin de siècle* influence of Aubrey Beardsley.

RANSOME, Arthur
(1884–1967) Author

Celebrated as the author of *Swallows and Amazons* (1930) and its sequels, about a group of children holidaying in the Lake District and on the Norfolk Broads, and their adventures on land and water. With their mixture of comic and exciting incident and their wealth of sailing lore, the books set a standard for children's adventure fiction which remains enduringly popular.

SAINT-EXUPÉRY, Antoine de
(1900–44) Author and illustrator

Most famous for *The Little Prince* (1943), about a child who descends to earth from the asteroid where he lives and describes his adventures on various other planets to an aviator he encounters in the Sahara desert (Saint-Exupéry was himself a celebrated aviator, who wrote several books about his experiences).

SENDAK, Maurice
(b 1928) Author and illustrator

Born in New York, Sendak is best known as the author of an outstanding trilogy of children's picture books, beginning with *Where the Wild Things Are* (1963), a comic fantasy about a small boy's dream-life, which was followed by the more light-hearted *In the Night Kitchen* (1970) and concluded with the much darker *Outside Over There* (1981). Other fine examples of Sendak's idiosyncratic style are to be found in *Higglety Pigglety Pop!* (1967) and his illustrations of *Grimm's fairy tales in *The Juniper Tree* (1973).

SEUSS, Dr (Theodor Seuss Giesel)
(b 1904) Author and illustrator

Best known for *The Cat in the Hat* (1957) and its successors – a series of comic reading books for children.

SHEPARD, E(rnest) H(oward)
(1879–1976) Illustrator

Best known as the illustrator of *Kenneth Grahame's *The Wind in the Willows*, and *A.A. Milne's *Winnie-the-Pooh*, in each of which the text is immeasurably enhanced by the delicacy and expressiveness of Shepard's drawings.

SUTCLIFFE, Rosemary
(1920–94) Author

Children's historical novelist, who began a long and distinguished career with several novels for younger children, before establishing herself with *The Eagle of the Ninth* (1954), the first of a sequence of novels dealing with the Roman occupation of Britain and its aftermath. She returned to the period for *Outcast* (1955) and *Dawn Wind* (1961), both of which are set against the background of the Dark Ages, and for the next twenty years or so continued to produce remarkable novels on related themes, many of them set during the author's favourite period of Ancient British history.

TENNIEL, Sir John
(1820–1914) Illustrator

A distinguished artist and *Punch* cartoonist, he is perhaps best known as the illustrator of *Lewis Carroll's *Alice's Adventures in Wonderland* and *Through the Looking-glass*, as well as for Thackeray's *The Rose and the Ring*.

TOLKIEN, J(ohn) R(onald) R(euel)
(1892–1973) Author

An academic by profession (he was Professor of Anglo-Saxon at Oxford), he is now best known as the author of *The Hobbit* (1937) and *The Lord of the Rings* (1955), ambitious sagas which incorporated much of the author's extensive knowledge of Norse myth and fable into an adventure story about the quest for a lost ring.

WALSH, Jill Paton
(b 1937) Author

A distinguished writer of fiction for adults and children, she is perhaps best known for her outstanding historical novels for children, including *The Dolphin Crossing* (1967), about the Dunkirk evacuation, *Fireweed* (1969), also with a Second World War background and *A Parcel of Patterns* (1983), which is set during the Great Plague of 1665.

WESTALL, Robert
(1929–95) Author

The author of over thirty books for children, Westall, who was born on Tyneside (the background for many of his works), is best known for his atmospheric novels about the Second World War, which convey the horror, occasional boredom and sporadic excitement of the war as seen from the point of view of his young protagonists. These include his award-winning *The Machine Gunners* (1975) and its sequel, *Full Fathom Five* (1979), *Blitzcat* (1989), *The Kingdom by the Sea* (1990) and *A Time of Fire* (1994).

WHITE, T(erence) H(anbury)
(1906–64) Author

Best known for the *Sword in the Stone* tetralogy (eventually published under the overall title of *The Once and Future King*, 1958) about the childhood and rise to power of the young King Arthur.

Index of Subject Categories

Index of Authors

Index of Titles